Farmland

River Bourne

Lakes

Caldwell
Manor

Farmland

Caldwell
Golf Course

Summerhouse
Knole Sett

rmland

Club
house

Motorway
Sett

motorway

Poplar row

Farmland

Farmland

Brushwood/
Poplar sett

ett

The Sett · Holly Tree sett

EPENNY
OOD

Sand Pit
Sett

use

THE CITY

GREEN-EYED FLO

GREEN-EYED FLO

The cat, the fox & the badgers

CHRIS FERRIS

FOURTH ESTATE · *London*

First published in Great Britain in 1992 by
Fourth Estate Limited
289 Westbourne Grove
London W11 2QA

Grateful acknowledgement is made to
BBC *Wildlife* magazine for permission to reproduce material from
Flo and Co. Also to the Leicester Badger Group for material from their
newsletter, *Faithful Attachment*. And to M. D. Press, Minster in Thanet, Kent,
for permission to reproduce the badger illustration by Katrina Walsh.

A catalogue record for this book is available from the British Library.

ISBN 1-872180-04-3

Printed in Great Britain by
Cambridge University Press

ASHCROFT WOODS BADGERS
Crisp and her cubs Pip, Squeak and Wilfrid
Missy, Mícheál, Meg, Bess, 'Bossie
Bessie' and her two cubs

NINEPENNY WOOD BADGERS
Old boar, Hazel and Hattie
Cubs: Harry (adopted), Moomin and her sister

List of Illustrations

Between pages 86 and 87

Badgers are good climbers – Hattie in one of the old apple trees.
Not too sure of the camera.
A common accident – a very young badger cub taken from its
  nursery chamber by a terrier being walked.
Karen drying Splinter the fox cub.

Between pages 150 and 151

Splinter spent most of his time watching, playing and sleeping
  on his grass-covered den-top.
Cage door open and freedom beyond, but it's a big world out
  there.
Splinter in his den-top, watching me at the kitchen window.
Ashcroft Woods.

Between pages 182 and 183

I might be busy outside the caravan and then look up to see
  Splinter close by.
Splinter waiting for Flo outside The Sett.
Ninepenny Woods.
Splinter waiting below the kitchen window.
A badger pawprint in soft earth.
A sett entrance between tree roots.
Badger claw marks on sandstone.
Splinter soliciting a game from Flo . . .

Between pages 214 and 215

. . . and the game in full spate!
The enclosure half hidden in the snow.
February 1991.
Flo coming home to be fed.

Introduction

CHRIS Ferris is not someone you forget. It's not that she is in any way imposing. Far from it – she is a slight, almost frail woman whom you would hardly notice if you passed her on a country walk. It's just that, when you meet her, she is one of those people whose physical composure, measured speech and power of eye-contact gives them an air of strength and conviction.

I first met Chris in 1985. I had been told about her by the badger expert Dr Ernest Neal and by a fellow editor, Juliet Walker, both of whom had felt that she was someone special, and whose writings should be read by others. She had, they said, kept a diary spanning fifteen years, which contained some extraordinary observations and some genuine revelations. They were right. But what turned out to be most unusual about Chris was that there was nothing unusual about her. She lived in a council house, in an ordinary neighbourhood, and had two children and an ordinary, part-time clerical job. The surrounding countryside, too, appeared to be ordinary.

Her diaries were special, though. They described the sort of intimate encounters with animals whch, as a child, I dreamt about having. That Chris had had no higher education and was totally unknown in the natural history world made them all the more surprising, until you realised that this was her secret – she had no preconceptions of how animals were supposed to behave, and no prejudices about how you were supposed to relate to them.

The fact that she had been able to observe what she has is, in part, the result of years of back pain, and therefore of sleepless nights, which led to her nocturnal explorations. But as so often happens, the joy that she has had from animals has been marred by the pain of seeing them injured and killed – for the sad fact is that many other humans get their pleasure by inflicting pain on animals.

Over the years, Chris catalogued horrifying and terrifying encounters with lampers, shooters and diggers, and built up a dossier that eventually helped convince the police and the public that many illegal practices involving wild animals, especially badgers, were growing in popularity. Her writings also gave others the conviction to do something about it, and helped to spur on the growth of local badger groups.

That she has been able to witness badger-digging, lamping and other such unpleasant nocturnal activities has not been without personal expense. A woman on her own at night is very, very vulnerable. And even though Chris's knowledge of 'her' woodlands and fields, and her remarkable nocturnal vision have enabled her to escape many a dangerous situation, she has been hurt, and in a couple of cases, seriously injured. Being a local who could point the finger, she was also in danger during the day, which made her shun publicity and therefore public recognition. But despite such precautions, she was threatened with physical violence on several occasions and once narrowly missed being run down by a car. Chris will not like me revealing these facts, because she is, by nature, modest. But such things need to be made public, if only to emphasise the brutality of other people's worlds and the need to understand what causes and motivates such activities.

As far as Chris's contributions to the magazine are concerned, they have not only been among the most memorable I have had the honour to publish over the past ten years as editor, but have also been ones that have influenced others and helped to change things for the better. I feel lucky to have had the opportunity to learn from her.

Rosamund Kidman Cox
Editor
BBC *Wildlife* Magazine

Chapter One

DRIFTING off to sleep to the distant sound of the tawny owls calling, I became conscious of a faint tapping against the wall of the caravan. This was a familiar enough sound in the wood, and I was beginning to doze again when I jerked awake; this time the tapping was accompanied by a loud scrabbling. Moonlight filtered through the window and the tawnies were still calling. I opened the little door and sure enough there was Flo, the tabby stable cat, balancing precariously on the metal step with Harry, the young badger – her partner in crime. Harry had been passed to me earlier in the year and, once weaned, was adopted by a cubless sow badger living nearby. But for Flo, I doubt that he would have returned to the caravan so often, but his feline friend believed in calling for me if I wasn't already out by 10 p.m. I left the door open whilst I donned anorak and boots. The tabby came in to investigate and outside a white head with tapering black stripes bobbed up and down whickering loudly – I was holding up the troops.

Walking under the tall beeches in the wood, I watched my two companions prowling ahead; in some ways so alike, in others so different. Harry was a forager, pushing his moist snout through the dead leaves and turning over stones in his quest for insects and grubs. He liked the area round the water bowl where he

1

could always find a slug or two. Flo was, at best, a hunter. Ears pricked, body poised, she constantly stared up into the leafiness of the branches far above – something a badger rarely needs to do.

A wood comes into its own at night as the creatures of the dark take over. Small squeakings here, a rustling there and the calling owls floating nearer on the wind till the trees seemed full of their yearning. Now came a rasping sound, as of someone wiping their feet on a rough doormat – Harry had found his slug. Badgers are not bothered by the mucus produced by small slugs, but this large black one required the removal of most of its slime before eating. Flo came to inspect her companion's work, sniffing delicately at the now flattened prey. I looked on with interest too. The slug's skin was unbroken. In spite of the harsh scraping with his forepaws, young Harry hadn't used his strength, but just carefully made the slug palatable. The tabby sat watching, tail neatly curled about her feet. A few quick chews and the delicacy was gone. Flo stretched upwards and began to wash the badger's ear, next his white face, dirtied from his foraging. Harry wore a sheepish look; they made a comic couple. When he was first brought to me, Harry had been catsize; now he dwarfed his fussy friend.

Something was moving through the dog's mercury towards us – Harry's adopted mother and her sister with the two sow cubs. One of the cubs nosed Flo, who spun round and boxed the other with soft paws, her claws well retracted so as not to scratch. Next moment the two were playing chase amongst the dead beech leaves, in and out of the smooth, grey trunks. Harry and the other young sow decided to join in the fun, whereupon Flo jumped easily on to a felled log nearby and left the others to it. Only the old boar badger made the cat wary. Probably something to do with his ponderous size and the powerful musk emanating as he passed, for he certainly wouldn't have harmed her.

Flo had been here two years prior to my arrival and must have known the adult animals for most of her life. A woman had stabled her horse in the meadow nearby and brought the kitten to keep down the mice. On her departure she had left the cat, who was well adapted to survive by hunting and sleeping in the straw bales. When I came to live in the caravan, Flo miraculously appeared and, in the casual way typical of cats, proceeded to take me over, whilst at the same time retaining her independence. I had converted the tiny bedroom into an office, complete with typewriter, telephone, books and the inevitable filing cabinet. On the top shelf sat Micky, a stuffed badger that went with me whenever I gave talks to primary school children on badgers and the countryside. Curiosity made Flo investigate the caravan, though she feared any sudden noise and if startled would rush into the office to be with the stuffed badger. It was only when sitting beneath Micky's head that she would ever consent to having her photo taken without making a dash for it.

She must have known he was a badger; after all, he was a replica of those she met almost nightly. There was a faint musky smell still clinging to his rough fur too. She would occasionally look up at his face above her, sniff underneath his chin, then the black fur of a leg, before squatting comfortably in the feline sleep position, purring contentedly to herself. Eyes closed, neat paws tucked daintily beneath the tabby body, Flo slept on whilst her guardian gazed into eternity above her head.

◊ ◊ ◊

Once I was settled at the caravan, soon affectionately dubbed 'The Sett', the place became not just a home, but an animal recovery centre as well. It nestled in a curve of the grassy path surrounded by small trees, hawthorn, field maple, aspen, young ash and wild service, that farther on joined a double row of lombardy poplars, remnants of an old drive. In the late 1800s, I was told, the owner of the property had planted them for his daughter to canter her horse along. They were planted too close together for a carriage or a trap, or even for two horses to walk abreast, so there was probably some truth in the story. Recently the gales had broken some and brought others down, but coming in from the farmland or across the meadow, the remaining slender pillars rising above the other trees seemed to point me the way. This poplar row disappeared into a small wood or shaw that I nicknamed Ninepenny Wood; it reappeared again as a hedge dividing the fields beyond.

Just inside the wood near the field edge was a small badger sett beneath a holly tree, and beyond that, under some brushwood in the poplar row itself, was another sett. Once there had been a

3

large family of badgers here, but they were now sadly reduced to three adults – the old boar and his two daughters – and three cubs. The rest of the clan had died when their main sett and one close by (the annexe sett) had been bulldozed some months earlier. Badgers are protected by law, but at that time their habitat and homes were not. The perennial activities of badger-diggers, together with development, reuse of farmland and busy traffic on once quiet lanes had decimated badger numbers locally. I often saw the family here now; at night they might snuffle round and under the caravan or drink from the bird's water bowl that I kept filled in the grassy verge. There were foxes too, as well as slow worms, lizards and herons; and one sunny day I watched a fallow deer lying up in the long grass under the orchard trees.

Harry had been the recovery centre's first occupant; now Vicky an orphaned fox cub lived in the cage. She would stay there till old enough to find her own food; by now she was about ten weeks old. I had no wish to handle her for if she was to be returned to the wild, wild she must remain. Housed in the quarters intended for a badger, however, I had no need to, for the cage could be cleaned with her in it. At the first sign of 'danger', Vicky would jump into the raised compartment, growl and hide her face. When I renewed the bedding, placed fresh pieces of discarded meat (we had a friendly butcher in the village) and changed her drinking water, I would sit by the cage and make the soft 'mmmmmm' contact sound of the adult vixen to her cubs, hoping that in time this might calm her.

The hot weather began in early May that year, with the cuckoo calling regularly near The Sett by 27th April. Pleasant at first, the intense heat soon lost its charm, and 1989 became known in the south as the year of the drought. By the first week in May everything was growing fast, helped by the heavy dews at night and hot sunshine. Already the ash trees' leaves were unfurling, though they are the last to do so, and on the farmland beyond the golden rape was in flower.

Vicky continued to prosper and would even hold a 'mmmmmm' conversation with me from the depths of the box as I cleaned her cage. Any human movement would send the fox cub into hiding, but Flo sat for long periods by the metal mesh communicating with her face to face. Before the fiery sun

4

climbed too high in the sky, green-eyed feline and amber-eyed vulpine stretched out together, one inside, one outside, the cage. Flo would not tolerate any other of her kind, savagely fighting all cats she might meet, but young badgers, and most especially foxes, she seemed to regard as her own.

◊ ◊ ◊

The police contacted me late one morning. Terriermen with spades and crowbars had been disturbed at a badger sett some miles away by a local man walking his dog. He hadn't been able to make out their van number, but could I check that the place was indeed badger-occupied? It was, with all the typical signs: bedding left to air by the animals themselves, latrine pits containing fresh dung and a recently used scratching tree, the claw marks clear and deep in its torn bark. A 'crowning-down' hole dug with the terriermen's pointed shovels to reach their quarry, dogs' pawprints in the moist soil and fast-drying blood on fistfuls of badger fur told their own tale. It was a large main sett and almost certainly, cubs had been present. Badgers are by nature, shy retiring creatures, but the sow defending her young is the most aggressive of mothers and will fight to the death – a great prize for the badger-diggers. We had found no evidence of recent badger abuse for some months, but it is never far away.

In spite of protection in law, badgers are still popular for sport. They may be dug out and baited with dogs on site if the area is sufficiently isolated, or taken away for future entertainment. Bets may be placed on the dogs game enough to fight in spite of injuries they will sustain, for the badger is a formidable adversary. Several dogs may be set upon it simultaneously. The baited creature may have its hind legs or jaw broken beforehand to equalise the fight. Young dogs are frequently given cubs on which to gain experience. Badgers are also used to ring the changes at organised dog-fights. Sometimes none of this happens. The badger is merely dug out with the aid of dogs, chopped viciously with the men's shovels or metal bars and stuffed back into an entrance of the sett. This has been sport enough.

The man who had stumbled across the terriermen showed me two other setts, both deserted. Not every badger home is occupied of course, for these animals will have several within their territory and some may be empty for long periods. He promised to alter his dog-walking in order to pass by each one at least twice a week, and he would keep a record of when they again became used now he knew the signs of badger occupation. I met his wife, who was horrified that badger-diggers should be operating in *their* neighbourhood – it was something she had heard of, but somehow never expected locally. I had pointed out to the husband old evidence of crowning-down holes infilled from past digs at all three setts he had shown me that day. In time the earth settles in these holes and though leaves and debris will cover them, one soon learns the tell-tale signs.

Indeed, all the remaining setts of the Ninepenny badgers had been dug several times over the years and only once had terriermen been caught in the act, charged and successfully convicted in court. Mr Ellis, the businessman who owned The Sett and allowed me to live there, had bugged the remaining badger homes on his land, by running a heavy-duty cable from each to his house. The sett under the holly tree was in a part of the wood owned by Mr Legget, a farmer, who agreed that the cable should run through his wood and be linked to the others. Recently, Mr Ellis had separated from his wife and now lived elsewhere. The cable still linked the setts, but was no longer used. Nevertheless, it was a deterrent for anyone seeing it and far too thick and heavy to be severed with a knife. I was here every day now and checked each occupied sett several times between dawn and dusk, besides seeing the badgers themselves at night. I phoned Mr Legget, whom I already knew slightly, and told him how well the badgers were faring at the Holly Tree Sett and asked had he noticed they had dug out close by under the brushwood in the bank between the poplar row and his part of the wood? Yes, he had wondered what that pile of sandy earth was and if it might be the badgers. I explained that since their main and annexe sets had been bulldozed, the Holly Tree Sett had become their new main home, with the one in the brushwood their new annexe sett. The farmer said he was surprised they didn't take over the motorway embankment, but I felt that until permanent cover such as trees grew up on it, the badgers were not likely to do so. Mr Legget seemed so pleasant and interested that I chided myself for my reservations. Of all the farmers, farm managers and landowners I knew with badgers

6

on their land, there were only three I didn't wholly trust – this man was one of them. Somehow, what he said and what actually occurred on his land didn't always tally. But fields are open, anyone has access to them, and in his case, footpaths and bridleways crossed them too. Perhaps I had judged too harshly.

Not far from The Sett was an old bath, partly filled with water, home to a Spanish terrapin. Terry had been found on a building site years ago when my daughter Karen was at primary school. Now she worked many miles away and lived in lodgings, so Terry had come to me. We had no idea of his age and these terrapins have been known to live up to 120 years in captivity, so I suspect he will outlive us all, possibly because he does so little. Activity is not his strong point! When the film *E.T.* was first shown, I was convinced the creator must have modelled his character on a similar terrapin, though events were to prove that our reptile hadn't E.T.'s gentle nature. Normally, Terry would clamber on to his rock placed conveniently in the centre of his home to bask in the sunshine, but that summer I had to move his bath out of the direct light as the sun was too hot even for his liking. Now I found a magpie drowned in his water – it did strike me as strange that such a large adult bird should have died in this way, but I thought no more about it. I took it out and placed it in Vicky's cage. It was the first feathered bird she had ever been given – as opposed to part of a carcass from the butcher – and a big one at that for a cub. Watching her from the caravan window, I noted she knew instinctively what to do with it, tearing the body feathers away as she shook her head to rid herself of the excess ones. Then she tore into the body and ate. The leftovers, as always, she tupped into a corner under the newspaper, then pushed dried grass over it with her nose. I cleaned her cage daily now, but took care to leave her a few of the largest feathers to play with. These were pounced on and tossed into the air, or crept up upon as if a live prey. How she loved the long grass clippings put in as bedding, pushing her nose through the pile and tupping over everything in sight – her big marrow bone, her toys and even her water bowl. She would watch me from around the wall of her box and 'mmmmmm' softly whilst I returned the compliment. She was three months old now and very foxy. Her string of a tail was bushing out and she carried it rather than it hanging limp. One night the resident vixen was calling and later I saw her watching Vicky. When the adult left, the youngster barked dismally, almost howling, and I felt rather sad. She was a good four weeks older than the vixen's two cubs.

Then one warm, starry evening I discovered a lone fox cub nose to nose with Vicky through the mesh. He was pitifully thin with unkempt coat and string-like tail tucked between his back legs. Yet the angle of his ears and the red guard hairs pushing through the puppy felting of his back and shoulders showed he was much the little vixen's age. Flo sat upright a few paces away with a smug expression on her rounded face – was this one of her foundlings I wondered? I kept a record of the fox families this area contained, but couldn't recall seeing this pathetic specimen amongst the other cubs. Where had he come from? The tabby had long since timed her appearances to synchronise with Vicky's meals, and from then on I put down three bowls, one inside the cage and two outside. Foxy, as I called the stranger, would creep off when I was in sight, but the moment I walked into The Sett and closed its green door, he would be eating ravenously from his bowl. Green-eyed Flo was never jealous of the feeding foxes for they ate virtually anything. *She* preferred to catch live prey and, except for a certain brand of catfood, anything put in front of her was treated with disdain as she stalked off. There was something about that feline back and the thick barred tail with its kink of offended dignity. I christened it her storming off act. 'You really don't expect *me* to eat that, do you?' her rear view seemed to ask.

Now the ponies' meadow was awash with golden buttercups, and orange-tip butterflies flirted along my winding path. Amongst the long grass, drooping white bells of Solomon's seal were opening to match the froth of hawthorn blossom above. Sweetly scented ghosts beckoned my night walks, as the barest of breezes touched each laden branch. Harry and his family were still finding food in spite of the hot, dry weather. Earthworms, their staple diet, were unobtainable now, but the heavy night-dews encouraged slugs, snails and insects. They spent all the short hours of darkness in search of these and foraged well into the morning light. Worms, when plentiful, are easily caught and an adult badger may fill itself in a couple of hours. Insects are a different matter. The water bowls under the beeches and in the path verge were their life-line now. If the nights became too hot for dew, I would need to put food out for them too. Nursing sows will allow their young to suckle long after the norm at such times, but if the mothers go hungry their milk will dry up. Many cub deaths are caused by drought.

Foxes catch grasshoppers and crickets by stalking and pouncing. Badgers lack this hunting ability, though I noticed they watched Flo's successful attempts with great interest. She would detect a movement or hear their stridulations then sit close by on all fours with back humped in her sleep position, though she was far from that. A deceptively soft, furry forepaw would suddenly land on the chirring insect – abruptly silenced as the unsheathed claws grasped. Then, turning the pads upwards, she would sit upright, biting off legs and body to crunch with relish. The badgers too would try this, and might indeed trap the hopper under a much larger pad, but now came the problem. How to transfer it to their mouth before it escaped? Retractile claws certainly have their uses.

Sometimes the badger cubs took time off foraging to play. Harry, by far the largest and most boisterous, was always leader and instigator of their games. The smallest little sow was much lighter furred than any others of her family I had known, and this prompted me to ask other members of our county's badger groups whether this was common. It appeared there were areas of albino as well as erythristic animals. The latter have a sandy or ginger appearance to the fur of flanks and back and the normally black parts are reddish; usually the eyes are brown, though they have also been recorded as red. I would need to watch this young sow in good light to make out how her colouring differed from the others. I only knew at present from my nightly observations that her facial stripes were clearly defined and her eyes were not pink, so she wasn't an albino.

A profusion of dog-roses were in bloom outside my office window, smothering the bird box where the blue tit incubated her eggs. The sun shining through the leaves gave to the room a greenish light; it was easy to imagine oneself up amongst the trees. Every view from The Sett was foliage backed, though it was not at all claustrophobic. At first light one morning the cuckoo visited, calling from the roof. I heard him land on the metal and wondered who it was . . . till he began his song. By

9 a.m., it was already hot with the turtle-dove crooning from a nearby oak. A mass of viper's bugloss stood in startling tiers of pink and vivid blue – the intense colours burned in the harsh light. It had been the hottest May on record. Something was knock-knocking nearby in the leafiness, but I couldn't make out what was busy there. Vicky was restlessly pacing up and down; it would soon be time to feed her. Collecting grass, cut and dried along the paths for her bedding, I watched a female orange-tip, not an eye-catcher like the male butterfly, but attractive none the less with her dappling of green and white blending perfectly into the garlic mustard on which she rested.

I continued to gather the sweetly dried grass on the path. Something followed, keeping parallel, but hidden beneath the low laden hawthorns' boughs. A shower of white petals touched the ground, and farther on another, as it passed beneath, and I smiled, knowing it was Vicky's friend. At her cage, I stuffed the dirtied bedding into a black binliner, then spread out the fresh as a small, sharp face timorously watched from a clump of ferns. Neither fox cub was old enough to find sufficient food by hunting, though they could forage for insects and beetles. If I now gave Vicky her freedom, she would probably starve. But with Foxy appearing regularly for meals, might they both return if hungry and so have the best of both worlds – food and freedom? It seemed cruel to keep her caged; I must make a decision soon.

◊ ◊ ◊

One morning, I strolled out to view the badger setts. It was too lovely a day to remain indoors and, who knows, a terrierman might feel the same way. From beneath the holly tree, great heaps of sandy earth sprawled over the fading bluebells and there, spread neatly on top to air, a pile of bedding. What it was made of surprised me. Not bitten-off bluebell greenery, grass blades or soft hay, but goosegrass. The tiny hooked prickles of this plant's stems and leaves cause it to cling to animal fur and human clothing; I had not seen it used for badger bedding before.

Standing in the trees' shade, I watched swallows skimming over the whiskered barley in their quest for insects. There were many about, with butterflies on the dogwood blossoms, woody nightshade and bladder campion at the wood edge. The hunters' sickle shapes twisted and turned in the sunshine as a distant wind raced through the poppy-strewn corn. A crow cawed above the other birdsong and long shadowy fingers stretched pointing across the field as towering clouds hurried by. Wetness from the showery night was fast evaporating; it had done nothing to relieve the drought.

One misty first light I walked around the green gate from the ponies' meadow and so along the winding path to The Sett. I could hear a gekkering and growling from Vicky. Peering cautiously round the corner, I saw Harry outside her cage gazing at the fox, whose back was arched like a cat's. She was not, I noted, cowering in her box from fear. I sensed that, though nervous, she was aware that Harry was like herself, only a cub. Farther off was the sow, snuffling amongst the long grass, home to many slugs and snails. But the old boar was under my caravan, sorting amongst the empty flowerpots and wood stored there. The latter he was trying to drag away with his claws and teeth. Perhaps there was something crawling beneath that he wanted. He lost interest and came to stand next to Harry, whereupon the little vixen did disappear into her box. Then all three badgers ambled off with that distinctive swaying gait towards the poplar row. I gave them time to get ahead before I followed.

Homeward bound, they paused beneath the trees, one to drink, the others to snout amongst the decaying mast. The wood seemed mysterious and eternal in the early morning light where a faint scent of bluebells still lingered. Bordering the trail that wound through the tall dog's mercury were patches of that curiosity amongst grasses, the wood melick. The ripened seed heads were hard and shiny, set on slender, branching stems that swayed gracefully above the bright green blades – a myriad of tiny gleaming beads. The misty night had crowned each seed with a perfect vapour bauble that fell on to three rough, grey backs as they passed through.

I sat on a log when they had gone, enjoying the solitude of the place. However, it was not for long! Three small characters came rushing madly through the undergrowth – Harry and his girlfriends were intent on their game. Round and round, each trying to grab the other's tail as they tumbled about. Their parents might have gone to bed, but they were staying up late. Unnoticed, I sat, chin in hand; gratitude that Harry had been so easily accepted by these badgers mingled with my pleasure in their play.

It proved to be one of those mornings. At 4.40 a.m., the first blackbird called from the briar rose next to The Sett and flew off when the cuckoo perched and sounded from a young oak just above. Then two herons passed my kitchen window, their heads jerking as they walked. Now it was the cuckoo's turn to fly away as the tall grey birds returned into my view. One was a juvenile, smaller and brownish. The pieces of meat I had left out for Foxy were picked up by the adult as the other gaped and begged for food. The heron stuck its long bill down its offspring's throat and the meat was swallowed by the youngster. I couldn't be sure whether the food was merely given or if some had been regurgitated, as more seemed to be swallowed than was picked up.

The drought continued. For days it was cloudy, but the promised thunderstorms never came. Returning from a badger-watch with Flo in good light, we met Foxy in the wood. I noted he was a far shorter build than Vicky, though his coat had developed a richer brown. On reaching the poplar row I called softly, but he had gone. Flo too had disappeared, but her absence coincided with a mouse rustling in the grass. Nearing Vicky's cage I found Foxy already there and talking to her. First I fed the vixen with her early morning meat, then her companion. When the bowls were filled with fresh water, I returned to The Sett, leaving the door open. The sun had pierced the clouds by now and was streaming through the doorway.

I began to type and forgot the foxes in my interest outside the office window. First a great tit, then a blue tit were finding insects amongst the pink wild-rose blossoms – then a pair of blackcaps and next a garden warbler. A faint noise made me peer round the corner into the kitchen. There, sitting in the doorway on the mat, grooming themselves and each other in the sunshine, were Foxy and Flo. He looked at me looking at him, his pupils elliptical in the brightness, yawned widely into the air and curled round to sleep. The tabby never condescended to glance my way but, giving his back a quick wash, sat upright beside him staring out into the trees. This incident convinced me that, if hungry, both foxes would return. I resolved to free Vicky that night.

It was 8.30 p.m. when Foxy returned. Looking out of my sitting-room window, I saw him nose-touching Vicky through the wire. Carefully I carried out their food; he moved a little away till I put his down near the cage. That evening I refilled my vixen's water, put her meat in and fastened open her door. Almost immediately she recognised the change, scented the air, but, ignoring the open door for the moment, ate her food. When both had eased their hunger, the dog fox put his nose inside the door towards Vicky, who sprang back growling and retired to her box. She had tupped over her remaining bones and, though Foxy could smell them, he merely sniffed in their direction and went to sit with tail curled round by the clump of vipers' bugloss. He drank from the water bowl and groomed patiently, but she spent nearly an hour coming to the opening, sticking her head out, springing back, putting a paw out, spring-ing back and retreating into her box in a tight little ball. She knew freedom was beyond that opened door, and she had longed to be free like her companion, but now freedom was offered she was fearful. Understandable really. I had kept her for nine weeks; how long had Steve, the RSPCA Inspector, had her? Vicky was now five months old. The dog fox grew impa-tient, gave a great yawn and suddenly bounded over. Poor Vicky hid her face in the box; a russet rump protruded out. Foxy grunted and ambled off into the greenery behind the caravan. Wait . . . a few more minutes and Vicky was out. No, she rushed back in again – oh, Vicky! – scented the air and cautiously came out. Quickly she ran in a circle and into her box. Only for a moment as her head poked around the box's side. Again she scented the air, poked her head out of the door . . . and was really out this time. The tall grass and ox-eye daisies waved – where was she? Ah, running through them, deep in their coolness, and they nod, nod, nodded at her passing. Now the dog fox was back; they touched noses, the vulpine greeting. She was no longer fearful for they were on common ground. She chased him and he chased her; up on hindlegs, forepaws on each other's shoulders. She licked his ear, he tweaked hers. She broke away, ran into her cage, crouched to urinate and ran out again to bump him sideways on. Twice more she went in, and each time came out again to play and explore. Now Foxy sat patiently whilst she searched carefully all round the back of The Sett. Satisfied, she walked over to him still sitting there and, she leading, both trotted sedately out of my sight. I still have the comments I wrote that night:

> Sure the young foxes are much of an age, but walking in single file like this, Vicky is noticeably taller and more rangy. She is lean though, not at all fat. She still has a great deal of white to face and coat. [This was to remain; she is easily recognised even at a distance.] The dark cross on her back and shoulders is well marked. In spite of relatively poor colouring, Vicky is very beautiful with great ears, very black and white markings on her mask and a well-formed brush. There is nothing slinking about her, she walks well upright in contrast to her smaller, more handsome companion. Really, this is rather odd since he is more experienced in the wide world outside. His coat is lovely, a really red young fox with a very busy tail. Vicky looks as if she will be the boss. [She still is.]

I soon found my foxes sheltered somewhere beneath the gale-felled geans, or wild cherries, in the deepest part of Ninepenny Wood. In those early days they regularly returned for food. Small items they ate on the spot, whilst larger pieces, such as rib bones with meat attached, they carried off to gnaw in their secret hideaway. I was careful to act as a parent fox would with cubs of this age, underfeeding rather than overfeeding to encourage them to find their own food. Insects were plentiful and highly nutritious. The co-ordination needed to locate and catch these would stand them in good stead for hunting larger prey. Foxy was skilful already, but Vicky had much to learn. They were too young to dig their own den, and in the south foxes only live underground in bad or cold weather, but the fallen trees gave them protection. I wouldn't hunt around and maybe frighten them; it was sufficient to know they were there.

Now the blue field scabious were open by my door, matching the cornflowers blooming against Vicky's old cage.

◊ ◊ ◊

I enjoyed watching the boar and Harry playing. There was such a difference in their size, yet the youngster would hang on to the other's tail and head-butt his legs – he was too small to do so to the adult's body. This the old male took in very good part. It was as if Harry and the other cubs had given him a new lease of life. I was fearful that the setts could be found by terriermen; it would be such a tragedy after all the little clan had been through. The RSPCA Inspector who had given me Harry came one day and we discussed the new blood the cub was bringing into the family. The level of man's persecution here was such that the dominant boar was father of the two adult sows. Not a good situation. Harry's arrival and acceptance was ideal.

We walked round together to view the setts. At the Holly Tree Sett, the fresh sandy spoil heap was covered in cub pawprints, but the Brushwood Sett out in the open was even more obvious and we were both rather worried. Several times I had encountered villagers walking their dogs at this sett. They had seen the bank with its pile of bright earth from the footpath two fields away and wondered like the farmer Mr Legget what it could be. At least these people would contact the police if they saw men with terriers there, but badgers advertise their homes too clearly I'm afraid. The Inspector commented on the solid dung in the pits; too dry for worming. It was yet another very hot day and there was talk of standpipes in the area. By now I was leaving food as well as water under the beeches and often came across the badgers feeding there. No leftovers were ever waiting for collection by the morning.

One late evening I went out meaning to cross the farmland and unexpectedly came across Harry and the other badgers searching for insects and beetles in the rotting bole of a long dead gean. It must have been an enormous tree in life, but now the soft reddish wood, honeycombed with tiny insect boring holes, was coming away in square chunks. I squatted down and made the contact 'Hhhhhhhhhhhhhharry' sound to the youngster without thinking. He hesitated and the others moved off at my approach, or so I thought. Harry came slowly up to me. Next moment I had a very angry sow rush between us growling loudly with her fur fluffed out to look much larger, as they do when roused. Clearly she was protecting him or afraid, perhaps, that I was taking him back. I jumped up and away just in time, for she meant business. I stood my ground as she and Harry hurriedly went into the wood. This, for me, had clinched the success story of young Harry. If his foster mother could guard him like that, then she had taken over the role of parent completely.

A phone call came from Mrs Ellis, the lady at the Big House, asking me to go round. Two of her dobermans were quarrelling on the patio, the other two I had seen earlier that day, roaming the village. She explained that the dogs were systematically killing her free-range chickens. She had been given these twelve hens by an animal sanctuary, together with an ancient rooster named Cedric. I had a soft spot for stately Cedric and his ladies and was saddened to find he had only two left. She showed me the growing mallard ducklings on the pond in front of her house. They were asleep all in a huddle on the tiny island in the middle, heads tucked under wings, tucked round into the owner's back or tucked into someone else's back! Their mother wasn't with them, but paddling quietly round and round on guard. It appeared that the largest dog had jumped in to get the brood, then had difficulty scrambling out as the water was very deep. Perhaps he wouldn't try again?

Would I take the latest dead hens for the badgers she asked, showing me three plump bodies. All had been fancy breeds – either speckled or unusually coloured. I agreed to take the two most distinctive and that night laid them carefully by the water bowl under the beeches. Vicky and Foxy had already been fed, so the badgers were more likely to find them. Would they eat them on the spot, perhaps quarrel over them? As it happened, when next I passed the spot that night, the chickens had vanished. Not even a feather lay there to tell the tale. So strange did this seem that the thought crossed my mind that someone might have come in from the farmland outside and taken them, but it was so unlikely, especially in the dark.

Chapter Two

IFFY must have been a born survivor, though I met him at a rather low ebb in his young life. One Sunday in June, I had a phone call to say that a badger cub had been seen earlier that morning lying in someone's back garden. It had since disappeared, but the feeling was that it was either ill or injured and had moved off, perhaps trying to get back to its home. The caller came and fetched me, and together we searched the friend's garden. Fourteen-year-old Jonathan from the house next door was interested in the badgers and anxious to care for them. He knew where the sett was and often went to look at it. Up on the hillside, in a hedgerow running parallel with the lane below, was an old main sett with many entrances, several of them well used. He knew the badgers had been coming into their back gardens to forage; one neighbour had a pond and Jonathan's parents put water out for the birds. I was to find this many times that summer. Badgers desperate for food were not starting for home till the sun was high in the sky. Cubs are always the weakest and, already exhausted by long hours of futile foraging, were unable to make the sweltering journey back. At first we hoped perhaps this youngster had made a delayed return, but looking now at the distance, it seemed unlikely. The brown grass between gardens and sett was grazed down to an all-time low and the cows had been moved. Great cracks ran across the hillside, telling their own sorry tale of the drought.

We found the young boar of about four or five months old where he had crawled into the concealing tangle of undergrowth and nettles, out of the worst of the sun. Jonathan and I scrambled round till we were close. He held the cage steady as I picked up the small mound of grey. It made one feeble attempt to bite, but the moment I lifted the body, I found it was only half the normal body-weight: big claws stuck on to matchstick limbs and loose floppy folds of skin where a rounded belly should have been. He made no further movement as I placed him in the carrying cage and secured the door. With snout hard and dry and eyes closed he looked very near death.

At the caravan I tried to get a few drops of glucosed water down the cub's throat every half hour. The easiest way was to have him lying on his back on my lap, dripping the water into the side of his mouth and stroking his throat to make him swallow. Some did go down, though much of it dribbled out. In between, he lay in the cage in the cool and dark, never moving, his breath quick and light. It was touch and go if he would survive, so Iffy the cub he became. Twice that afternoon he appeared to stop breathing. It seemed a cruelty not to allow him to die in peace. On the second such occasion, I laid his head down and went out into the blazing sunshine, my conscience troubled. The grass round The Sett was long and still green, for unlike the cub's field the only grazing was by a few rabbits. The badgers here foraged successfully for snails and slugs that crept from this long undergrowth to feed in the dewyness. There were at least five thrush's anvils within a few metres where these birds used protruding flints to hammer snails' shells into pieces and extract the soft bodies. There was water too for the birds and animals. I looked at such an anvil dotted around with vari-coloured shells and, on impulse, returned to my charge. He lay limp where I had placed him; the grey flanks no longer moved. Carefully I tried again with the glucosed water and a forepaw came up weakly as if to push my hand away! From then on there was hope, and by 10 p.m. that evening I knew he had a good chance of surviving the night.

Monday, the cub was lapping and eating a little, as well as sleeping normally. That evening the skies were darkly overcast, though the rain didn't arrive until midnight. It was heavy until 5.30 a.m. Tuesday morning, but soon the sun climbed the blue sky to dry the earth once more. That morning I moved Iffy outside to the recovery cage where he had more room. Butter-flies, bees and birds were all busy in the moist, warm conditions as the badger slept on in his new surroundings. A green-eyed tabby came to inspect the new arrival, found no response and walked off with dignity to more interesting things. That evening I replenished the cub's water. With humped shoulders and half-closed eyes, a striped face rose from its dried grass bed and growled warningly. Iffy was on the mend. By Wednesday he actually appeared to enjoy his scraps from the butcher mixed with moistened terrier meal. Little and often seemed advisable. That evening I looked in at him before leaving. For many years I had watched and studied a clan of badgers several miles away in Ashcroft Woods. Now I lived too far away to visit them often, but with the drought on my mind I had been walking over to check them three nights a week. There was something not quite right about Iffy. The same humped shoulders and small eyes half-closed, but drops of fluid ran from his snout and the grey fur stuck out at odd angles. He protested as I carried him back indoors and swung his head round to bite. This was a good sign and I fervently hoped I was mistaken in my first impression.

I returned in the morning with my thoughts on the badger cub I had left behind and lifted the cover to look in. If I hadn't known better, I might have thought he had been out drinking the night before. Iffy had all the appearance of a hangover. The little eyes were bleary, the slack mouth dribbled and he seemed to sway slightly as he rose up on front legs to look back at me. Then I saw that his food was untouched; the level of his water was still high. Definitely a case for the vet.

In the waiting-room, I put the covered cage down carefully on the floor and gave my name and address to the receptionist. 'What is it?', she enquired. 'A badger', I replied quietly, hoping the rest of the tiny room's human occupants wouldn't hear. I sat carefully away from the other patients: a doberman sporting an inverted lampshade round its neck, a pug with a down-turned mouth sitting on the lap of an equally morose woman and a basket containing an incessantly yeowling cat held by a thin, nervous man engaged in non-stop conversation with the lampshade's owner. All talk – apart from the cat's – ceased as I took my seat. Intent on keeping ourselves to ourselves, I lowered my gaze to Iffy's cover, half-closed my eyes and, humping my shoulders more than usual, thrust hands into pockets.

Time passed, the lampshade was seen to and went; likewise the others. Then my name was called. I walked in and put the cage on the floor under the friendly gaze of a fair-haired young man. 'That's a big container for a bird, you've got there,' he breezed pleasantly. Startled, I opened my eyes wide and straightened my shoulders. 'It's not a bird; it's a badger,' I retorted. 'Oh, sorry, she's written down budgie on your card.'

I donned leather gloves and offered to hold the cub whilst the vet gave young Iffy a 'thorough examination'. His heart and chest were sounded and the thermometer carefully inserted into his rectum. 'Oh, he's growling,' remarked the vet. Momentarily my sympathies were firmly with the badger. 'Temperature and heartbeat normal and no sign of chest infection. Mmmm, looking at his teeth in your glove, his gums are rather pale. That's a sign of shock.' I strove to appear casual. 'Actually, his teeth are also embedded in the thumb in my glove. Have you finished?' Just an injection if I could hold on a minute. More accurately, it was Iffy who held on – willingly and for an indefinite period. Injection over, I gradually wriggled my numbed digit free of the glove, leaving a contented badger under the impression he was still doing battle with me.

The little chap lay on his back, gripping the glove as if his life depended on it. We both stared down at him, pitying the floppy folds of skin and the ridiculously big paws with their long claws set on the twig-like limbs. Iffy gave a heavy sigh as two fleas wandered on to the fur above his snout. With one hand I carefully squeezed the life out of each in turn as another two did a slow waltz on his balding belly. We discussed the drought, the probable near starvation of the other members of Iffy's clan and Jonathan, the boy who had promised to look after them. I had intended to release the cub the following Sunday evening, in three days' time. But did he think I should continue to keep the badger in an attempt to put weight on him or might it be better to return him to his own kind? The injection was partly an anti-biotic and partly antishock. By midday I would notice the difference in Iffy and the effects of the injection would continue for forty-eight hours. If on Saturday morning he wasn't 100 per cent fit, I was to return him for another injection, and it would be best to keep him longer. However, the vet felt fairly sure that the badger would be fine and stay that way. In his opinion, a return to the badger clan, especially if Jonathan was prepared to care for them, would be preferable. We discussed this feeding of badgers and my normal reservations and concern that the animals shouldn't become dependent on humans' handouts. The vet agreed and recommended that the terrier or dog meal that I used, soaked in water and placed near the sett, would be a source of bulk, moisture and nutrients without being preferable to the badgers' normal diet. When conditions were dry with little to eat and drink, they would take the dog meal; as the weather improved, however, they would forage for more interesting food. The meal also had the advantage of not becoming foul if left. Fruit was always acceptable too; this kept badgers off the sweet titbits, whilst ensuring their survival during drought conditions.

By now Iffy had gone to sleep, the released glove lying next to him. 'Have you got something safe to get rid of his fleas?', I asked. 'No, no, they're all right, quite normal. Nothing to worry about.' Well, perhaps I *was* being a bit over-sensitive and I let the matter drop.

Back home my young badger slept all morning and well into the afternoon. Coming into the kitchen to make a mug of tea, I had a shock. The cage stood on newspaper in the darkest corner, partly covered to resemble as closely as possible the 'safe' conditions of a sett. A regiment of fleas were practising formation drill over badger and cage. Normal they might be, and who was I to quibble over the odd shared flea, but Iffy's collection was another matter. My shattered gaze fell on the cooker, carpet and fridge top – metaphorically speaking, they had left no stone unturned. The warm conditions, the cub's lack of grooming and lack of others grooming him had triggered off a population explosion, but no way was I willing to put him outside. I wanted to be around to see he was progressing.

At the pet shop I selected a flea powder in a puffer container meant primarily for cats and dogs. There was no ideal kind for wild animals and my heart sank at the thought of upsetting the patient. I returned almost convinced I wouldn't use it; after all, what were another three flea-infested days? Nothing had altered indoors except that they had now found my office. Fleas balanced with delicate panache on phone and radio, whilst others hopped on and off the typewriter keys. No, Iffy would definitely have to be defleaed.

Right from the word go, Iffy fought. He had no intention of being held still and even less intention of being defleaed. He was also aware by now that I had only one pair of gloved hands. As I sat in the outside doorway with him on my lap, his scruff held in my left hand and puffer in my right, he sunk his teeth into my trousered leg with all his young strength. I continued carefully puffing, telling myself that he was only a cub and a convalescing one at that; his jaw muscles were not yet properly developed; his fleas weren't good for him in such quantities and he *must* have a good start when he returned to the wild. Iffy for his part continued to hang on to my thigh as if he had waited all his short life for this moment and was going to savour the experience to the full. I placed the canister carefully on the floor and looked down at his now sweet-smelling, dusty back, wondering how to get him to release his hold. There was nothing for it. A deep breath and I released my hold on the back of his neck and slowly stood up. For agonising moments, he hung suspended from my thigh, then I caught him as he dropped. Back in his cage he gazed at me, little eyes narrowed, shoulders humped. His tongue came over his snout and I had a glimpse of blood. He hadn't hurt himself, surely? Immediately concerned, I bent lower to peer more closely and he snorted forward in a rush. At the same time I was aware of something warm and wet on my leg, and looking down I saw the torn denim soaked in blood. 'Idiot', I thought in relief, 'it's yours, not his', and with that, turned to check the time. In another thirty minutes I would have to comb that flea powder out – happy days!

It was like struggling with an animated bottle brush – a bottle brush with teeth. This time, however, I was taking no chances. I placed him on the ground, held him by the scruff and briskly combed out his fur against the pile. Iffy did not enjoy this and told me so in no uncertain terms, continuing steadily till back in his cage. Fetching fresh water and food, I noted with great satisfaction the bodies of deceased fleas falling through the metal bars as Iffy shook himself. Ten minutes later, I was a little

Flo, with Micky for company.

Vicky, the orphaned fox cub.

Old bedding turned out on to the spoil heap at the Holly Tree Sett.

Flo had come a long way from roughing it in the stable!

less enthusiastic as heaps of them continued to appear . . . and still they appeared. That evening, I had a grand sweep up and emptied them in triumph out the door. I looked at Iffy just finishing his meal and Iffy looked back at me. I could have sworn he smiled – or was it just a leer?

◊ ◊ ◊

The creatures with which we are familiar sometimes surprise us the most. Terry terrapin was no exception. Algae discoloured his water quickly in hot weather and, being busy, I had neglected to renew it as often as I would have liked. Now a young magpie stood drinking from the centre rock. Terry was a dark shadow beneath the water against the rock and slightly behind the bird. It finished drinking and turned away to preen its feathers. The reptile slowly climbed up behind, his webbed feet getting an easy purchase on the stone, and grasping the unsuspecting bird by its right leg, dropped back into the water with it. The terrapin stayed impassive on the bottom still holding the leg as its prey's flutterings ceased. I could hardly believe what I was seeing, yet it was all so obvious. I recalled how often in our garden, birds had 'drowned' in Terry's pool and I had wondered how it could have happened. This seemed to occur mostly when the water was cloudy. Not surprising really, for otherwise the prey would probably have seen the predator. How many times had I taken pathetic bodies out and renewed the terrapin's water, unaware that I was doing him a disfavour? That evening I found the surface littered with feathers and Terry tearing at the head. All the years we had had this terrapin – true, he lived at the bottom of our garden – I had never witnessed this before.

◊ ◊ ◊

The last afternoon of Iffy's convalescence, I thought to check his water and, opening my door, nearly tripped. The commotion startled something that had been sunning itself in the long grass opposite. Two erect, black-backed ears pointed my way as their owner registered her disapproval at my noisy exit – Vicky. She turned and sauntered off under the hawthorns. Neither young fox was regularly returning for food as there were many baby rabbits above ground now that were very easily caught. Later, I followed Vicky's trail through the undergrowth and found fox scats containing insect chitin, which I photographed. I was collecting pictures to compare fox with badger and these were particularly distinctive.

The rural policeman had suggested he collect the badger cub and me that Sunday evening in order to return young Iffy to his home. It wasn't merely a kind offer, but a wise way of getting to know Jonathan and his family and where the sett was situated. Graham came at 9 p.m. as promised, and with Iffy in his cage in the back of the patrol car we drove to the outskirts of the next village where Jonathan lived. It was a mellow evening with long shadows making the hillsides golden with their near-ripening harvest. The distant shaws were darkly green.

We got out and I introduced Graham, who was very friendly, first chatting to Jonathan and then to his parents. We all trudged up the hillside taking it in turns to carry Iffy. I said perhaps the cub should get out and walk, but no one took me up on that. It was hot work, for the hillside was steep as well as stony and cracked. I had warned everyone that the badger might stay in the opened cage for up to half an hour, as sometimes they are suspicious of their new-found freedom. I need not have worried, however, for as soon as it was open, out trotted Iffy. Under the barbed wire, into the hedge, he did a neat left turn ignoring two well-used entrances before disappearing into the third. We could almost hear him saying, 'Look, Mum, I'm back!' I showed Jonathan how to mix and spread the terrier meal, then dug a hole deep enough to take the big water bowl, for badgers often tip a bowl after they have drunk from it. The boy promised to keep it well topped up.

Now the dusk was deepening, and looking out over the distant hillside with the lane below us it was a breathtaking view. That lane winds into a steeper landscape some miles further on and I mentioned the people who had told me of the lamping of badgers there. This hunting at night with a bright light and dogs had continued for two years with none of the locals who saw it thinking to tell the police. The badgers had been systematically wiped out. Jonathan spoke of the men with terriers at the sett that his neighbours had seen off, and this led us to talk of badger-digging and baiting. Graham gave the lad the police phone number, saying that if ever he or his neighbours saw such people around the sett again, or suspicious vehicles parked off the lane, to phone the local police immediately. If, on the other hand, he had a problem with the badgers themselves, he was to let me know.

Driving home, I asked the policeman who owned the land, with the view to checking for more setts which must be in the vicinity. He knew the farm manager well and would get us permission to look for other setts. Back at the caravan I cleaned out Iffy's cage before catching a few hours sleep and going out. I hadn't cleaned it that day as I hadn't wanted the smell of me upon the cub when he returned to his family.

Young Iffy proved to be the first in a long line of cubs I was to handle that summer. There were reports of deer fawns approaching humans; extraordinary behaviour for timid creatures whose instinct is to freeze when we are close, but they too were starving and dehydrated.

The sun was slowly sinking behind the caravan as I prepared the Ninepenny badgers' food one evening. The molten rays piercing the foliage outside speckled the table top on which I worked with drops of gold. Flo was bored. She had come in through the open window, requesting my attention. The tabby had done rather well recently for my sympathy after playing with a wasp. What happened to the wasp I know not, but a subdued cat with a swollen face and forepaw twice the normal size suggested it had gone down fighting. Fit and well again, and my attention diverted, Flo took herself off to the sitting-room. Cat-like she enjoyed sitting up high and the top of the curtained wardrobe seemed an inviting spot. She had occasionally jumped up there before and, close to the ceiling, liked to look down on me from her superior height. She had not as yet discovered that the caravan roof sloped gently to allow rain to run off, so the space between wardrobe and ceiling was much less at the far end. That evening she sat on a chair-back gazing up, ready for an easy jump on top. The first sign I had of her problem was a frantic scrabbling, then a muffled yeowl. Flo had her head stuck in the tiny gap with the rest of her flailing into space; her neck was stretching longer every minute. Something had to give, and it did – the flimsy top was not intended to take her weight. She fell, ricocheted off the floor and jumped back out of the window . . . which I had shut a few moments earlier! Poor Flo. It took much coaxing and cajoling to persuade her from behind the bookcase where Micky the stuffed badger was a cat's only friend.

At nightfall I took out the soaked terrier meal with a ruffled tabby shadow following on behind. Under the beeches I left both and walked at the side of the rustling corn. The badger cubs were playing on the huge spoil heap of the Brushwood Sett; it made a wonderful hill down which to roll. Harry went first: tucking his head with those ridiculously tufty ears between his front legs and grasping his wiry tail with his teeth, he bounced down like an animated football amidst a cloud of dust. Then came the little sows, jostling to be next, whilst Harry galloped up the bank for another go.

I decided this field was sown with wheat, but there were also many barley 'volunteers' that had sprouted after a previous harvest and a great many patches (some of them metres across) of wild or false oats. It was rather a messy field really. All three cubs had played in the field, but fortunately it was the wild oats growing profusely below the spoil heap that were flattened. The wheat beyond was upright and untouched, which relieved me for I didn't want Mr Legget to have an excuse to complain about the badgers. Now the boar had appeared, so abandoning their game the three youngsters played chase around him. Then the light-coloured cub tucked under his body and hid there; her sister saw and tried to chase her out. Next Harry began to worry his foster-father's tail. The adult sows who had been foraging in the wood turned up to see what all the commotion was about and Harry went too far. He head-butted the dominant sow who boxed his ears for his cheek, and a rather subdued cub was put in his place.

Now the mothers returned to their searching under the trees. There came the sounds of claws tearing above us. Oaks had been planted at regular intervals generations ago at the very edge of Ninepenny Wood, as boundary markers. Now old and gnarled, the big tree nearest the Holly Tree Sett was often climbed by the badgers, for two metres up was a gap where once a branch had broken off; this gave access to a hollow cavity where lurked such delicacies as mice and beetles.

In moments, all the badgers except Harry, who had vanished, were in the tree. The sows had discovered a bees' nest and were quarrelling over the contents. It was still dark and the bees lethargic. Although some of them must have stung, it didn't deter the sweet-eaters a jot. Pieces of comb and rotting wood dropped on to the ground and the light cub jumped down to retrieve them. She was the smallest, it was crowded up top and her elders were squabbling; she probably gleaned as much as the other four plundered.

Now a shaft of light lay in the eastern sky and all was still. No leaf or blade quivered, no rustle was heard. These are the most precious of moments, neither night nor day, when time itself seems to stand still. Even the badgers were silent, as if awaiting the new morning. Then a lark began singing from within the wheat and, the spell broken, another called from on high. Light slipped slowly over the land, pushing the shades of night back into the wood where they languished till the sun rose. Soon there would be enough light to see colour, but for a while longer I could savour the many tones of the dark. Now a pheasant called his strident challenge and the new day was come. The badgers gone, I looked at the pieces of comb scattered below the old oak where a few bees still crawled amid the ruins of their nest. A few metres away was a wasps' nest beneath a rotting stump that, as yet, the badgers had not found. Did the smell of honey help them to locate the bees I wondered?

At The Sett I saw a huddle of fur in the long grass nearby – Flo and Foxy were mutually grooming. This had practical advantages. The constant heat had encouraged unusually high insect numbers, and harvest mites in particular were assuming plague proportions. The most favoured parts of their hosts are the ears, and they can't be dislodged by a wet paw passing over them. Flo's rasping tongue could keep the young fox's ears free of these parasites and he could tend to hers.

◊ ◊ ◊

It was time to clean the badger reflectors placed at both sides of the busy road leading out of town to the next village. Before the reflectors were installed, several badgers had been killed crossing the road at this spot. They had come from the main sett on the bank that faced away from the traffic. It was one of several on private land owned by a woman with a livery stables. She was very interested in her badgers and had long ago given me permission to go in and watch them or check the setts at any time. These reflectors were made of dimpled steel fixed at badger height on short wooden posts on each grass verge; there were eighteen in all.

Badgers use regular paths which they squat on to and scent-mark at intervals as they pass. Each member of a clan does this scent-marking, which has a two-fold purpose. It warns strange badgers that the territory is already occupied, but more important still, it enables a badger to back-track its way to the home sett under any conditions, be it a mature animal or a youngster out on its own. Through vegetation, these scent paths become well-worn trails that are visible to us. The posts with their life-saving reflectors had been carefully positioned so that light from oncoming vehicles was reflected from one side to the other on to the path of a badger about to cross. Quietly approaching one night, I actually witnessed a sow temporarily dazzled by the lights of an oncoming car. It was only when the vehicle disappeared that she crossed. I have since seen this again with the dominant boar there. The dimpled steel needs regular cleaning and grass and weeds have to be well cut back to prevent them obscuring the reflectors. These reflectors would be of little use where vehicles exceed forty miles an hour, on sharp bends, or between steep banks. Indeed, there has been much speculation as to whether they are even effective under ideal conditions, but I feel these are well worth the cost of their installation and the small effort required to maintain them.

Cleaning the reflectors that morning, I spoke to the grounds-man mending the barbed-wire fence. The stables were broken into frequently. No tack was left there overnight now, but certain things could not be transported back and forth every day. At one time, ducks and chickens had been kept in the adjoining field, but these too had been stolen. The main sett in the bank had been dug by terriermen several times, for once off the road no one could see or hear what was going on through the trees below.

Throughout the drought, water was regularly left in the stable yard within easy access of the badgers who came down to forage on the pickings left by the horses. Any wisps of hay found lying would be carefully gathered up by one young sow in particular, to be carried backwards to the sett. Such bedding is held between chin and forefeet against the chest with the animal shuffling backwards on its front 'elbows' and back legs. It must be by following the scent trail back to home base that such bedding collectors manage to travel with surprising speed and yet avoid obstacles *en route* with amazing accuracy without looking behind them as they go. I enjoyed coming to watch these badgers, and I hoped that their cubs this year would thrive and take the place of past losses. It is true that much of my pleasure lay in the knowledge that the landowner and her family were concerned for their welfare too.

◊ ◊ ◊

At last we had some rain and it became cooler. Sometime after midnight it was cloudy, with a fresh wind disguising any sound as Flo and I slipped through the wire of Ninepenny Wood and walked alongside the ripened wheat. Harry and his foster-mother had dug out two entrances of the Holly Tree Sett and were started on a third. I sat in the contorted ash tree and made myself comfortable with my back against one of its trunks. Badgers are so easy to watch when they are occupied. The tabby purred at Harry as his earthy rump appeared out of a hole, dragging the soil beneath him. She sniffed at the busy back whose owner was too preoccupied to notice. Next moment a shower of sand and small stones engulfed the small figure as the youngster pushed the excavated soil on to the spoil heap with one or two hefty kicks of his hind legs. Poor Flo, he never even saw her, but promptly went below again to dig out some more! She came up in the tree with me, her dignity as ruffled as her fur, and began grooming. Really, these badgers, her humpty figure seemed to say.

The sky was clearing and pale moonlight relected on the glossy leaves of the holly at my side. A passing fox paused briefly at the mounds of fresh earth and went on its silent way. The badgers were still below ground. The sound of digging would come clear on the quiet air, then silence before the bomp-bomping of earth dragged backwards along the tunnels. Now the boar came and watched, grunting and whickering for their attention. He solicited a game from Harry, not that by now the young boar needed much persuading, and the sow was left to finish by herself. Harry was growing too large to run in and out of his foster-father's legs, but chase and hang-on-to-your-tail seemed popular with both. Game over, the boar was grooming the cub's ears and neck when a very muddy Mum appeared and he groomed her. One by one they disappeared into the field. Their trails to and from the sett entrances were very clear through the ground ivy and grass. I left Flo, who seemed interested in a rustling higher up in the tree, and went in search of the badgers. Rounding the curve of trees, I stopped to watch, for there was the whole family ahead. The cubs were pulling off the heads of wheat and biting out the ripe grain. The adults were far more proficient. They reared up on hind legs and, bending the stems down, ran the ears through their teeth. Most of the ripe grain dropped into their mouths, though a little was foraged for afterwards on the ground.

Badgers tend to forage within very small areas of corn, concentrating on a few square metres rather than covering an entire field. Only in severe drought conditions do they take unripe grain. They will glean dropped grain after a harvest for as long as it is there. Modern harvest methods can be very wasteful and where a combine has overfilled the lorry or temporarily missed it, large piles of grain may become regular feeding grounds for rats, birds and badgers alike.

The cubs were interested in the piles of wild oats that, the day before, the women had pulled up, folded over and left at the side of the field. This is a regular occupation in these parts just before the harvest. The cubs tried extracting the grain from these wild oats, and in fact did so, but the seeds are far smaller than the cultivated variety and are easily lost.

It had been a good night. At dawn I sat in the shade of the beeches of Ninepenny Wood and wrote my notes. The turtle-dove still crooned, but the cuckoo had flown away. To my right amongst the dappled dog's mercury were two stinkhorns with their attendant flies. Most of this fungi's dark gel had already been eaten so the flies were concentrating on the few spots left. A wren and a great tit called, gnats danced in a sunbeam that shafted through the moving canopy far above as I continued to write.

That same day, I walked out with Flo again and was concerned to find a man's bootprints on the fresh soil of both the Holly Tree and Brushwood Setts. No damage had been done, no humans or their vehicles were in sight, neither were there dog prints anywhere. However, this so concerned me that I returned several times to check all was well. In so doing, I met one of the farmer's men standing smoking by the holly tree. He said Legget was very annoyed at the damage the badgers had done to the field; they were a f—— nuisance. Yes, it was his bootprints I had seen earlier. I pointed out that the main flattening had been to the wild oats, which had saved them having to be pulled out, and the wheat damage was to a very small area.

Two miles away was a golf course in the grounds of what had once been Caldwell Manor, recorded in the Domesday survey. Bordering the well-trimmed turf were three woodlands. The land sloped gently down to the stately home with its lake dammed from the waters of the meandering Bourne, which wound its way through the valley. It had been a deer park and though the high fences had long since disappeared along with the deer, the fallow and their fawns occasionally glimpsed at The Sett were descendants of the escapees. Once badgers too had flourished, digging their homes below the fastness of the mighty oaks and venturing out beneath their shelter to forage. On damp, mild nights, the golf course, site of the ancient parkland, was their favoured place, for here the earthworms were most easily caught as they rose to the surface at night to feed.

Diggers had steadily removed most of the badgers and the 1987 hurricane, casting down some of the massive oaks, had destroyed setts and their occupants with part of the woodland. Since then, cubs had been born and family numbers would slowly increase if the persecution could be arrested, but the whole area was huge and difficult to patrol. A club house was situated near the entrance gate, but no other building over-looked these hundreds of acres, no roads passed through them and the whole expanse was surrounded by farmland.

One curious badger home was dug into an artificial mound called Summerhouse Knole, created in the heyday of landscape gardeners, follies and gazebos. The summerhouse had gra-dually disappeared. Nettles, elder and that pretty umbellifer *Conopodium majus*, or pignut, had taken over. From the top of the knole grew two Scots pines which, rising out of the smooth turf, were a distinctive feature of the place. It had become the main sett for the Caldwell badgers who at dusk would steal out on to the golf course for a night's foraging. In the annals of badger history such idylls rarely last – man sees to that. Now lights were seen at night; a courting couple reported dogs hysterically barking and snarling. Sometimes the evidence was left, like the young sow's body that was covered in dog bites and thrown into the wood. Only part of her head remained. This was exceptional, however; normally there was nothing to suggest anything was wrong. Odd tufts of badger hair, perhaps, lying on the smooth turf, or dog's fur – but badgers do fight each other (though generally only when overcrowded) and people walked their dogs here and dogs will fight. Of the lampers themselves, their dogs or even their parked vehicles, nothing was ever seen.

None the less, Caldwell was a wonderland and the golf course had helped to preserve it. The three woods were all quite distinctive, one containing the ancient pollarded oaks, another mainly chestnut coppice and the third, on the edge of the Manor, running down to a road. It was here I first watched badgers digging for pignuts. *Conopodium majus* is related to the carrot family. It has fine, filigree leaflets and small, white flowers. The root is a thick, brown, nodular tuber that pigs were once trained to smell and snuffle out for human consumption, rather like truffles. Badgers love these pignuts too. With their acute sense of smell and long digging claws, they will soon fill themselves on these delicacies.

Now the nettle-leaved bellflowers, enchanter's nightshade, traveller's joy, wild marjoram and St John's wort were all in flower and the flat-sided berries of the wayfaring trees had changed colour. Taking photos by the Holly Tree Sett, I noticed someone had left a small bundle of grass outside his front door. Harry and his foster-mother had been collecting bedding well into the dawn, till a certain young badger grew tired of housework. On the far field, the straw was already baled and stacked in groups of eight waiting to be towed away. All was turned to gold in the strong sunlight: stubble, straw and something else. One of the distant piles wasn't quite flat-topped. Camera in hand I crossed the open ground keeping bales between myself and the stack I was stalking. Yes, I thought as much – Foxy, Vicky and a small tabby were lying outstretched worshipping the sun. It was the vixen who sensed me first and, speaking softly, I turned and walked away without my picture. It seemed a shame to disturb them.

That night a beautiful orange crescent hung heavy in the velvet sky. The old boar was climbing a tree, digging his long front claws deeply into the fissured bark. He quickly reached the first branch on to which he scrambled, then padded out carefully along the limb, stopping here and there to pick up something. At times it would be crunched, a beetle perhaps, and at others merely chewed and swallowed. Occasionally a rasping sound would disturb the quietness of the night. Slugs travel up trees in the cool hours of darkness to feed on lichens growing there. Badgers are good climbers and can tackle sheep fencing and dry stone walls with ease.

Tasselled chestnut catkins littered the paths with the remains of the geans' cherries. Both foxes and badgers enjoyed the blackberries and the yellow and red cherry plums from the old trees in the walled garden. These plums were small and very sweet, no wonder they enjoyed them. Flo looked on very puzzled. She sniffed at one, then sat down regarding the others stuffing themselves. Badgers are noisy eaters, slurping, chomping and burping with gusto. I picked Flo up and cradled the small body in my arms as we watched. I could feel the vibration of her purring. She turned her head to look full into my face. The two foxes ate a few metres away from the badger clan, who might have chased them off if the drupes had been scarce, but there were so many plums that the grass was littered with them. A breeze gently pushed the branches and sent more to the animals below. Sounds of eating hid the soft wind and the distant motorway traffic. The cat gave a sudden miaow, but only one head looked up briefly. Was she saying, 'Pass along the trough'? If so, I agreed!

It was the last night of July and already the acorns were falling though they were very small and green. Their stems had dried and withered because of the drought. The beech mast was ripe though and the squirrels were taking it. There was a good supply of plump hazelnuts which Harry and his foster-mother were eating. The cub tended merely to crunch them up, but experience had taught the adult differently. She took one in her mouth, bit and dropped the small cob; then nosed about and ate something in the grass. When both had gone, I searched and found many neat halves of shell lying there with the kernels missing. This seemed a remarkable achievement for such a large-jawed mammal, so I was not at all surprised by what I witnessed some time later.

Several magnificent walnut trees grew in the ponies' meadow, their bold masses of foliage thickly punctuated with the green, fleshy husks containing the unripe, soft-shelled nuts. Rooks, crows and squirrels were eating these and leaving many more on the ground for the badgers to find the following night. Later in the year, the remaining husks split naturally and the walnuts, encased now in tough woody shells, drop to the ground. These too, were easily split open by the badgers' bite and, like the cobnuts, the neat halves left in the grass. The tasty kernels were savoured with noisy enthusiasm, which had to be heard to be believed.

◊ ◊ ◊

It was after the harvest and well into August when I came face to face with lampers on Mr Legget's land. The older man dazzled me with his light, but not before I recognised one of his companions. This lamper had skinned a fox alive for a £20 bet. He had been guilty of no legal offence since foxes, like most animals in the wild, are not protected. It shows the nature of the man, however, who sees nothing wrong in such an action but, rather, boasts of his 'skill'. These men and their lurchers had caught rabbits that night so were merely 'trespassing in pursuit of game'. I ignored their threats, secretly relieved for the badgers who were still foraging in the old garden well out of sight. Yet it left me disquieted; what was happening at Caldwell and further afield? I let the rural constable know and he promised to alert the other officers.

There were days when the temperature touched 32°C and the nights were so hot that no dew formed. A badger cub was found dying under a half-full cattle trough it had been too weak to reach. Somehow that symbolised this hottest summer of the century with its prolonged drought. Most of the dehydrated badgers I was called to were cubs and usually they were too far gone to save. How many died in their setts or hidden above ground there was no way of telling.

All the food I left by the water bowl for the Ninepenny badgers was regularly taken and I noticed their dung contained insect chitin too. The only field not yet harvested was that facing their two setts. When eventually it was, I discovered the wheels of a heavy vehicle – probably the grain hopper or a tractor, had passed over the spoil heap of the Brushwood Sett so as to completely obliterate the lower entrance and a greater part of the heap. I walked all round the field before dark that evening, but in no other place had anything similar occurred. This could not have been an accident: Legget was trying to make the badgers move. Approaching the small outliner sett by the motorway where the old boar denned, I startled a family of grey patridge from the stretch of Japanese knotweed nearby. Till the last field was cut they had sheltered within the wheat, so this was home now to the adults and their three youngsters. Fortunately badgers are slow animals, or their new-found shelter might have been shortlived.

One evening I left food and water early in Ninepenny Wood and discovered the three cubs had forestalled me. They moved away whilst I cleaned the bowl and replenished it, but jostled one another to be first when I tipped the food nearby; badgers always eat as if each meal is their last. Now I saw the light-coloured cub in good light and saw she was erythristic, although not red or sandy, but a deep creamy colour and her facial stripes were more brindled than pure bands. She was very unusual. The father had mated with his daughter owing to the shortage of badgers here and interbreeding is more likely to produce unusual colouration. By now I had known several generations of this family, but this was the first strangely coloured one. Watching them eating reminded me of the words of a boarding-school caretaker a few miles away. He was feeding the badgers living in his grounds and these did well on the children's leftovers. Recently the kitchens had turned out a quantity of individual Christmas puddings, which he left with the other food and fresh water near the sett. The cubs found them first and gathering as many of the curranty cannonballs as they could under their bodies, growlingly threatened their elders as they approached. Fortunately, the adults were not very interested, merely eating the other food before going on their way and leaving the youngsters to feast on their find.

Having eaten all they could that evening, my little sows began teasing Harry who needed no encouragement. One tweak of his ear and they were chasing in a close circle, snout to tail amongst the limp green of the dog's mercury and dead leaves. Too fast for the eye to follow clearly, the group swirled over the dead log and into the far undergrowth, then suddenly they were back again, just as Harry's adopted mother appeared. She backed on to and musked each of the young badgers in turn, before eating some of the remaining food and swaying into the open field with the youngsters scrambling after.

That was the night the tawny owlets practised flying from a branch near their nest hole. I had heard the two wing-flapping to strengthen their muscles a few nights earlier, but this was a great moment. Their squat shapes and round, fluffy heads were grotesque imitations of the graceful birds they were to be. Anxiously, the first fully opened its wings, talons gripping hard the branch beneath. Instinct told it to launch into space; fear held it tight to the limb. Wings moved in a frenzy that lifted the owlet, but its claws refused to release their grip. Many times it repeated the lift-off, only to remain glued to its branch, when something shot past, hovered a moment and flapped uncertainly to the ground. Its sibling had made the descent and, unhurt, was exploring a great new world. Encouraged, the first tried again, and this time released its hold. It also stopped flapping and executed the best gliding first flight I've ever been privileged to watch. Two dumpy figures flat-footedly padded about amongst the beech mast that littered the ground. They came to the drinking bowl now half full. How often must they have watched bird and beast drinking and washing here? One tipped a beak and spluttered – the other grasped the smooth porcelain edge owl-like first with its beak, then with its claws. For a moment it swayed, then belly-flopped in, soaking both. If the first drink wasn't a success, the bath was. They shuffled around like two solemn dancers, big feet plonking and big heads bobbing. Another attempt at drinking was now impossible – no water left! Owlets might lack beauty, but these two certainly had appeal.

Something glided by, a drifting phantom above my head; in its curved beak danged the long tail and rounded body of a mouse. The parent landed in a flurry of activity; its fledglings falling over in their haste to be out of the bowl and first to the meal. Glad that I hadn't been too close to her offspring for her to attack me, I stood in the shadows watching the departure and return of both adult tawnies as they fed the hungry pair.

◊ ◊ ◊

The farm managers who worked the land surrounding Ashcroft Woods were putting out food and water for the badgers there, so the cubs would survive. Now one was on holiday and I could pick the plums from his garden and take water from there. On my way, I also collected damsons that were growing in the hedgerows. A few more weeks and these, together with apples and pears, would begin to fall and life would be easier for the badgers. Crisp, my special sow, came purring to greet me, then backed on to my shoes to scent them thoroughly with the musk gland beneath her tail. However infrequently we might meet now, I was not forgotten. She made no attempt to eat the moistened terrier meal mixed with scraps, nor the fruit, but sat on my lap as we watched her three little cubs take their fill. She could no longer suckle them for her milk was quite dried up, and though she might roam far in search of food, they had not her stamina. Last time I was here the smallest, a boar, had repeatedly nuzzled whimpering under his mother in vain and I wondered if he would survive until the autumn, that season of fruitfulness. I knew she regurgitated food she had foraged for them, but there must be limits to her doing this and remaining healthy herself. My Crisp was four years old now and this was her first litter. That night she and I sat watching together, my arms round her rough fur, my head against hers. She was a good mother and wonderfully protective towards her young. When another adult approached the food her cubs were eating, she growled a throaty warning and it hastily backed off. Only when they had eaten their fill did she relax her guard. The few healthy cubs I had seen that year were all abnormally small like these, but provided they could forage well in the autumn to put on fat for the winter they would survive. Now it was the adults' turn to eat. It was good to watch their big, moist snouts pass over as everything down to the smallest morsel was vacuumed up.

It was long past dawn when I returned across Legget's land, and checking the setts I had a surprise. The Ninepenny sow with her two cubs had turned out bedding on to the spoil heap and amongst it were many feathers from the hens killed by the dobermans at the Big House. These feathers were so distinctive – one hen had been black with tiny zig-zags of colour, the other a pretty golden brown. Badgers undoubtedly do carry back food to their cubs, although this is not usual. I also picked up five partridge feathers amongst them. Birds were moulting and growing new feathers. A combination of trying to get airborne and a badger creeping up in the barley could easily have been a partridge's downfall. I ran my hands through the soft feathers; there were so many on the spoil heap, some half hidden in the sandy soil, some in large clusters. It seemed wisest to return with a black binliner and collect all the feathers I could find. In times of prolonged drought, badgers have been known to take free-range chickens till the rain comes, when the killing will cease. I knew the dobermans had killed these hens, but the farmer seeing the feather-strewn soil could be forgiven for thinking the badgers had made the kill.

I went out to check the Ashcroft badgers one night and was also eager to see the lunar eclipse. I have seen partial eclipses before, but never a total one and I hoped it would be visible in the clear sky. It was, and an experience I will never forget. The usual full moon was visible until 2.20 a.m., when a dark 'bite' appeared on the top left-hand section of the curve. Gradually, as I crossed Legget's fields, this dark portion crept deeper. I walked through the tunnel under the motorway and so out past the field of cleared oilseed rape until the track turned and ran parallel with the traffic. Now I was walking with my back to the moon and at regular intervals would turn and raise the binoculars to stare. There was delight and awe in seeing the mysterious beauty of the lunar eclipse that has enthralled man through the centuries. What surprised me was that up to the previous evening, scientists hadn't known whether it was to be a total eclipse or not.

I stood till 2.55 a.m., when three-quarters of the moon's reflected light was obscured, though I could still, through the binoculars, see the outline of the full moon as a background. Sensing something was behind me and with binoculars still raised, I turned round and looked along the track – nothing. I happened to look directly down and there was a very cross-looking boar badger staring straight at me in horror! He was very large and his eyes were old and rheumy. This was well beyond the territory of the Ninepenny badgers. I think he was probably trotting along nose to ground at peace with his world and minding his own business when whoops, he nearly walked into the back of my legs. The wind was blowing from him to me and though he stretched up straight with his left paw off the ground (what lovely, long dark fur he had on his chest) he couldn't scent me. Brockie turned and trotted back the way he had come and I squatted down to train the binoculars on his receding back. However, it didn't recede very far before he turned and had second thoughts. I made the low 'mmmmmm' sound through closed lips and he came trotting back. I could almost hear him tut-tutting to himself; he wasn't a bit frightened, just somewhat put out! He hesitated on facing me and then, gathering speed, went round. Slowly I turned, still squatting, to see him travelling at his old pace along the track. He turned a moment as if to say 'What, is it still there? It'd better not be when I come back!' and continued on his way.

I took the lane through the harvested barley fields till I reached the warehouses at the motorway junction. There is a police parking space there for observing the traffic. I passed a stationary patrol car and could see that its two occupants were watching the eclipse too. By now there was only the lower edge of the moon visible with its light almost squeezed into a solitary ray that went across the sky. On impulse, I offered them my binoculars, but the nearest man produced a fabulous pair, far superior to my own, and invited me to try them, which I did.

By the time I neared Ashcroft Woods the eclipse was total and stayed so until 4.25 a.m. The moon was still visible although the night was now dark. It had a peculiarly hard, solid look and was a pink, creamy colour. All the badgers except Crisp, the sow with cubs, were on the nearest irrigated fields. I walked the length of the woods for the pleasure of it. The dusty paths were strewn with sweet chestnut catkins, which made a soft carpet underfoot. Out on the meadow above the main sett, I saw three little cubs busily foraging over the heavily dewy field. Their mother was digging out amongst the elmbrush of the bank. I watched her shaggy, grey rump and smiled to myself. Altogether, it had been a good badger night.

Walking home I saw the earth's shade continue over the moon, revealing the sun's reflected light from above. The same top left-hand edge was being disclosed again. The moon set and disappeared before it was completely clear. A wonderful experience and, as the 6 o'clock news stated, it was the clearest sky for many years, making the eclipse freely visible.

Chapter Three

THE entrance of the Brushwood Sett, broken and crushed during the harvest, was soon re-opened by the sow and her cubs. Towards the end of August, masses of bedding were spread out to air in the noon-day sun, quite the largest amount of bedding material I had seen for a long time, with grass, ivy, leaves and bracken amongst it. I strolled over to the boar's sett by the motorway to find all was well and quietly returned. Within Ninepenny Wood there was a movement under the holly tree and I saw some of the bedding had been taken down again in my absence. Then first Harry's head appeared as he stretched out, gathering the grass and bracken below his chin and against his chest, and silently backed down again holding it. A few moments later and his foster-mother was doing the same. So intent were both on their freshly aired bedding, that neither noticed me standing quietly to one side.

Their dung was dotted with elderberry and blackberry seeds as well as damson stones. The weather might be dry again and the earth turned to dust, but this fruit compensated. I was still leaving out water under the beeches and by The Sett. It was a joy to watch the three little cubs playing in the stubble. They would sometimes be joined by the adults – and Flo – and all would have a silly half hour in and out of the trees of Ninepenny Wood. The bowl was often turned upside down and bomped about, and was even used as a dung pit! I wondered which badger was responsible for ill-treating my bowl in this way – it had to be an adult because of the weight. Fortunately, its surface was slippery, so it couldn't be carried off.

Earlier that year an artificial sett had been made near the empty lake. Apart from the farmland, most of the earth was chalk, thinly covered with soil. The Tank Sett, as it was called, had three curving tunnels cut out of the solid chalk leading to a single, large bedding chamber. Badgers are conservative creatures and apart from exploring its tunnels, had largely ignored it. Now Harry and his two little girlfriends found it, and from that moment made it their own. This was a healthy sign; the cubs were confident enough to wish for some independence, though if frightened would undoubtedly hurry back home to Mum. I left a large pile of hay by the lake and for once the cubs spent more time working than playing. Harry's foster-mother came to investigate, but she seemed to be getting in the way of all the activity and went away. I felt rather sorry for her.

Acorns, the last of the blackberries and many windfall apples littered the ground, though the pears were poor and shrivelled. There were many slugs and larvae to be found so there was plenty for badgers to eat. They and the foxes still came to drink in the wood. The farmland was ploughed, which gave both a chance to find insects and grubs in the up-turned earth. Many leaves had withered and fallen early owing to the drought and crackled underfoot; it was difficult to walk silently beneath the trees. The path that wound its way to the Sett was lined with wild cherries, whose red leaves glowed in their dying glory.

Now it was September and the start of the hunting season. Life in the badger world seemed suddenly to have gone mad. A phone call came one Sunday to say a sett had been attacked by badger-diggers. The crowning-down holes had been made with shovels and a fork. This last I had heard of, but not come across myself. Obviously when the earth is very hard, shovels might have difficulty tearing through soil and tree roots, although some have a serrated edge to cope with this. I met the landowner, a farmer, and together we joined the police at the site. They had already found a crowbar hastily pushed under some bushes by the terriermen when they were disturbed. We split up and checked each entrance hole of this large main sett, as sometimes tools or nets are pushed well into them to be recovered later. It was an officer who made the find, though not of equipment, but of the body of a sow cub horribly mutilated. So at least one badger had died that day.

I returned to The Sett as the phone rang again; this time a badger discovered in a wire snare. I took the reinforced carrying cage and a grasper and met the patrol car in the lane. These were the city police and from an area unknown to me. We drove to a piece of waste ground near a railway. The snare was fixed in a gap in the wire fence and probably intended for a fox. There were badger and fox hairs caught on the barbed wire and doubtless, rabbits passed along this well-used trail too. It is not an offence to set a free-running snare for rabbit or fox, though it is to use a self-locking or stop snare. In theory, the free-running snare tightens only as long as the victim struggles; when it rests from its exertions, the tension eases as the wire slackens. A stop snare has a metal angle that prevents the tension from easing, so is considered inhumane and is therefore illegal. In practice, most free-running snares do not relax their tension when the exhausted animal ceases to struggle, for by then it is well embedded in the fur and skin. Simple snares can be home-made and more elaborate ones bought from sporting shops and catalogues. These latter often have the ability to self-lock as the sporting man has only to alter the angle of the metal fastener.

The law requires that those putting down snares shall check them at least once every day. Such a requirement cannot be enforced, however, and, as many rotting carcasses bear witness, it is often totally ignored. It *is* an offence to snare badgers, deer or domestic animals, but snares, of course, are blind and do not differentiate between species.

The snare that morning was a commercially made one of several strands of thick wire twisted together. The metal angle hadn't been altered to make it self-locking, but it was embedded deep in the badger's belly none the less. An indication of its agony was the deep circle of earth it had clawed up around it in its efforts to rid itself of its torture. Now it lay at the bottom of the pit, well below the level of the surrounding ground. She was scarcely recognisable as a badger, let alone a sow, for the dirt had

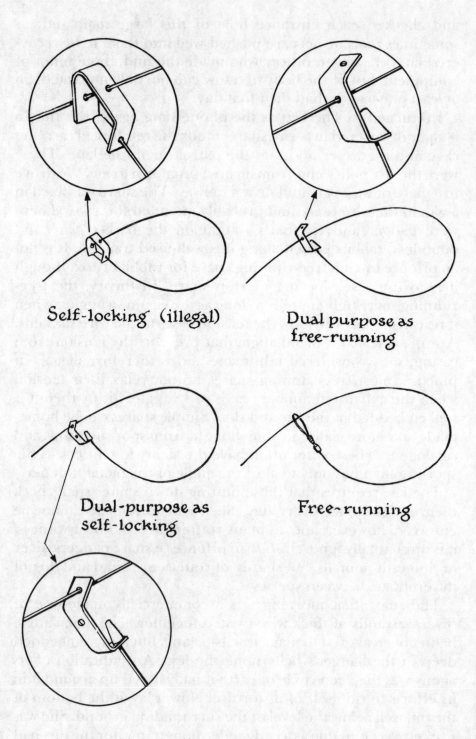

Self-locking (illegal)

Dual purpose as
free-running

Dual-purpose as
self-locking

Free-running

dried on her blood-soaked body. At least Death was merciful and had reached her before us.

This wasn't the first time these police had encountered snares that summer, and in each case those responsible had not had the permission of the landowner. As one officer commented, 'We caught a fellow the other week taking a fox out of a snare and he claimed he was controlling vermin. When the farmer turned up and said he didn't allow any snaring on his land, the poacher still protested that he was doing the other a favour and we nearly had to separate them!' The price of fox fur has dropped in recent years, but it is still a worthwhile trade and 'vermin control' is as good an excuse, if caught, as any. The price a farmer can pay may be heavy too. One poacher, snaring in a hedge, caught and severed the tongue of a browsing cow. Bovines take herbage into their mouths by curling their long tongues around it, so this Friesian, a valuable milker, had to be destroyed.

In my locality, snaring has occurred in parks, at the back of gardens, and on school playing fields and although the intended victims were probably foxes or rabbits, it is often dogs and cats that fall victim. Poachers frequently refer to the latter when caught in their snares as 'feral' cats. One farmer I know who lost a favourite cat in this way commented bitterly, if ever he caught a feral poacher snaring on *his* land, he would enjoy practising a bit of vermin control on him!

The evening sun was low in the sky when I returned, and I slept for a while before the phone rang again. A badger had been spotted by a passing motorist as it struggled on a bank, apparently caught in a snare. Complete with cage and grasper, I again met a patrol car in the lane. This turned out not to be a snare, but wire bundled together and thrown up on to the bank of a wood. I caught the badger with the grasper – a hollow, metal tube a metre long with a plastic-covered cord running through it and forming a noose at one end. Graspers were first made for the RSPCA to catch dangerous dogs and enable the animal to be held firmly at arm's length. They are not ideal for badgers, who tend to tuck head between front legs when fearing attack. An adult brockie has massive shoulders with muscles developed through digging that can take a fair amount of punishment. Many an inexperienced terrier has gone for those shoulders, only to find the badger's head suddenly whip out and teeth fasten on the attacker's face. This night's badger, however, was not on the defensive. He was large and cross and throughout the entire operation told us deafeningly what he thought of humans and their throwaways! The wire was well and truly tight around his stomach and hind quarters with one end caught amongst the brambles. This last probably saved the boar a long and agonising death – for no way could the wire have worked free. He insisted on struggling and trying to turn his head to get at me, but with the grasper held steady by one of my companions and my forehead pressed into his back to stop him bucking, he could only vent his anger vocally on the two policemen standing in front. I would never have succeeded without their help. With the last of the wire untangled, I stood back as the noose was slackened and lifted off. The badger never hesitated to shake himself or turn around but charged, still bellowing, at the men standing there. One fell over, but was up again and running with the other almost before he touched the ground. Horrified, I was left to pick up cage and grasper as the sounds of the pursuit receded into the distance. It seemed a long wait by the patrol car wondering if they would find their way back in the dark, although it must have seemed longer to them!

◊ ◊ ◊

Woodpigeon are undoubtedly agricultural pests, as anyone watching them on farmland must be aware. Shooting them is popular and I am told they make fine eating, which is as good a reason as any for having a dog to retrieve those you may maim. The men Mr Legget sent on to his land to shoot woodpigeon, merely parked their van and car on the footpath, draped them with camouflage netting and shot from there into each flock of woodpigeon that settled. Some were within range of their shotguns, though most were not. A few were shot outright and many received the odd piece of shot. Then the men would drive on further, park again and repeat the performance. They had no dogs.

Legget wasn't popular, but villagers are practical people and this was a normal autumn occurrence. I had known the farmer slightly for many years, but was a relative newcomer to this area and had sound badger reasons for not wishing to fall foul of him. For the next fortnight spent chasing and killing wood-pigeons with trailing wings, a leg blasted away or holes shot into their sides, I privately cursed the man for his lack of humanity, but kept, as they say, a low profile. Not so the people of the village, however, who that autumn decided they had had enough.

Steve came one day to tell me that the RSPCA had received complaints from people who had found maimed pigeons crawling on roofs, in gutters and in gardens after the latest shoot-up. 'As you are friendly with Legget . . . ' continued unsuspecting Steve, and for once I forgot myself and told him exactly what I thought of the man. The RSPCA Inspector was in an awkward position because the farmer wasn't condoning anything illegal – it is not an offence to cruelly ill-treat pigeons as they are pests, though birds not classed as such have good protection in law. A man from one of the farm cottages had showed him a living pigeon with a gaping hole in the back of its head, but understandably had asked not to be named. I had a suggestion. At first sight of the shooters, I had spoken to a PC I knew and confirmed that the men were committing two criminal offences: carrying an unbroken, loaded shotgun in a public place (public footpath) and shooting from the same. I was also aware from reading BASC publications, that the British Association for Shooting and Conservation wouldn't have approved of what occurred on Legget's land. Legget and his son were keen shooting men themselves and probably belonged to this association. Might not Steve go to see the farmer, point out people were upset at the number of crippled birds (I had found eleven myself in and around Ninepenny Wood), and mention the criminal offences and the ethics of 'clean' shooting. Some people, it transpired, had already contacted the local press, so he could mention this to the farmer too. Steve also had another complaint to make to Legget: a small badger sett farther over on land he rented had been found to have many spent fresh shotgun cases stuffed into its main entrance completely filling the hole; how many had dropped below it was impossible to say. The farmer agreed to be more circumspect in future. This was Steve's first meeting with Legget – 'Seems an educated, decent enough sort of a chap' was his comment. I merely grunted – time would tell!

◊ ◊ ◊

My resident tawnies found a short-eared owl in their territory. One evening the male tawny was calling from my roof – deep in a telephone conversation a few feet below him, I was at first more concerned with what the caller at the other end was saying, and the competition was considerable. Once I put the phone down, there came a different sound – a triple hoot that wasn't the answering tawny. An owl with long wings soared and wheeled over the scrubby trees before uttering a harsh, barking note and flying away. Each time a tawny called, the short-eared owl would answer. It was a less bulky bird than the tawnies, its underwings and wingtips had dark patches and its yellow eyes were a contrast to the deep brown of the resident birds. Short-eared owls also hunt by day and for perhaps a week I watched its effortless, buoyant flight above the ponies' meadow hoping it would stay, but in vain.

The cream-coloured sow cub was beautiful, and now that the youngsters were settled in the Tank Sett, she often came round to my sett to investigate and meet Flo. It was rather a case of 'Are you coming out tonight?' The unlikely couple seemed to enjoy ignoring the bigger cubs, especially if Harry's games proved rough. A small striped feline with long upright tail, side by side with the pale rounded brockie under the moon. Watching them go off one night down the winding path a name came to mind, and Moomin she remained.

The two adult sows came to live with their offspring – I could almost hear the cubs groan! It was the largest sett in their whole area now and the single bedding chamber was very spacious. Before it was covered with earth, I had half-filled the tank with hay and the youngsters had carried in more. So, after some initial disagreements, all five settled in. The businessman had always intended to have the lake bed puddled with clay to waterproof it and then filled to make a long shallow flight-pond for geese, but now he was gone that dream would remain just a dream. However, the margins of the place, occasionally cut, but mainly kept short by grazing rabbits, were ideal worming pasture on damp nights. The badgers had only to emerge from their home and they were on to the inviting turf. The Tank Sett's one drawback was that it couldn't be dug by the animals themselves – the tunnels couldn't be extended, or more made, as the whole area was solid chalk going down several metres. The instinct to dig is very great, their claws will grow long and eventually turn under if not used, and this desire is particularly strong in the autumn when they prepare their winter homes. Would the badgers stay there? They would be safer in this place, for no human could dig manually through such chalk either, but of course the animals themselves couldn't know this.

Geese and swans were much in my mind now. There was a great joy and wonder in being out and alone at night this time of year. All was still, all was quiet. Just myself and the land – a sense of belonging, of unity; a feeling of oneness and peace. Then faintly would come a mere suggestion of sound; from which direction, impossible to judge. As I turned my head trying to decide, the sound would become a beating of wings. It might be a V-formation of white-fronted geese, their flight punctuated with cries not unlike a beagle pack. Often great flocks of Canada geese passed overhead, and one unforgettable night I heard the higher-pitched whistling wing beats of whooper swans. Sometimes majestic mute swans came on deep, throbbing wings, their phantom shapes crossing the face of the moon giving them an illusion of immortality; but sadly swans proved the most mortal of all. Why some should plunge to their deaths on the wet lane wasn't immediately obvious, until I was told they had poor eyesight. They had passed the meandering Bourne, still dry from the summer's drought, and it seems likely that the shining tarmac at night was mistaken for its water.

It was moonlight when I stood watching the badgers foraging by the empty lake. The scene had a fairy-tale quality – a wide expanse of short turf through which a multitude of the fungus *Coprinus comatus* had pushed its way. The stately ranks of long, white woolly caps well deserve their country name of lawyer's wigs. Harry was in playful mood and head-butted his foster-father. The boar merely looked at him hard, then continued his search for earthworms. Harry then tried the same with the sow cubs, but they growled and ran off to forage a short distance away. Standing idly by the hawthorns and listening to the tawnies, I suddenly received a painful blow to my shinbone – Harry was trying it on me. He was as bad as the Ashcroft cubs – no respect! I made the contact sound, but he wanted a game not

49

a fuss and went over to worry at the lawyer's wigs. When these toadstools first appear, they are edible and tasty, but soon the white gills become pink, then black, and rapid liquefaction affects the entire cap, which continuously drips black liquid containing thousands of minute spores. This liquid was once used as writing ink. The stain takes some time to wear off, as the Ashcroft cubs found when they lost their handsome white faces after nosing about amongst this fungus. That night Harry became somewhat ink-stained too.

Now Harry came up whenever he caught sight of me. I would squat down and make the contact sound as we touched snouts! By now – mid-October – he had grown into a very handsome young boar. His foster-mother didn't seem to mistrust me anymore, probably because he was older and nearly independent. Now came a period of gale-force winds and heavy rain. The Sett stood up to the 90-mile-per-hour gusts, as much due to its positioning as to its construction. The badgers foraged beneath the sheltering trees; their diet was almost exclusively of earthworms. The weather remained mild in spite of the high winds and each sett was being cleaned and renovated in preparation for the winter. Walking round checking the setts by day, I would sometimes meet villagers walking their dogs and though I never mentioned the badgers, most of them would tell me these were occupied setts which they too kept an eye on. Occasionally, Mr Legget drove by in his landrover or, more recently, on an ATC or auto terrain cycle – so useful and popular for driving over rough ground. I first met his son on the ATC with his shaggy black dog gamely running behind. It had just been delivered and Paul was trying it out. I had to admit, I trusted the lad far more than his father.

Gale-force winds and torrential rain were whipping the last leaves from the trees. We needed water badly for the level was low county-wide. Everywhere the spindle berries were bright splashes of pink against the darkening sky. This dainty tree, scarce more than a shrub, embodies all that I treasure most in our countryside. Yet it is common, has insignificant white flowers and for most of the year grows unnoticed in our woods and hedgerows. Once autumn comes it declares itself. The slender pointed leaves change to a pink that deepens until they drop. It is only then that its four-lobed green capsules begin to ripen from pink to vivid coral. Each lobe opens to reveal an orange seed and the slender branches are transformed. Man has reason to be grateful to this small tree. All through the ages, until the invention of the spinning wheel, spindles were made from its dense, white wood – spindles that drew the loose wool into thread. Today we still use spindle wood to make fine quality artists' charcoal, but like our countryside in general, the spindle tree is taken for granted. The best things in life we use unthinkingly, only appreciating what we had when it is gone.

Mrs Ellis, the woman from the Big House, contacted me. Bruno, her year-old doberman, was causing problems and she was very distraught. Two of her dogs lived indoors, but Bruno and his mother were kept in the courtyard. They slept in an extension of her house originally intended as stables and at present empty, apart from some bales of straw. These dogs were never walked and, in boredom, Bruno had recently chewed his way through to her laundry room. Now, in spite of repairs and reinforcements to the wall, he had done so again. To crown everything, he had chewed a pair of her son's expensive new designer-labelled jeans.

She didn't mention what we both knew. Until recently, she had allowed her four dobermans complete freedom, merely opening the front door and letting them go. To do this with one guard dog is irresponsible; to do so with four is criminal, but I could scarcely tell her so. My stay at The Sett and care for the animals on her ex-husband's land was dependent on her goodwill. I also felt sorry for her. She was wealthy, lonely, bored and very unhappy. Complaints were made as the dobermans roamed the village and nearby allotments; all except young Bruno had bitten people and other dogs. Without catching the dog in question, however, it was impossible to prove who was the owner. It was understandable that no villager was anxious to do so and risk being badly mauled. At present she was keeping the dogs in until the latest furore blew over.

I noticed that she had little genuine affection for her dogs, though she professed to be an animal lover. If one came up to her, as dogs do, for a fuss or to be stroked, she merely pushed it away. If it persisted, she shouted so that it slunk off. In her husband's day there had been two dobermans for security. He enjoyed their company and liked to walk them when he wasn't away on business. Then his wife had taken in a doberman bitch that had badly bitten its owner's child. This bitch had duly mated with one of the Ellis's dogs. Looking at Mrs Ellis now, I remembered her confiding to me how she intended to keep all eight puppies from that mating! Fortunately, common sense prevailed and only Bruno remained with his mother. Now Mr Ellis was gone and there were four dobermans. It would, of course, have been more practical to have installed a good burglar alarm and perhaps keep one dog, but you can't organise other people's lives.

I suggested she walk Bruno. She had a new large car and there were several woods and pleasant places not too far distant where he could be exercised. It was also a way of getting to know other dog-walkers and making friends. There were local dog-training classes; why not take him to these? It was in vain – the interest wasn't there. It was a tragedy for the young dog; he was more sinned against than sinning. I offered to walk him myself, though not often for I hadn't the time. Bruno was large, strong and unused to a lead or walks, so he might be hard to control, though like all the dogs he knew me well. We would have to see, but it might encourage his owner to take an active interest.

I was shocked to find that he was terribly nervous. At first I trained him in the grounds, but at the slightest reproof in my voice he cringed and cowered. He hated being parted from his mother too, for he ran everywhere with her. The quiet lane leading to the footpath was a torment, with each person, bike or car to be feared. It took great perseverance and, above all, patient kindness to persuade him to walk quietly to heel, but we battled on together for some weeks and eventually got there. His owner showed not the slightest interest, however, and after a while I had to cease the dog-walking for I hadn't her spare time. I was sorry though. True, her dogs were her problem, but I had a sneaking suspicion they might become mine.

◊ ◊ ◊

Flo always accompanied me whenever I left The Sett. Most mornings would find me taking fresh water to clean and replenish the bowls. If I walked across the meadow to the village or out to the farmland by day or night, the neat, striped figure would suddenly shoot past and up the nearest tree. If my hands were full, I would merely call her a greeting and she would pad up to my side purring hers. If they weren't and my way was woodwards, I might pick her up and carry her, still purring, along the poplar row. Flo loved this; it gave her extra height and a clearer view. Her rounded, furry head, stuck owl-like on an equally rounded body, suddenly grew a long neck that turned this way and that, intently. Was that a squirrel or weasel, high up in a beech? What was the greyish bird up to, creeping headfirst down that oak? We always parted at the end of the wood or meadow. It seemed to be accepted that beyond was out of bounds. If I left via Ninepenny Wood, I would return through it and at whatever time of day or night, the same small figure would be waiting – perhaps at the water bowl or else darting ahead of me. I'm sure she didn't spend the interval waiting; rather, she had a happy knack of predicting my return. Independent, yet friendly, this little character, companion of Harry, Moomin and Vicky, became very dear to me.

I sometimes walked the footpath to Caldwell at night. It came out at the first wood with the ancient oak pollards. By day with the sun slanting through their branches it was an awesome place, but at night it had a different mystical quality. These pollards were part of an ancient form of wood management, rarely practised today. A young, broadleaved tree was cut off at about six to ten feet from the ground. By the following year, it would send up fresh shoots that in time formed a bushy crown. (The word pollard comes from the Norman-French *poll*, meaning head.) In time these shoots grew to thick trunks themselves, well out of the way of browsing stock or deer. Then the tree was repollarded and the valuable crop carted away. This practice thickened the original trunk and prolonged the life of the tree indefinitely. It continued up to the First World War, which altered so many things, but probably the greatest enemies of woodland management were the advent of plastic and, more recently, the import of much cheaper woodpulp from countries such as Poland. No one knows whether an ancient pollard that has remained uncut for many years can be safely repollarded, so most have been left. Ancient pollards are as much a part of our heritage as ancient monuments, and looking at Caldwell's oaks that night I would say more important. But then I am biased.

The Caldwell oaks were of enormous girth, their trunks

twisted into bizarre shapes. Contorted and knotted with age and covered in lichens, several had ferns and other plants growing from the gnarled bark. One spectacular oak even had a young oak growing from its bushy crown.

It was a mild, damp, windy night with a crescent moon struggling behind moving clouds. I wandered out on to the golf course and for a time stood watching a fallow doe browsing the rough. It was taking fungi too, though I couldn't have said what kind.

The badgers were also foraging well out on the fairway for the inevitable worms. Their short, squat figures were dotted about at a good distance from each other. The nearest was slowly moving my way. The wind blowing his fur backwards was also blowing in my face. His scent was coming to me had I the ability to smell it, but more important, mine was blowing away from him. I sat, chin on knees, with great pleasure. A worm fed on the surface, with its tail end anchored in its burrow. It lengthened, finely stretched to reach the next piece of decaying leaf, as the badger grasped it by the head. He didn't pull as his victim tried desperately to retract – rather, he moved forward giving a little, so that the worm relaxed its hold on terra firma. A sucking sound, two quick chews and it was on its last journey. There was another busy worm by my boot. The boar moved softly nearer.

At that moment a bright light appeared near the farthest badger. Something ran along the beam, tall and rangy like a greyhound and as fleet of foot. Another light came from our left and more lurchers. I had forgotten *my* badger till it blundered into me in its haste. Its fear was a cloud of musk I could almost taste. There came a great cry that lingered, borne on the wind – men's voices and dogs' snarling. All the badgers seemed to have gained the safety of the nearest wood or their sett in Summerhouse Knole – except the one that didn't get away. There was no phone or dwelling for at least two miles and no way to bring the police to intercept them. Only a ruse that had worked once before, years ago near Ashcroft Woods. I ran down towards the little group shouting, 'Get the police John, quick, quick and I'll try to keep them here.' For precious moments they stood, turned to stone by my noisy, unexpected appearance. One long, lean dog with an alsatian's head forgot its sport and turned on me, as did another. Then amongst the shouts and confusion,

Terry terrapin exploring.

A spoil heap from a sett entrance beneath tree roots, and a trail through bluebells.

Iffy in the recovery cage.

Harry.

The spoil heap of the Holly Tree Sett, with the hollow oak to the right.

Any snare can inflict
appalling agony.
(Copyright: League
against Cruel Sports)

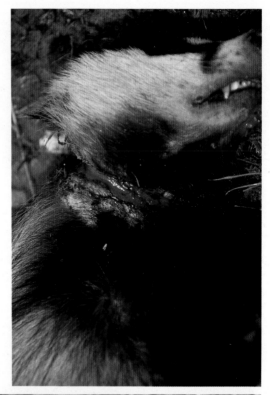

Wilfrid the Wimp!

bless the god of all brockies, this badger melted away into the night. Threats and abuse followed, but one lamper, more nervous than the rest, urged his friends to get out of it quick to the van. I didn't follow, having done that once before and suffered the penalty. But part of me was singing; the badger had got away!

It wasn't until long after, when I returned to The Sett and phoned our local police, when green-eyed Flo jumped on to my lap and sniffed, then licked the bites, that I realised I *had* been bitten. She stared into my face and miaowed. 'It was worth it,' I answered her.

It was returning from sett-mapping in Caldwell Manor one grey, foggy January day nine years earlier, that I first discovered the Sand Pit badgers. As I left the golf course and followed the track to the park gate, the sunken lane continued for half a mile before making a sharp right-hand turn. On each bank were clear animal trails leading to and from a small beech wood, through a stretch of overgrown chestnut coppice. A well-used badger path wound back and forth amongst the coppice till it came unexpectedly to a near-sheer drop. The place had once been dug for sand, but time and nature now hid the scars and badgers had made the pit their own. Majestic beeches with fluted trunks stretching gracefully skywards like cathedral columns, soared from the sandy sides, securing the crumbly earth. A feature of beeches is their exposed root system twisting into the ground; underneath these sentinels the badgers dug out their homes. Generations created these vast spoil heaps that dropped far down into the quarry floor, now covered with holly, hawthorn and young oak. These heaps were much higher than the sett entrances; no wind would whistle down *their* tunnels! Trails through the dead beech leaves linked each hole with its neighbour. Here was an elder, the soft bark torn away by the dominant boar to expose the white wood beneath. At many setts this feature is absent and once it was believed that badgers did this merely to clean their claws. It is generally accepted now that it is a visual marker of the principal boar's dominance and a warning to trespassing boars. He stretches upwards on hind legs to tear downwards with his long front claws. Often he will complete the operation by backing on to and hand-standing up the whitened trunk to leave drops of his musk upon it. Usually only elders are treated in this way and rarely other trees, and it is only the elder that exposes such whitened wood.

Several times, when passing, I knocked at the cottage nearby hoping to find the owner and ask permission to go on the land. No one was ever in. Eventually I asked Graham, the rural policeman, who gave me the name of a farmer I already knew. This man in turn gave me the phone number of another and, at last, I could go on to the land freely. The farmer was only the tenant, however; the land was owned by the county council. Yes, I was welcome to watch the badgers, but if I used a light at night (which I didn't) it would be advisable to let the lady in the cottage know. The badgers came into her garden – she and her husband were very protective and kept an eye on 'their' sett. I found out much later that this couple had unsuccessfully tried to buy the land to protect the badgers. It was good that people were interested in what was one of the largest setts I had seen in this part of the county.

The Ninepenny badgers deserted the Tank Sett and returned to their homes in the wood, not wholly because they could not dig through the solid chalk to extend the sett, though this probably had much to do with it. The deciding factor was the doberman guard dogs who, on finding the sett badger-occupied, spent much of their time running round and round it barking, scratching at its metal-ringed entrances and defecating over the dung pits. Bruno even temporarily had his head stuck in one hole, but this didn't deter him or the other three. There was little I could do. True, the sett had been made for these very badgers, but the businessman and his enthusiasm had gone. Mrs Ellis merely remarked that she liked to see her four dogs running around together enjoying themselves and she was in charge of the land.

Harry and the two young sows took over the Holly Tree Sett and spent much of the night hours renovating their home. The sandy spoil heap grew and grew under the holly tree, spilling out over a wide area and covering the undergrowth. The older sows denned together at the Brushwood Sett, a few metres distant, with the old boar still in his earth by the motorway. All were digging out and extending their homes as if their lives depended on it: the youngsters were like three small JCBs! It was at this time that I saw Moomin near the water bowl in the wood one night and discovered she had vomited a pigeon's foot, complete with claws. I was still occasionally finding those maimed by the shoot and it would seem from this that so were the badgers.

Steve came with some concrete slabs to reinforce the floor of the large badger enclosure. Later we discussed the badger situation and bovine TB in the Republic of Ireland. In Northern Ireland, bovine TB is not considered a problem, but there they enforce strict regulations on cattle hygiene and cattle movements. Over 80 per cent of the human population in the south is agricultural with only 20 per cent urban or industrial. It has a history of bad husbandry, illegal cattle movements and tag-switching. When a bovine is tested and found to be TB positive, it is ear-tagged for identification, then sent to be destroyed. The system of testing is not reliable. Should the beast going for slaughter appear healthy, it is easy to understand why tags are often removed and fixed into the ear of a scrawny but otherwise healthy beast which is sent in its place. A southern bovine changes farm three or four times; there is a huge trade in cattle transportation.

The first bovine TB eradication attempt was made in Ireland between 1954 and 1965, after which the country was declared free. Obviously, they spoke too soon. In 1963, when Irish vets were on strike, there was a movement of live cattle from Ireland to Britain. These cattle went unchecked on the English side. Our vets do now check, but the damage had been done. The first English badger found to have bovine TB was in Gloucestershire in 1971. It is interesting that a deer was also found to have it, although our Ministry of Agriculture, Fisheries and Food (MAFF), took no account of this. MAFF vets decided that to ensure cattle remained healthy, badgers should be eliminated from areas where bovines were found to have the disease: a policy of extermination by cyanide gassing of setts began in August 1975. The Zuckerman Report of 1980 recommended that the efficiency of this gassing should be investigated, and after testing it was discontinued in 1982. The Minister of Agriculture admitted that his department's gassing procedures had been inadequate. Almost certainly many thousands of badgers had died slow and agonising deaths. Cage-trapping has now taken its place. There was no live test for badgers; they had

Poster designed by Martin McGarry for Badgerwatch Ireland

to be killed and a post-mortem carried out. There is a live test now, but its success rate is poor. In 1989, 206 badgers were killed in Gloucestershire alone, with only 37 found to be carrying the disease.

I showed Steve the recent report citing that the disease in deer had now spread to Scottish farmed herds. The fact that only 20 per cent of the Republic of Ireland's badgers carry TB indicates that they must have a very high degree of immunity, since they breathe one another's air and grub about in the soil. It has been proved under artificial conditions that cows can contract TB from badgers, but only after a long period and under unnatural proximity. Such proximity is unlikely in the wild under natural conditions. Undoubtedly the greatest carriers of bovine TB are bovines. The Department of Agriculture in Northern Ireland had just produced the results of a ten-year survey. The report concluded that spread of infection from neighbouring herds (by nose to nose contact) accounted for 70 per cent of all break-downs, and that infection was commonly introduced by pur-chased animals. It also concluded that the presence of a substantial population of infected badgers is not associated with bovine TB in cattle.

Eighteen months earlier, the results of a three-year study in Devon and Cornwall had shown that there was no connection between badger population density and the incidence of TB in cattle. There did, however, appear to be a link between out-breaks of the disease and the population density of cattle. None the less, MAFF seemed content to continue with their familiar pattern of badger extermination in affected areas.

By 1987 the cost of this eradication programme to the tax-payer had reached £7.1 million; we were now in 1989. If only that money – or even some of it – had been channelled instead into research. There are microbacteria in the soil and there are scientific methods to analyse them, but this is expensive. Why is it that some areas have never had the disease and in others it is present and can never be entirely eradicated? In yet other areas the disease had disappeared, apparently of its own accord, which implies it has produced a natural immunity.

Now the Republic of Ireland seemed anxious to repeat our mistakes and was actively considering gassing badgers. This was decided earlier that year, but public opinion had stopped it. As in Britain, their badger is protected, but unlike here, so was its habitat or sett. However, that year had seen badgers snared, shot, poisoned and lamped, and their setts bulldozed or filled with slurry by farmers wishing to rid themselves of what they saw as a threat to their livelihood, while the authorities turned a blind eye.

Fortunately, the Irish badger was not without friends, including the four local groups known nationally as Badgerwatch Ireland and the Irish Wildlife Federation; but its greatest champion was undoubtedly Dr Jim Barry from Cork. For his pains, he has had to suffer the contempt of the wealthy and voracious agri-business interests and farming journalists anxious, on the one hand, to put the blame on the sacrificial badger and, on the other, to silence its leading advocate. He was undoubtedly a thorn in the side of Irish political policy for it was scientific fact that governed his speech.

There was talk of badgers losing their protected status; they could then be classified as vermin – the same status as the rat. There would be nothing to stop everyone digging them out, poisoning, gassing – whatever they chose.

Chapter Four

NOVEMBER ended with dense fog. Small, shrouded ghosts snuffled for rotting apples in the overgrown orchard. A sudden head, raised to listen, showed with startling clarity in the greyness. Slugs and insects eating the soft pulp were eaten in turn by the badgers. Most of these aged trees leant in all directions, their untrained limbs twisting this way and that. The youngsters as well as their elders clambered easily amongst the branches, seeking out slugs feeding on the algae-covered bark and beetles living beneath it. These arboreal badgers – Moomin especially – gave a touch of unreality to this forgotten spot. They left neat, conical snuffle holes in the moss by the old pigsties. It was an eerie place in the heavy mist, the hanging ivy constantly adrip amidst the distorted trees. An eerie place made comic by the sudden sight of a striped face poking out from a sty.

Returning homewards through Ninepenny Wood, its badgers loitered. They sampled the parasol mushrooms and *Boletus edulis* growing beneath the trees, and the old boar caught a mouse as he foraged amongst the burnished beech leaves. It was more by chance, for he was a ponderous animal, but it darted out under his snout. Harry and the young sows stayed long after the others had retired for a well-earned rest. I enjoyed watching them run in and out of the trees. It had to be Harry, of course, who found hanging on to the twining stems of traveller's joy such great fun. He reached up, got a good tooth-hold and swung! Flo watched them in disgust and went home. 'These badgers' her stuck-up tail seemed to say. I stayed until they disappeared into their sett and then I returned to change into dry clothes.

It was good that I had taken photos of the setts in the area I covered before everywhere had disappeared in the fog's clouded grip. It was something I did seasonally with occupied setts. Then if terriermen should be caught digging one out there was visual proof it was occupied before the incident occurred.

The 1st December I was away. It had been a day of particularly thick, freezing fog. I went out with Flo about 11 p.m. and soon found the old boar. We watched a tawny watching us from his perch on a beech. His feathers were glistening with moisture from the clinging mist. We were probably spoiling his hunting, so cat and I stole away. The mist muffled his quavering call that followed us back along the poplar row, the tree-tops cut off in the greyness.

The following night I again went out and saw the same badger snuffling for grubs in the ponies' meadow. Where were the rest of his clan? I searched all the Ellis's land, then moved out to the fields. By now it was well into the Sunday morning. It seemed strange, for young badgers are more likely to be above ground than adults these cold, misty nights. In March 1987, I had found a sow dead in a snare on Mr Legget's land, but it was difficult to credit this could have occurred to five animals! It was so quiet; even the motorway noise was muted. Sometime before first light I came round to the far end of Ninepenny Wood to find just a gap and a smouldering fire where the Brushwood Sett had been. Because of the fog, I came on it quite suddenly and for a moment thought I had lost my sense of direction, so alien did it seem. The bank with its heavy cover of brushwood lying across, the great sandy spoil heap dropping down to the field edge were gone. It was impossible to take in the nightmare. The dull, glowing fire seemed to mock. A sudden thought jerked me alert. The cubs under the holly? That too, was as if it had never been. The tall holly tree with its long, hanging greenery and bright berries and the sett beneath were no more. Only the raw, bare earth compacted under a caterpillar tread, the marks showing clear. Numbly, I followed them round, a scattering of red berries lining the trail, and realised that the holly and undergrowth must have been piled up on what remained of the Brushwood Sett after the same machine had flattened it and the whole thing fired. Holly's waxed leaves burn intensely; for a brief time it must have been like a towering inferno. Then the thought that a badger might still be alive galvanised me into action. By now it was 7 a.m.

At The Sett, I phoned the police. Graham, our rural constable, was the only one who knew exactly where the setts were. They would leave him a message to phone me at 10 a.m. when he came on duty. I explained that badgers might still be alive, so I would try and dig them out. We all knew it was an offence to dig for a badger and technically I was breaking the 1973 Badgers Act. It does contain a 'humane' clause, but that doesn't cover digging or every badger-digger would swear in court that he had seen an injured animal go to earth and was digging it out to take to a vet. Indeed, stranger tales have been told! The police couldn't give me permission, but by saying what I was going to do I was clearing myself. I also phoned Steve, who I knew was due to take part in some surveillance with other RSPCA inspectors that morning. He would come when he could.

Then I took the pointed shovel (left at the site of a dig years ago), and returned to the scene. Everywhere looked so different; where should I start? The mist seemed worse out on the fields as I stood by the still-glowing fire, then slowly walked the ground. No sound at all where the cubs had denned, but there seemed to be a faint bomp-bomping some distance away from the fire embers and slightly into the field itself. Kneeling down, I laid my ear to the ground – yes, there it came again. I dug straight down and found the ground below the surface was hard and dry. It was not far, however, before the shovel's pointed end broke through to a cavity. It was a dead end, or rather a sleeping-chamber with bedding and one, yes two panting, sweat-covered figures. It appeared that the sows had crawled as far away as possible from the crushed entrance of their sett and the fire made on top of it. I scruffed the first head I saw and dragged the badger up with the bedding, then leaned in and grasped the other (Harry's foster-mother); her neck and head were slimy with excreta and saliva and she was very distressed.

After a few moments, the first sow scrambled to her feet and disappeared slowly across field into the mist. I tried removing some of the muck from the remaining sow who, by now, had staggered to her feet. At first she seemed too dazed to heed what I was doing, then she twisted away from me and finally snapped at my hand. I released her and watched her wander into the wood. Twice she stumbled into a tree, obviously lacking co-ordination after her ordeal. Then she too disappeared into the mist.

I stood for a long time where the Holly Tree Sett had been, then knelt and put my ear to the compacted earth. There was no sound at all, though I did this every few paces and made the contact sounds I used to make to Harry. Nothing. I tried digging down with the shovel, but the ground was so crushed by the machine (a tractor-shovel parked a short distance away at the far side of the wood) that I could make little impression on it, in spite of the shovel's pointed end. Unless I opened up a badger tunnel, no way could I get to the youngsters crushed or suffocating below.

The rural constable phoned just after 10 a.m. and straight away came to inspect the destruction. I took photos of the area and one of the officer standing by the crowning-down hole, complete with the dragged out bedding, I had made to rescue the two sows. Some time later, Steve came with another Inspector. They noticed two disused entrances at the side of the destroyed Holly Tree Sett and suggested the three cubs might have exited from these. We saw a man at the tractor-shovel who told Steve that the machine had broken down and he had been called to repair it, but he knew nothing of what had occurred. The only part of the wood that was cleared was that which the Holly Tree Sett had occupied; the only part of the ground outside that was cleared was the bank that had contained the Brushwood Sett. If it hadn't broken down, would the tractor-shovel have been trundled away? How coincidental that this had happened during a period of thick mist, when villagers walking their dogs would not have seen it. Before the RSPCA Inspectors left, I said I would check that night to see how the rescued sows were and also try to find their cubs. However, when I later went back, knelt down and really examined the disused entrances, it was obvious from their choked and cluttered state that no animal the size of a badger had passed through them. Both these holes were beneath the tree, so I couldn't dig back from them to trace the tunnelling.

In their weakened state, the sows would have been incapable of foraging long for themselves. Indeed, it was 1a.m. the following morning before they came to take the dog food I had left by the water bowl the previous evening. Such a bitterly cold night. Both seemed very poorly and unkempt – a sure sign of a badger in bad health; they are normally so meticulously well-groomed. Harry's foster-mother still had signs of excreta round her head and neck. The sows ate for a while then moved slowly away in the Tank Sett direction. I didn't try to follow for I was concerned they might hear me on the deeply frosted grass, which made a crunching noise underfoot. The boar stayed to finish the left-overs.

For two hours I walked the entire territory of this little badger family, but found no trace of Harry and the young sows. In my heart I knew they were dead. Hard to put into words the numbness I felt; the place seemed so empty. Never to see them again. At last the fog had lifted over the fields that seemed to stretch to infinity. Rows of regimented barley stood in neat white formation – promise of the harvest to come. At least Legget wouldn't be bothered with three badgers in his barley next year. The thought came to me that it was just as well he didn't know I had rescued the two sows. He would think he had wiped out the entire family – accidentally, of course.

I spent most of that winter afternoon till dusk, digging where the compacted earth was workable in what had been the Holly Tree Sett area and slowly made four crowning-down holes. Again, the earth below was dry and hard. I thought I struck a tunnel on the last attempt, but it had caved in so that I couldn't follow along it with the shovel as I had intended. I left the holes open with a pile of excavated earth next to each. Mist was closing in with the darkness as I trudged back to find Steve had arrived. We sat and talked over mugs of hot coffee – could the RSPCA get permission from Legget to dig for the bodies? It was highly unlikely as it would prove he had killed them. No one had witnessed my rescue of the sows. I hadn't taken photos and hadn't waited for someone to witness it. In truth, that was the last thing that had been in my mind, but of course in court there would only be my word for what had happened. Steve, like myself, was disheartened by the tragedy. We had both been so proud of young Harry and pleased his acceptance into the badger family here was so successful. Why had we bothered? The Ellis's land seemed such a secure haven when I was first invited to use The Sett and Legget seemed reasonable enough, for all my instinctive distrust. It was Steve who remarked wryly 'You always doubted that man, didn't you Chris?' And the badgers had suffered. Perhaps one should heed one's intuition.

That evening I again put out dog food and by 11.30 p.m. the three adults were eating it. No sign of the cubs. It was a much milder night; they would certainly have been there if still alive. Much later I walked through Ninepenny Wood and found the two sows already there on the site of the Sett where their cubs were buried. Harry's foster-mother was frantically digging inside one of my crowning-down holes. Every so often she would scramble out and wander over the raw earth, snout to ground, whining. Like this she bumped into her sister who was also trying to dig down a short distance away. The two stopped short staring, one groomed the other's face briefly, before continuing their hopeless task. They well knew where their offspring lay entombed, but it was all much too late.

Before leaving for Ashcroft Woods that morning (I had promised to help its warden that day), I walked round to the area to infill my holes. One of the sows had made a dung pit and defecated in the earth I had excavated.

It seemed best to infill the holes, for though I had permission to be on Legget's land day or night, digging holes (even in good causes) is rather different. I left a large flint on the site of each hole, however, in case the RSPCA should get approval to dig. The crowning-down hole I had made when rescuing the sows I left open of course, as both had gone in and out that night and one could in fact, be denning there. These badgers had lost four of their setts now to human demolition in the last two years; they were becoming very short of homes.

I had promised to phone the rural constable at 9 a.m. sharp that morning, so nearly at Ashcroft Woods I knocked at the farm manager's door and asked if I might do so from there. When Graham had come that fateful morning, I had asked him to request that the farmer did nothing further to the wood, not to burn any more at the fire site and to leave the hole open at the Brushwood Sett. Now Legget had contacted him with a view to continuing clearing the wood. The policeman had to give a reason for these requests, so told him I had rescued the two sows who were still denning there. He also told him of the three missing cubs in the wood. This took me aback enormously, for one of the golden rules one always follows is to never volunteer information when an offence, or possible offence, has been committed. Whilst I well appreciated why Graham had done this, there was nothing legally to stop Legget digging up the bodies and disposing of them. I suspected he had hoped to simply demolish the setts and take away the tractor-shovel under cover of the fog with no one, for a time at least, being any the wiser. He had no idea how regularly I checked the setts or how well I knew their occupants. But I had found out soon enough to rescue two of the badgers and *actually knew there were three still missing*! This must have shaken Legget considerably. Now obviously the story would be that he was in the process of clearing his wood, but the machine breaking down had stopped him going any further.

Then Graham dropped a bombshell. 'When Legget contacted me, he was talking of suing you for trespass. He also gave me the impression he might ask the police to do so. If he does, I shall tell him that trespass is a civil offence and nothing to do with us. I'm sorry; I seem to have put you in it, but I thought I had better warn you.' It's strange. Up to that moment I had been very depressed and sad at losing Harry and his two little girlfriends, but suddenly I was furious . . . and pleased. Let Legget try to make out I was trespassing; let him sue me. Nothing would please me more. But, boy, wouldn't he give himself some bad publicity. For the moment, thoughts rushed through my mind of how we could alert the local newspapers. What a marvellous way of showing the public that badger setts were not protected, what an ass the law was! I had photos of Harry as a small cub, Harry climbing up my leg, Harry . . . On mature reflection, however, I suspected that Legget would have second thoughts. He was not a stupid man and must realise that by taking me to court he would play right into our hands and expose himself not only as a destroyer of occupied badger setts, but as vindictive and vengeful as well.

The farm manager's wife gave me a welcome coffee and we stood discussing Legget. They were not only angry on the badger's behalf, but his behaviour reflected badly on farmers generally. This couple had a sett belonging to the Ashcroft clan on their land, which they faithfully watched over. Earlier that year, the husband and I had accosted men with two terriers down it. The breed was brindle whippet crossed with pit bull! They protested they had merely been ferreting. The ferret was lost and the dogs had been sent in to find it. Did I mention before that strange stories are told? But you only need one man like Legget to give the whole farming community a bad name.

I met Ray, the warden of Ashcroft Woods, and together we set about making a brushwood fence between Briarmead Lane and the trees, where lads with motorbikes had pushed through to rough ride round the woods. This ancient woodland was a Site of Special Scientific Interest (SSSI) and a protected place; such activities damaged the flora and the paths and made the badgers vacate when done over the steep slope of their sett. Ray chain-sawed two storm-felled ash trees, whilst I took the toppings and started on the fence. It would also protect a huge clump of grey iris growing nearby. The sun came out and who should drive by up the lane but a farmer who once helped me enormously here with the woods, its badgers and all the problems, long before they had been granted a warden. The farmer had moved many miles away and we hadn't met for over a year. I introduced Ray and we stood talking – of the past and the future. The farmer still rented a field called Little Chantry, which made an enclave of land into Ashcroft Woods. It was poor land and its difficult access had caused it to be left uncropped for several years. It had always been my cherished ambition to make it into a wildflower meadow, and the farmer had promised that one day we would, but like so much in this world the dream hadn't become a reality. Could Ray and I have his permission to do so now? Several species of flora grew there already and it wouldn't need to be grass-sown. It would require cutting twice a year, however, to prevent hawthorn and invasive bramble taking over the area and to give the existing wildflowers sufficient light. Some gale-felled trees lay across it at present, but these could be chain-sawn and moved to the edges, both as a haven for wildlife and as protection against the weather. Little Chantry Field overlooked the valley and was often windswept. The farmer said certainly we could, provided it was done in his name, for this small field was part of his agricultural tenancy. A local man managed the rest of the land for him and he came from time to time to see all was well. This promise of the field shone like a bright star amongst the darkness of Harry's death.

That night I again put out food for the badgers of Ninepenny Wood and watched them eat and drink. The sows looked better, but I would continue to leave them something for a few more nights. They dug about half-heartedly in the vicinity of their cubs' burial place and Harry's foster-mother again made a dung pit there and used it, close to one of my infilled holes. In good light next morning I returned to photograph it as Steve had suggested and noted that the small flint markers were still in place.

Gradually the tractor-shovel that was clearing Legget's part of Ninepenny Wood had been getting closer to the Ellis's boundary and now I could hear it constantly as I worked at The Sett. That afternoon at about 1.30 p.m. I stood watching the men through my binoculars from the cover of the trees, looking diagonally across the field. The farmer appeared in his landrover and work stopped whilst the men stood talking. Then the tractor-shovel went back into the part containing the destroyed Holly Tree Sett. It was driven straight in and remained stationary as it worked – it seemed to be digging. Time went by with occasional stops. The farmer's landrover was driven off in the direction of the farmyard and returned soon after. The driver of the tractor-shovel got down and walked over to Legget and they stood talking. Then the farmer drove off leaving the other to make good the ground he had dug. I walked back to The Sett very thoughtfully.

The man left at dusk with a fire brightly burning in the cleared part of the wood. The moment he had gone, I ran downfield to see what had been going on. The flint markers and the badger dungpit had all disappeared, and looking carefully I could see the area of the Holly Tree Sett had been re-covered completely. Undoubtedly the dead badgers had been taken. When Steve returned from a busy day of call-outs, I phoned to tell him what had happened. It would be a waste of time trying to get permission to dig for dead badgers now. Mind you, I suspect Legget would have given it! Yesterday, Ray had suggested using a root fork on a JCB to lift anything like a body carefully out of the earth. It was too late to think of that now.

The three surviving badgers returned to wander under the remaining trees of the cleared wood and snuffle in the bare, raw earth. They made no further attempt to dig out the destroyed sett, or to go into the crowning-down hole I had made to rescue the sows the previous Sunday morning. It all seemed so very sad.

That Thursday morning the men arrived before 8 a.m. and continued to clear the wood. I could hear the sharp cracking as trees were uprooted and fell. There were two large fires now and birds (including two pairs of partridge) flew up into the Ellis's part of the wood, out of the way. Later I walked past the Big House and surprised the grey heron fishing in the pond. He wasn't unduly bothered, however, but rose with slow wingbeats to the conifer nearby till I walked a little down the drive, then flew back and commenced fishing once more.

That last evening of the clearance, the woodman didn't finish till it was well dark at 4.45 p.m. and I again walked out to see what had been done. The embers of a fire were glowing on top of what had been the Brushwood Sett and the hole from which the sows were rescued had gone. Someone had filled that in too, but it no longer mattered for the badgers were not there, but denning with the boar at the sett by the motorway. The requests of the police and RSPCA to leave certain things as they were had been completely disregarded. However, it was all far to late now. I stood in the desolate wood grieving as the near-full moon rose high in the sky. Only 5.30 p.m., but how quickly night comes in winter; soon it would be the shortest day.

Steve was keen for the RSPCA to make a court case of the sett destruction here. This could only be brought under the 'cruelly ill-treating' clause in the 1973 Badgers Act. In the past, his organisation had brought cases under this clause when active setts had been deliberately slurried, gassed, poisoned or destroyed, knowing they were unlikely to be successful, but using them to highlight the inadequacy of the law. Under the Protection of Animals Act 1911 the badger may not be baited, and the Badgers Act 1973 states: 'If any person wilfully kills, injures or takes, or attempts to kill, injure or take any badger, he shall be guilty of an offence.' There is also the offence 'if any person shall cruelly ill-treat any badger', but for this to be proved in court regarding sett destruction, a dead or injured badger would normally need to be produced as evidence. It has also to be proved that the offence was done knowingly and deliberately to protect anyone accidentally destroying a sett.

Unlike Northern Ireland and the Republic of Ireland, our badgers had no sett protection, partly because we only granted habitat protection to endangered species and partly to safeguard the sport of foxhunting. All that you could not legally do to a badger sett here was to dig for a *badger* in it. You might dig for rabbit, fox, your lost terriers or anything else you care to name, but the onus was upon you to prove beyond reasonable doubt that you were not digging for a badger. This was not difficult for badger-diggers to do if they took a ferret or fox net along with them. A dead fox, conveniently stored in the deep freeze till needed, was also popular. If you were a terrierman working on the instructions of a foxhunt, then that was proof enough that you were not after a badger. Foxhunts regularly put dogs into occupied badger setts when foxes were thought to have bolted into them. Hunts have also destroyed occupied setts when dogs have become trapped inside. A Gloucestershire hunt bulldozed and destroyed a thriving badger sett in search of two dogs their terrierman had entered into it. They weren't looking for badgers, so they were not breaking the law. Foxhunting doesn't control foxes, but it does provide a living for many; it is a thriving industry. Indeed, when any criticism is raised against the sport, a favourite argument in its defence is that it provides numerous people with work. So, of course, does war.

Since the 1973 Badgers Act, there has only been one successful case of cruelly ill-treating and that was quashed on appeal. For this clause to work, it has to be proved that the accused was aware it was an active badger sett and that a badger was actually inside it when the offence was committed. The police have no powers to allow a sett to be excavated without the landowner's permission and no landowner who has just destroyed an active set is going to give it.

◊ ◊ ◊

Early one morning the wind rose to gusts of hurricane force, screaming under the metal roof of The Sett as it tried to carry it away. The large sitting-room window was sucked in and out with great ferocity as if a giant's hand was working it loose. At each gust, Terry terrapin's aquarium on the sideboard moved and jolted as water slopped out. It was too cold for him to survive outside, but he must have felt he was being shipped back to Spain! At the first movement, green-eyed Flo crouched down growling and asked to be let out – cat deserting the sinking ship came to mind! Soon water found its way through the ceiling to drop, drop, drop on the sitting-room floor. At least it wasn't over my office, where books and papers were stacked. Outside, the wind and rain made it difficult to stand upright. Every badger – and a certain cat – was safely below ground. Flo's liking for the badger life came as a surprise. Sometimes she inhabited Harry's old bed, the packing case under my home, now made snug and draughtproof. At others, she frequented the derelict summer-house where pony nuts, hay and straw were stored. This pro-vided a warm bed, with mice and rats as a bonus. Sometimes she graced me with her presence on a wet night or day when I was indoors, but holes in the ground seemed a strange resting place for my feline friend. When the Tank Sett had been briefly badger-occupied, the tabby had taken little interest apart from calling into a tunnel or rubbing chin and face against the entrances' sides. She may have found the cold chalk passage uninviting – who knows? When it was vacant again she disco-vered the partly hay-filled tank chamber and from then on considered it another cat-den. The dobermans running round it and barking didn't bother her. She was dog-wise and knew they couldn't get in. Late-born young rabbits sometimes took refuge a short distance into one of the entrances, but they rarely survived to stay long! This could have cemented her liking for life underground. True, her ancestors denned under tree stumps or amongst rocks, but taking over a set, artificial or badger-made, I had not experienced before. Except on short-cropped turf, her striped coat was ideal camouflage. Sitting under the beeches amongst the dead leaves, I would often not see her till she turned her head my way. Flo's sense of smell might be indifferent, but her vision and hearing were excellent. She was happiest in Ninepenny Wood. Returning from the farmland one afternoon, I heard her call, but couldn't make out from which direction it came. I copied the call to excite her, or I would still have been searching now. Happening to glance up, I caught a movement about three metres above in an old oak pollard. It appeared to be hollow where a limb had broken off and this became another of her dens. She merely ran up it to go in and, more cautiously, walked down, jumping the last metre with ease. Retractile claws are a great asset; so is a striped coat on a shadow-flecked bough. I decided to give Harry's foster-mother a name, so christened her Hattie and her sister Hazel. Cat and sows were often together; Hattie and Flo seemed to have a marked preference for each other's company. She was still apprehensive in the old boar's presence, however, though for his part she didn't appear to exist.

Christmas would soon be with us. The remaining Ninepenny badgers often foraged around my home. It continued wet and windy with very strong gusts and occasional bright periods. I walked round before dawn accompanied by my striped shadow and looked at the place not far from the destroyed Brushwood Sett where the two sows had dug out the previous night. Now the brushwood was gone I renamed it the Poplar Sett, for it was in the gap at the end of these trees and the wood edge. The badgers had dragged much of the storm-washed debris away and opened up a tunnel into the sett. One of the fires was still smoking though the men hadn't been near it for nine days. The tabby poked her head into the new entrance and called. Rather shocked I said 'Flo!' with disapproval in my tone, but she merely sat upright and stared me out. I left her there and continued to Ashcroft Woods, but had barely gone a mile before it began to pour. The forecast had been heavy showers with bright periods, but this particular shower lasted five hours!

That afternoon, Ray had a visit to make, so I picked up rubbish and wardened until he returned. A young man in his twenties came over to me. He and a friend had played as children in Ashcroft Woods and carved their initials and date on one of the trees. His friend later died in a road accident and he had moved away. It seemed so strange to see their initials still there together. I suspect he was normally a reticent man, but his return had opened old scars. 'Do the woods seem smaller?' I asked and he nodded, surprised. 'Things always do when you return to the places of childhood, perhaps because you were a child and smaller yourself. I always feel that the woods will endure long after me and mine are gone and somehow that is a comfort. Something stable in a changing world.' We looked at each other and he smiled. 'Thanks, that's a good thought – I'll go and have another walk round.'

Now it was 3.30 p.m. and becoming dull and cold as the winter sun hung low in the sky. Long tree shadows wandered weakly over the woodland rides and a twittering bevy of long-tailed tits hunted amongst the prickly teasel heads for their last meal before dusk. With that evening came steady rain that continued for several days. We needed it, for the council were making more standpipes for the following year. However much rain we would have between now and spring, it would not be enough.

At 7 p.m. on Christmas Day I heard the owls calling and went out into the night, with Flo following on behind, to stand under their beech tree. Tawnies are marvellous birds; how I wished that my tape-recorder was working. To tape the calls and play them back is an excellent way to encourage these night callers to come closer and investigate. Flo lost interest after a while, so we walked out on to the farmland and along the last furrow at the wood edge. There was movement at the Poplar Sett: the movement of three badgers digging out. One was now far inside the crushed tunnelling, which had been opened up once more, another was at an entrance collecting the earth her sister was dragging up and the boar snuffled and snorted around, awaiting his turn below ground.

I was very uneasy when I saw how much the badgers were opening up the destroyed sett. They had dragged out charred pieces of branch, diesel tins and other metal on to the steadily growing spoil heaps. I could only think these had sunk into the original entrances on the now non-existent bank when the holly tree and other debris were piled on the fire about their home. Hattie had flecks of blood on the white stripes of her face, caused by the piece of barbed wire in the freshly dug out earth. When I picked a piece up and bent it, the burnt wire easily snapped. Mr Legget was scarcely going to be pleased. Before the sett had been bulldozed and then fired, the badgers' entrances had been under the brushwood on the bank and neatly out of the way. These brand new entrances based on my crowning-down hole were some metres into the field, and it would be tempting to 'accidently' crush them with the next piece of heavy farm machinery that happened to pass this way. Now the brockies were greatly enlarging and re-opening the crushed tunnelling and making new passages too. After some thought I told Steve of my worry and he phoned back later to say he had warned the farmer to be careful; that was a relief.

My mail contained a letter from RSPCA headquarters on the sett destruction in Ninepenny Wood. They hadn't been able to contact Mr Ellis regarding his bugging of the Holly Tree Sett some years ago. He was the only person we knew who could confirm that Legget did know of at least this sett's existence; otherwise it would be my word against his. Understandably, perhaps, Mrs Ellis had no desire to be involved, though she had seen her husband and friend put the thick cable in place and jointly received a thank-you letter from the farmer. This letter, which was now in my possession, duly dated, had come about in an unusual way. In gratitude for allowing the sett to be protected, Mr Ellis had sent Legget a copy of my first book, *The Darkness is Light Enough*, without saying he knew the author, merely commenting that he might like to read more about badgers. Legget's reply hadn't mentioned the bugging, however, so in evidence it might not be of use.

◊ ◊ ◊

It is not usual for a young vixen, introduced into an area that already contains a dominant she-fox, to emerge high up in the pecking order. Some zoologists believe that by the time fox cubs appear at the mouth of their dens aged four weeks, their place in the litter hierarchy has already been determined below ground. I have no way of proving this, but certainly some cubs seem to be underdogs and others assertive and 'boss' from a very early age. Cubs are generally only born to the dominant pair, and subdominant vixens in the area may help with the feeding and care of the dominant's family. These subordinate vixens are mostly the daughters of the alpha couple from previous litters. A dearth of young vixens may cause them to disperse to less crowded areas, but often they stay in their home territory, at least for the first two years. If a young dog-fox wants to mate, however, he will have to find an area of his own and be prepared to defend it. Many foxes are killed by traffic in autumn and winter as they wander on unknown ground, searching for a permanent territory.

From her earliest days with me, Vicky had been an assertive fox. As an adult, she now stood half as tall again as any other fox the area contained. Good regular feeding accounted partly for this, but not altogether. I often pondered her history before she arrived at The Sett. Foxy was the reverse, but in her shadow seemed to be accepted by the other vulpines. The two were always near each other now and I suspected Vicky would soon be in oestrous. Would the pair mate or would the dominant dog-fox assert his right to do so? Vixens are receptive for only three weeks of the year and of this period, they can only be fertilised on three or four days. Mid-January would probably be Vicky's fertile time and I resolved to lessen my badgerwatching and try to observe these foxes instead. She had dug out a den under the Japanese knotweed near the motorway, with Foxy taking over the work when she paused to rest. Fox paws, unlike the badgers', aren't well equipped to dig, which is perhaps why they prefer to enlarge rabbit burrows or take over part of a disused badger sett. These two extended the tunnelling so that one hole was hidden amongst the brambles while the other was within the secluded gloom of the tall, crowded knotweed stems. On cold days they denned together for company and on mild, slept above ground in the fox way. Across the fields, they attracted little attention from humans and their dogs and none from the resident foxes.

Now came a time of deep frosts, with the temperature -9°C at night for much of the time and days when it never rose above freezing. Birds appeared larger as they fluffed up against the cold, and the badgers remained below, warm in their bedding collected on mild autumn nights. The foxes often hunted by day, foraging frozen apples and softening walnuts, or high-pouncing on mice and voles in the long meadow grass. The Sett's green exterior stayed ghostily frosted with a delicate tracery of twiggy branches all around. By day the herons came, not to catch fish, but field voles and beetles around my home. Near the wild service tree I picked up heron pellets and found a fresh one with the mummified hindquarters of a field vole protruding. At the time I thought this unusual, but similar remains of voles, rats and water voles are not uncommon. In his article *The Food of Birds* (Trans. Highland Agric. Soc., 1912) L. Florence described how he found a partly digested rat still in the throat of a grey heron that already had a full stomach. This could explain how these dried-out bodies occur.

A fine white pattern of interlacing branches stretched overhead and the dead leaves crunched even beneath a tabby's soft paws. After five bitter days, the sun was melting the night's frost from a young ash tree scarcely taller than myself. As its leaves began to drip moisture in the warmth, each leaflet, complete with stalk, dropped softly to the ground. One moment the stripling was in full leaf – five minutes later it was bare! The cat had deserted me, bored with my inactivity. The sun rose higher on wings of flame and the wood was filled with a steady plop-plopping. Birds drank at the sheltered bowl under the beeches and a daring robin elected to have a bath. I was just thinking that a certain cat would be impatiently awaiting my return to The Sett, when passing the opening by the grassy sided lake I spied a movement ahead. It was Vicky, but what was that in front of her? I stared in surprise. The beautiful young vixen lay in the sun-touched grass, her head raised and looking my way. One tall ear was upright, the other was being thoroughly washed by Flo. Even as I watched, Vicky moved slightly and the cat firmly placed a restraining paw on her shoulder as if saying 'For heaven's sake keep still and let me finish!' The other's attention to me communicated itself to the washer and the cat turned, saw me standing quietly a short way off and came trotting through the short, rabbit-grazed grass. I knelt down and stroked her as she wound herself around me, purring and marking my legs. Then back she returned to Vicky, still lying in the grass, and I left them to their grooming.

◊ ◊ ◊

Steve and his family came on the last day of December and together we went to see what the badgers were doing. The children loved the wood and their father said he sometimes took them to the far larger Ashcroft; there was so much to see and explore there. I wanted Steve to note for himself what the badgers had done, in case any further evil should befall them. The amount of digging out clearly showed they were active and well.

That night I sat finishing the last fieldbook entry of the old
year. 1989 had been a strange time with sad events and happy
ones. Great social changes were taking place in eastern Europe.
The Berlin Wall had come down, and in Romania the people
seemed to have triumphed over oppression, but at a great cost.
We in Britain are fortunate to live where we do.

Chapter Five

AFTER two days' absence, Flo appeared one morning as I was cleaning the water bowls outside The Sett. Accompanying her was Vicky. The tabby jumped lightly in through the door, followed hesitantly by the other. I wandered back and forth indoors tidying up quietly, whilst fox and cat went walkabout. It was as if Flo was showing her companion around. Then the phone rang – it was a call-out to a badger road casualty and I took down the location and name of caller. In the middle of this came a screech and I turned to find three of the dobermans had been let loose and were chasing (I thought) both cat and fox. I saw Vicky streaking up the path towards the poplar row and wasn't too worried, for she was quick, long-legged and light. But oh dear, poor Flo; what had happened to her? She was nowhere to be found, though I looked in all the obvious places inside The Sett and out. Then gathering up the carrying cage and grasper, I locked the caravan door with a heavy heart. I had become very fond of a certain green-eyed cat.

Amongst the dehydrated cubs and adults that had convalesced with me last year, there had been several road-casualty badgers. Normally an injured animal was seen by a vet and if the damage was severe, it would be painlessly destroyed. However, if after treatment it needed somewhere quiet in which to recover and gain health and strength, it came to me. It was important to note exactly where the injured badger had been found and to check the area for a nearby sett. Usually, there was one at no great distance. In theory, the animal should be returned to the place it was found. But leaving a confused badger, who had been confined for some days or even weeks, next to a road could lead to a recurrence of the accident. And there was the danger of returning it to the wrong side of the road, so that it would have to re-cross in order to reach its home.

This morning's casualty seemed to be stunned and was slowly coming round. Aggressive badgers I held by the grasper and placed in the cage. Groggy ones are capable of biting just as hard, but you never quite know what internal damage you are causing, so for these and unconscious brockies, I prefer to don leather mitts and pick them up. This one was a lactating sow, so there were hungry cubs somewhere below ground.

X-rays and a check of chest and heartbeat revealed this casualty to be unharmed, except for a glancing blow to the skull. It would have been ideal to have kept it for a couple of days before release, but the vet and I knew those cubs would already be hungry. He gave her a shot against shock and infection and pronounced her to be strong and sturdy. The lady who had found it drove me to her home, where we left the sow in her darkened cage in the warm kitchen. Then together we went back to look for a sett. There were three near the vicinity: two in a bank on one side of the road, one in a wood on the other. Which one? The big, main sett in the bank seemed most likely, for it showed more activity than the others. Only at this were there signs of fresh digging out and one recently created spoil heap had been heavily musked. The smell hung on the still air. We agreed to return the badger at dusk that evening.

Back at The Sett I opened the door to be greeted by a little tabby who had been hiding inside all this time, and judging by the warmth of the armchair seat she had made herself at home!

At 4.30 p.m. I was met in the drive, and complete with badger we drove along the road where the sow had been found. We parked the car as near the sett as possible and got out to begin the slow trek in the gathering dusk. It was beginning to rain and mist was making the lights of the busy traffic behind us glow murkily through the gloom. We skirted bramble bushes and hawthorn that strove to tear us as we passed with our burden, anxious that she shouldn't be jolted or frightened too much. As the sow moved, her weight altered the balance of the cage and several times she growled ominously. Inwardly we were pleased; it was, after all, a healthy sign. Somehow the darkness, rough ground and trailing undergrowth that seemed intent on tripping the unwary, made us feel like two conspirators, hell-bent on fulfilling a secret mission. Panting but triumphant, we found the chosen sett and put the bucking cage gently down. Whispering to my companion to stand well back, I opened the door. A large moist snout was raised to catch any scent, a pause and the sow was out. Straight as an arrow she padded into the nursery entrance, without a backward glance, a growl or sign of any kind. She seemed completely unaware of us huddled against the chill. A pause and there came a high-pitched trilling from below – Mum had returned to the family. We who had been strangers eight hours ago, silently hugged each other in delight. Really, badgers have a lot to answer for!

It was raining heavily as we found our way back still whispering, then laughing as we realised quietness was unnecessary now. A police car stood by ours and a big, burly figure appeared by its side. We must have seemed like lunatics, two middle-aged and soaking-wet women laughing together, one holding an empty cage, oblivious of their state. 'Oh, it's you,' called the man seated at the wheel. 'Badger business, is it?' We strove to explain about the sow and cubs, then sat in their car as I drew a sketch of the three sett locations. 'We'll keep an eye on these; stopped two terriermen parked where you are the other Sunday morning – early it was, only just light. Didn't know any setts were about here.'

Driving home, we promised to keep in touch. Now she knew of the setts' existence, she would walk her dogs in the area whenever she could. 'I'll make sure they are on leads, though, near the badgers,' she said. 'Especially since you have said how small cubs are often taken accidently by dog-walkers' terriers, whose owners don't even realise what has happened.' This has occurred several times in my experience and usually the sow is unaware, sleeping as she does a short distance away from the nursery chamber. The terrier scents and hears the tiny cubs below and carries the nearest one out, having mortally punctured the hapless creature with its teeth. One cannot blame the dog, for many like Jack Russells have been bred to enter holes. I hope that dog-owners are becoming more aware and caring.

That evening it rained steadily well into the night and I was glad the roof was mended as I worked through my photos of Ashcroft Woods. I rediscovered several beautiful ones taken some years ago and quite forgot why I was doing this in my pleasure. There was an investigation afoot regarding damage caused to active badger setts during tree-felling or coppicing operations, and some before-and-after photos were wanted for the Old Cherry Sett in Ashcroft Woods. Lucy, my unfortunate badger, had been killed there on 9th February 1989. As a result of her death, we had been given Ray, our warden, to care for the woods and its flora and fauna, but the incident had sparked off reports of similar cases where setts had been demolished by heavy vehicles crossing and re-crossing them, especially in wet weather. Lucy may have died, but her death seemed to be helping others of her kind. Flo was bored and showed it by walking over my photos. Clearly it was time we went out!

As we left, there came sounds of quarrelling from the stable yard direction, and moments later the two sows appeared. Quantities of parsnips and turnips had been thrown with other household rubbish on to the huge manure heap there. Badgers seemed to have a particular liking for turnips, so it could have started through this. Yak-yak-yaking loudly, but with no apparent physical contact, the sisters disappeared from view under the hawthorns opposite The Sett, the sound of their discontent fading into the night. Until the arrival of Harry as a cub, his foster-mother Hattie had always been the underdog; now she seemed to have found the confidence to hold her own. Something crept from beneath the caravan and wound itself round my legs. Flo might pick fights with other cats, but she didn't like badger arguments one bit!

That night I observed Vicky and Foxy mating. He had trailed her with increasing obsession for eleven nights, soliciting her with his paws and muzzle, and always she had rebuffed him. Foxes couple like dogs, the male turning to face away from the vixen, and they remain locked in this position for as much as half an hour. Foxes only den below ground when the weather is excessively wet or bitter and when the vixen gives birth and suckles her cubs. The belief that they spend all their sleeping lives below ground is quite untrue, though the idea may have taken hold from their habit of bolting or going to ground when pursued as in foxhunting. Unlike badger sows, vixens do not take in bedding for their expected litter, but give birth on the bare earth of the den. Fox cubs or pups, however, are born covered in short, dark fur. This, together with their mother, who remains for their first few weeks in their nursery chamber, ensures they stay warm as their coats continue to grow denser. The gestation period is fifty-two to fifty-three days, so I would expect Vicky's cubs to be born about 8th March. Now they were always together and twice I saw Foxy offer his vixen food – once a woodpigeon and on the other occasion, part of a rabbit. As she grew heavy with her pregnancy, he increased his offerings until the birth of their cubs. In those early weeks, he would hunt for them both. Unless he was killed, she would remain almost entirely with her offspring, rarely leaving them for long.

◊ ◊ ◊

Tim, the chairman of our badger group, spoke to me of a sudden upsurge in casualties on a stretch of BR line currently under repair. I was surprised when he said that many of the badgers weren't badly injured, but merely suffering cuts and bruising, till I recalled the mobile canteen used on the line at night and the machinery that moves along laying the rails. These both travel very slowly and could easily slightly injure, whereas a train would more likely kill outright. I remembered the Ashcroft badgers' interest in the mobile canteen some years ago – or, rather, the savoury smells coming from it – in spite of the noise made by the workmen. This work was normally done during winter nights when little food is about and I could well imagine brockies *and* foxes appearing in the vicinity.

◊ ◊ ◊

Fluffs of scudding cloud raced in a blue January sky. Bluebell greenery was well advanced, competing with the glossy wild arum leaves. There were catkins on every hand. The hazel's golden ringlets glowed in the sunshine that, from a distance, gave each tree a haloed look. The aspens' long, speckled tassels moved gently in a soft air filled with the busyness of insects. The nights too were mild. Although the badgers here were well used to my presence, I had a desire to watch them unbeknownst, so climbed up into the oak pollard at the end of Legget's wood. A waning moon, orange and heavy, hung in the silken sky. There were little rustlings to my left as a bank vole ran in hurried fashion along the branch towards me, then vanished into a hole scar left from some long-dead limb. A fox barked somewhere across the autumn sown barley and the sows were out from the Poplar Sett below me. How they enjoyed a good scratch when first they came above ground. Stretch your back legs, then your front and turn far around to nibble at your shoulders – ah, that's better! The sows backed on to each other in turn with tail raised to musk each other, then mutually groomed. One went a short distance along the row of stately trees and used a dung pit. Returning, she was met by the old boar who had come across the field from his home by the motorway. With much purring and whickering, they passed beneath my tree and came face to face with Flo, who earlier had followed me out. She was still slightly nervous of the male, but that night they had a good sniff at one another, and thereafter the tabby accepted him as she did the sows. Though the wind was blowing the wrong way, i.e. from me to them, my scent must have wafted far above their heads and I enjoyed the sensation of looking down. From that angle, their foreshortened bodies reminded me that once before, when I first watched this clan, I had climbed this same tree. Then the cat looked up at me and bounded into the oak purring. The badgers looked up too, but myopic as they are, couldn't really see what was making her purr. They snuffled around just below us turning up acorns, grubs and tubers hidden under the dead leaves, whilst Flo rubbed herself round me and walked out on to a branch over their heads.

Now came a wild, wet day with gale-force winds. Great gusts buffeted The Sett, and the trees growing nearby rasped and tore at its walls. The 6 p.m. radio news reported at least twenty deaths in the south with inland winds of 80 mph and 105 mph on the coasts, rivalling the hurricane of October 1987. We in the south-east were not as badly affected as we were in the Great Storm of 1987, though some roads were blocked and motorways temporarily closed.

That night the badgers remained below ground. There were

some trees and branches blown down with much twiggy debris, but nothing really bad. The following night the badgers were out in the company of green-eyed Flo. It was walking round at first light, then about 7 a.m., that I spied the boar badger searching the moss-covered branches of an apple tree, about one and a half metres off the ground. I slipped back to The Sett and returned with my camera to take several pictures in good light when he looked up for a moment from his foraging to listen. Later he scrambled down and I heard him in one of the pigsties nearby. Walking back through the old orchard, I again took some photos – this time of his head poking out of a doorway. Their black and white masks show very clearly even in poor light or mist, though the grey body tends to blend into its surroundings very well.

◊ ◊ ◊

Going through the village one day, I heard a commotion ahead and found one of the Ellis's dobermans attacking a dog on a lead. Another doberman had been driven off and disappeared. A mother and child with their dog had just approached the local shops when the incident occurred. I grasped Bonnie, Bruno's mother, by the collar and heaved her off the other dog – a family pet, and an old one at that, who clearly wasn't used to being attacked by guard dogs. The child's screams abated and I found myself surrounded by angry onlookers who, understandably, thought the doberman was mine. It was an elderly man who came to my rescue. We often met walking to and from Oakley town and the village; he knew full well that I had no dog. I liked the villagers, normally a friendly crowd, and suddenly, everyone present recollected that I always walked on my own. Admittedly I did know the dog, but was reluctant to say who owned it. Meanwhile, Bonnie had twisted out of my grasp and headed for home. That day I privately vowed not to get involved again with any of Mrs Ellis's dogs. It wasn't worth the unpleasantness, and although not bitten this time, I had been bitten in the past. Things were strained between myself and my landlady already because of them. Several times my water had been cut off, only coming on again briefly when her lodger went to feed and water her ponies at the stables. My water and electricity ran from her house to the stables and then to the caravan 250 metres distant. I had no way of turning either off myself, even if I had a pipe leaking. Mrs Ellis professed to know nothing about the loss of water and was acting very strangely.

In a way, I was sorry for her. Months ago I had suggested she join the local badger group and introduced her to several of the other members when we went to a fund-raising barbecue together. Tim had even taken her badgerwatching, and the previous winter I had shown her how to leave food closer and closer to the house in order to watch the Ninepenny badgers. Floodlighting was installed in order that she might sit comfortably indoors to watch them feed – badgers soon become used to artificial lights. I had encouraged her to do voluntary work, which at first she seemed to enjoy, but like everything she undertook, the novelty soon wore off. I recalled my first meeting with her some years ago; though still married, she was bored and unhappy even then. Mrs Ellis confided she had never liked the Big House they had built and regularly took *Country Life* in her quest·for another, more agreeable, property. House hunting and shopping seemed to give her the greatest pleasure. However, money isn't everything and until she came to terms with herself, I doubted that she would ever find true happiness. One of her sons still lived there and her young woman friend lodged with her too, so she wasn't alone. As the house was alarmed now against burglars, four dobermans to guard the place seemed scarcely necessary, especially as she had no interest in them as dogs. I resolved to say nothing about this most recent incident for fear it would trigger off something worse than lack of water. Cowardly perhaps, but we lived at a distance from one another and rarely needed to come into contact – a case of letting sleeping dogs lie!

It was a lovely morning when next I walked to Ashcroft Woods. There I met Ray and together we went to see what the contractors had been doing at The Chantry, the highest point overlooking the valley. For me this had always been a special place. The tall, straight beeches soaring overhead had been planted at the end of the 1700s by Francis Bathurst, a relative of the famous Lord Bathurst of Cirencester Park and friend of Alexander Pope. Francis had lived and died in the great Elizabethan house by the river Bourne, which wound its way through the valley below. My love of these woods had driven me to search

Badgers are good climbers – Hattie in one of the old apple trees.

Not too sure of the camera.

A common accident – a very young badger cub taken from its nursery chamber by a terrier being walked.

Karen drying Splinter the fox cub.

the local, county and national archives to find out more of this lover of trees and landscape architecture, but in vain. No papers, no letters were in his name. Even the tablet to his memory in the church by the river had been erased by his daughter with an inscription to his second wife over it. That surely must have created a scandal in its day, but was now rarely noticed except by a sharp-eyed vicar. Somehow, Francis seems to me to have been a sad and lonely man. Thoughts of him had often been with me when I came here at night and laid my cheek on the bark of one of his trees. Nothing remained of him now but the gracious house with its gardens, and The Chantry with most of its beeches toppled by the Great Storm – 'Man to dust and trees to timber fall.'

It had grieved me to see his trees lying one atop another like a giant's game of Jack Straws. For more than two years beech had sprawled across beech in hideous confusion. No seedling trees could grow to maturity in these conditions, there was not the room. The contractors had cleared The Chantry very carefully under the worst possible conditions – rain and mud. Now the enormous root balls were buried.

There were several bomb craters in Ashcroft Woods left from the Second World War. A nearby farm had the dubious distinction of being the most bombed in Kent. German planes unable to reach their targets in the city had to jettison their bombs before returning home. Craters in built-up areas and on farmland had long since disappeared, whilst those in the woodland remained. In time, trees rooted in the fresh, upturned earth, seeds settled and grew. Few knew or cared why the hollows were there, and two craters the Ashcroft badgers had made their own. The Chantry one had been Old Joe's sett; badger-diggers had taken him from there to be baited. No other badger had stayed there under the beeches for long since his going. The hurricane and its subsequent uprooting had undermined the old sett and one of the contractors working here had suggested they infill the hollow with the remaining root balls and debris and cover it with earth. Should the badgers return and dig out again, they would have a more stable structure for their new home with no fear of it collapsing. This had seemed an excellent idea and now all was completed.

At present the earth was raw except round the remaining

trees where dog's mercury and bluebells flourished. We leaned against such a tree in the bright sunshine and watched a pair of great spotted woodpeckers searching for insects amongst the criss-cross ribs of an old oak's bark. The cleared beeches, Ray told me, would be sold for mining and railway timber, such as pit props and wedges, and any good oaks for gates and fences. We both agreed that in another year, by the spring of 1991, this bare earth would be covered once more with verdant growth. Nature abhors a vacuum – it would not remain bare for long. A brimstone flirted by in the sunshine and I notice a smooth conical snuffle hole – the badgers had been here already. Their thick, rubbery snouts dig down into the earth for a juicy titbit with its owner turning as it does so. Unlike a fox or rabbit scrape, the hole shows no signs of claw marks. Some day a badger would come again to make this place it's own.

Steve came one afternoon and we walked round the setts discussing the deaths of Harry and the others. I had seen the two adult sows mate with the old boar the previous year, but it seemed now this wouldn't result in cubs, probably through the stress of all that had happened. Badgers normally mate soon after they give birth, within a few weeks in fact. They will also mate throughout the year, though birth will only occur in the spring. After mating, the fertilised eggs, known as blastocysts, remain in the uterus and don't implant into the wall of the womb and begin growing, i.e. gestation, until sometime in December. This delayed implantation, as it is called, also occurs in other mammals related to the badger, such as stoats and martens. Gestation in the badger takes two months after implantation and birth occurs between January and March, though February is the most common.

Steve's boss had intimated that a prosecution had been considered, but there was a problem. Mr Ellis had been traced and could be used as a witness, but he had made a statement and then retracted it over another case concerning badgers on his land some time ago. Through his actions, this case had to be dropped, but not before a great deal of time, money and energy had been wasted over it. Thus the solicitor acting for the RSPCA didn't feel the businessman could be relied on to make a statement regarding Mr Legget's permission to bug the Holly Tree Sett. With no independent witness it would be the farmer's word against mine in court and the case would be lost. Never mind; perhaps it was for the best.

◊ ◊ ◊

The following morning was a pleasant one for checking the local badgers, having first cleaned the reflectors and cut back the grass. Although still early in the year, the mildness and frequent rain had encouraged the plant growth to be well advanced. On the lane's verge stretched the rayless, lilac flowers of butterbur. I photographed a glorious patch of winter aconites, each petalled cup on its ruff of green a golden ball opening to the sun. There were many bees in attendance.

By the afternoon, now overcast with a strong wind, I reached my homeward stretch with only the Ninepenny badgers to check. At the Motorway Sett, home to the old boar, I had a shock. Two well-used entrances had been hard-stopped. The top of each hole was broken down with the spade marks clear and the fresh earth trodden hard into each opening. The wind was beginning to dry the moist earth, so it had been done that morning. I looked around. Below me were the recent tracks of a vehicle that had come in from the direction of the distant road. It had parked on the grass verge of the motorway bank near the tunnel, then reversed and returned the same way. There were pawprints in the fresh earth and along the side of the field. Were the terriermen disturbed by horse-riders or dog-walkers on the footpath or farther bridlepath? Or had they merely sussed out the place intending to return tomorrow? Walking back thought-fully to The Sett, I was greeted by my striped shadow. There I phoned the police and asked them to let Graham know. If diggers had returned to my area there was a good chance they were tampering with setts farther afield, so I also warned Tim.

It was a beautiful, round, orange moon that rose slowly in front of my kitchen window that night. Two hours later there should have been an eclipse visible, but heavy clouds soon obscured it. Flo and I walked out in wonderful visibility to meet the three badgers in Ninepenny Wood. The boar seemed unaf-fected by the disturbance at his sett. There were still some chestnuts and acorns to be found in the leaf litter by the foraging animals, as well as walnuts in the lush grass of the meadow. Sows due to cub are busy digging out and taking down fresh bedding now, but neither of these females seemed inclined to do so, though the weather was mild and the ground damp and soft. Flo was very skittish with the sows, especially Harry's foster-mother Hattie.

Now I left the cat at the boundary fence and crossed the fields to Chalkpit Wood near Legget's farmyard. The sett here had been empty of badgers until last spring, when two sows and then a boar appeared. They dug out the old entrances, together with several badger skulls and bones. I knew where these three had come from – the clan living on the land of the livery-stable lady near the reflectors. The overflow of animals from her property was beginning to repopulate some of the surrounding setts, deserted through the activities of terriermen.

There was a movement ahead and a rustling. One of the sows was collecting old, dried grass beneath a crab apple tree. She pulled some out with her long claws and tucked it up with the small amount she already had against her chest, then backed several paces with a bucking action before selecting some more. The ground was littered with tiny yellow apples that rolled about as she snuffled through them. Slowly the bedding increased until a satisfied badger backed along the trail to the sett. So absorbed was she in her work that she quickly passed me quite unaware. The humping noise of her progress died away, leaving me to the soft sounds of the shaw, its branches moving gently in the breeze and the faint call of a tawny, far over the distant fields.

Now she was out again so intent on her task that she bumped into the other sow and swung round on it aggressively. For moments the two stood facing each other, then lost interest as the first continued her work. Now there were sounds of clanking metal coming from the Chalk Pit direction. What creature was moving about on the rubbish dump there? I slipped away carefully, crossing the grassy space to the top of the deep pit and looked down. This place was used as a farm dump, with anything from old cars and bedsteads to unsold produce thrown down. Once Legget had ventured into market gardening and surplus lettuce and vegetables had found their way here too. These, as they rotted, attracted insects, which in turn brought birds, mice, rats and, eventually, a buzzard that hunted and roosted nearby until it was shot. A black and white head moving

below me interrupted my thoughts; there was a badger searching amongst the debris.

Coming to the village one morning, I met a member of the
parish council who asked if I had seen what happened to the
badger setts on Legget's land; had they been empty? I explained
and then was told something that startled me very much. A
member of the local footpaths association had been walking the
path by the Motorway Sett one Sunday morning, when he
disturbed men with dogs who were digging there. He had
hurriedly returned home and phoned the farmer who said it
was quite all right – he had given them permission. I duly
contacted the local man who couldn't remember when the
incident occurred though it was some while ago now. At the time
he had thought the sett badger-occupied, but from the farmer's
words concluded they must have been after fox. Later that
morning Graham phoned and in passing I mentioned the Chalk
Pit badgers, and also the digging incident at the Motorway Sett.
Should Legget be told there were badgers well settled so near his
house or would it be better to keep quiet? The constable felt that
at this stage it would be better to say nothing, but there were two
people from the village he knew that could be trusted to keep an
eye on the sett there.

◊ ◊ ◊

I was still having convalescing badgers in the cages, especially
the large one, most of whom were recovering from road traffic
accidents (RTAs). I had never heard of these RTAs causing
damage or injury to humans however, which surprised me as a
fully grown badger is a sizeable animal to drive into. The only
human injury sustained was reported in a local newspaper and
subsequent badger-group newsletters, and read something like
this:

Cyclist Injured by Hit and Run Badger

Mr Rainer of Colhill had to receive hospital treatment after
a road accident in which he was knocked off his bicycle by a
hit and run badger who failed to stop or leave his name,
address and insurance details. Mr Rainer, who had not
been drinking, was returning home after dark when a large
badger ran into the road and collided with his front wheel

damaging the machine and causing him to be thrown on to the road. The badger left the scene of the accident at high speed, leaving Mr Rainer to make his own way home suffering from a broken collarbone and multiple contusions. Mr Rainer can now been seen around Colhill with his arm in a sling, but is not currently well motivated towards the protection of badgers.

◊ ◊ ◊

Slowly the mornings were growing lighter. Now first light was 6 a.m. An hour later I watched the rising sun staining the sky all shades of red. I stood in the rutted lane noting long curls of wood smoke touch the far horizon. A pheasant stalked out from a sheltering hedge, saw me and remained thoughtfully poised on one leg for a moment, considering his next move. There were field scabious in bloom nearby, their splashes of blue a welcome surprise. It was a lovely day after recent rain and the poplar catkins looked newly washed in the clear air. There were yellow lesser celandine with forget-me-nots and sweet violets, with their deep mauve blooms. What lovely harbingers of spring they are.

I walked home in the sunshine as a small tabby cat came to greet me and the telephone rang as I walked indoors. It was Steve to say he would be around later as he had some papers to return. Then Mrs Ellis appeared asking if I could find two of her dogs. Bonnie and Bruno had gone off and not returned since she let them out nearly two hours ago. I was becoming very tired of her dog problems as three, no four, times recently I had been asked to do this, and on each occasion had traced them to the village. Fortunately, this time they were close at hand, chasing squirrels in Legget's part of Ninepenny Wood.

The next morning she phoned again with the same request, adding that as she was going out for the day, when I found the dogs I could leave them shut in her back courtyard. This time, however, I could honestly say I was about to go out myself to help in Ashcroft Woods. I went the field way so that I could check the homes of the Ninepenny badgers at the Poplar Sett. I found it very dug out, but not, I was sure, by the badgers. There were many pawprints in the damp earth, so many one upon another, that I couldn't be certain it *was* dogs' work. Could it have been the dobermans? Had they found the sett?

It was the following day that I heard the dogs being called from the stable yard. With sudden foreboding I went out to check the Poplar Sett. It was the warmest February this century and another gloriously sunny morning. To my horror there was Bonnie digging furiously at an entrance, now grossly enlarged. Close by, where the other entrance had been, was a gaping hole and Bruno was down it and almost hidden. I shouted at them and they both went running back as I surveyed the damaged sett. What on earth would the badgers do now? The inner tunnels were exposed to the wind and rain; with a heavy downpour they would be flooded out. What a good thing they hadn't had cubs this year.

I took a deep breath and walked to the Big House to let Mrs Ellis know. After all, once she had shown an interest in these very badgers. I asked that she come to look at the sett and we began to walk that way. What did I expect her to do, she said, keep the dogs locked up day and night? She was fed up with complaints from the village. At least if they were going on the farmland now they were less likely to bite people there. If I preferred, she would let them out after dark. That might be better, for people wouldn't see them then. What did I think? I stared at her in amazement, at a loss to know what to answer, but seeing my expression, she became abusive. She had never before spoken to me like this, although I knew the local police and others had been treated so. I tried to reason with her, but the more outrageous and silly she became. She turned back to the house shouting and screaming, and that was the last I saw of her for some time.

I had a word with Steve and, although he promised to speak to Mrs Ellis he rightly pointed out that the digging by the dogs at the badger sett wasn't an offence. Her lack of control over them was though. A printed notice warned of guard dogs near her house and the law states that these must be kept under the control of a competent handler at all times. It was therefore a police matter, rather than one for the RSPCA. He suggested that I keep a record of how often I actually witnessed the dogs interfering with the sett.

A phone call came regarding a possible badger-dig arranged

for the coming weekend. Lorry drivers working at a site on the Kent coast had apparently invited friends from Wales to try their hand at a certain farm. A friend of one of the badger group had overheard the event being discussed in a local pub. Later that day I had a call from the group's chairman confirming this. Tim, with other members of the group, the police and RSPCA would all be taking it in turns at the farm's setts that weekend. They had radios and the use of the farm telephone. The farmer was very sympathetic towards his badgers.

I went out after midnight that Sunday to see how the Ashcroft badgers were faring. Crisp and her three yearlings still had their home in Cliffords Bank, out beyond the woods on the farmland. Crisp was a big, untidy-looking animal with fur that never seemed to lie flat; she was also my favourite. No cubs, it seemed, would be born this year either to her or the other sow, Missy, but I hoped next year would be different.

I had dubbed the yearlings Pip, Squeak and Wilfrid. Wild animals have individual characteristics, just like domestic ones, and I could only describe Wilfrid as rather a wimp. A good description really for he seemed to whimper at everything. Even the few flakes of snow we had that winter caused him to whine and beat a hasty retreat underground, whilst his sisters ran around trying to catch them before they fell. Poor Wilf the wimp, but he was improving!

First light found me in The Chantry looking out to the winding Bourne and its silvery lakes. All eight badgers were with me, snuffling about in the disturbed earth left by the contractors. Mícheál, the clan's only adult boar, came nearer, backed on to and musked my boots. He rose up on hindlegs against me and I stroked the handsome striped face and tickled behind his neat ears. Thoughts of Old Joe came to mind and the other boars that had followed. Old Joe, Sam and Jude. All had come to violent ends, but now there was Mícheál, called after the Dublin lad who loves badgers. (It was Mícheál and his younger brother Aodhán's concern for the plight of their country's badgers that had caused their mother to form Badgerwatch Ireland.) The king is dead; long live the king. This clan would survive and flourish.

I had promised to warden that morning, and once the badgers were underground I walked the main paths picking up litter. I am partially deaf in one ear now, so find it difficult to locate the direction of sound. I could hear a shotgun occasionally fired and although shooting, camping and snaring are offences in Ashcroft Woods, I couldn't be sure whether the sounds were coming from outside the trees or in. I picked up some bright green cartridges, however, along one of the rides, then encountered the shooter wearing camouflage gear and face netting and explained that he shouldn't be doing this here. He merely moved away without comment and shortly after I heard the firing again. Most of the weekends in this nature reserve are quiet and pleasant, but this proved to be one of those other days. I followed the smell of wood smoke and came across four young men camping with tents and a fire. They groaned on seeing me for we had met in similar situations before. Tucked away, they had hoped to go unnoticed, but though my sense of direction may be poor, there is nothing wrong with my sense of smell! By now it was 9.15 a.m. and giving them time to douse the fire and pack up the tents and rubbish, I asked them to be gone by 10 a.m. or I would have to get Oakley police. They knew this was no idle threat, having tested it before.

Meanwhile I walked out on to the fields again to Cliffords Bank and, lo and behold, met two men amongst the trees there with terriers and a lurcher. The latter, with its pit bull head, was becoming a common greyhound cross in these parts. One man carried a pointed shovel, the other a metal rod. The rod didn't appear to be a crowbar for it was too thin; more likely a probing bar which is pushed into the ground to trace the line of the tunnels beneath. The man with the rod picked up another shovel as they ran off. Annoyed with myself for letting them see me, I tried to grab the lurcher, only to find this easier said than done. The dog was as anxious to get me as I was him. Only the black binliner of rubbish pushed at him and then a distant whistle from his owner saved the day. I ran in the direction of men and dog, but too late to get the full registration number of a green van that bounced off across the farmland towards the main road. Was the sett unharmed? On returning I found it was – what a relief. Then a small, brown fell terrier ran out of an entrance, through the elmbrush of the bank and so across the field to the woods. Again, I tried to catch it with no luck, but obviously the terriermen would be back later for it.

By now the sun was well up. It was going to be another

beautiful day. I ran down to the bottom of Briarmead Lane and its houses from which I could phone Oakley police. Shortly after, a patrol new to the area drove up. First we checked the campsite to find the men gone and Ted, another warden, collecting up the rubbish they had left. This reminded me that mine was still lying strewn about at the top of Cliffords Bank. Of the shooter there was no sign, but the PC wasn't busy so he was in no great hurry to leave. Like the police farther down in the county, ours had been alerted to possible trouble this weekend. We agreed this was probably unconnected with the Welshmen. We are not short of such people ourselves and fine Sunday mornings at this time of year, when cubs may be present, are popular with badger-diggers and baiters everywhere. He was interested in the badgers and their signs, as well as the ways on and off the land. We drove round looking at all the routes on both farms and the two well-occupied setts, then said goodbye. The missing terrier was bait for its owner to return, probably in a different vehicle. An unmarked police car would come up and down whenever possible till nightfall; perhaps they would have some luck.

I still hadn't collected up that rubbish. I had scarcely re-entered the woods to cross to the farther farm, when I encountered two local brothers well known to us all, with their terriers and lurchers. There is no offence in walking Ashcroft Woods of course, but I did notice they looked even more unhappy at seeing me, than I probably did at seeing them. These two dig and lamp everything that moves, be it rabbit, fox, badger or bird, and have been picked up by the police so often that it is surprising they haven't both ceased hunting now. Ashcroft Woods and the surrounding land is generally considered by local enthusiasts to be a 'hot' area, so I doubted they would try anything here. However, just as they had a right to walk their dogs, albeit under control, I had a right to trot after them to see what their latest vehicle looked like. It was a blue Bedford van I hadn't encountered before, in the car-park at the top of the lane. It also transpired that the other warden here that day had warned them off already!

By now a strong wind had arisen and I found my rubbish well dispersed over the field. It seemed to have been a long day. Slowly I made my tired way home struggling against gusts that were nearing gale force and a lowering sky. Reaching the poplar row on Legget's land, I spied two men with dogs at the Motorway Sett over the far field. They saw me, of course, as there is no cover and these fields are flat. Oh no, it was the Squire brothers with their blue Bedford van parked under the motorway tunnel. I checked the sett, but no digging had commenced and there appeared to be no dog left down it. By now it was raining heavily and the wind nearly blew me off my feet. I struggled in to find my daughter Karen patiently waiting for me and a green-eyed tabby purring from the best armchair. Now there was a wild storm with thunder and lightning that continued till late into the afternoon. At dusk I walked out to the Poplar Sett, which was flooded with water up to the top of the ground. Drat that woman and her wretched dogs. Poor badgers – they had enough trouble to survive without this treatment.

That evening a friend phoned to say they were having badger-digging problems in their county and did I know that the previous Friday in Shropshire, two badger-diggers/baiters had been successfully convicted and their dogs confiscated? One of the offenders was the area representative of the Fell and Moorland Working Terrier Club, an organisation created to promote the welfare of working terriers. He was removed from office following the case in which he was convicted of eleven charges of badger-digging and causing suffering to six dogs. He was sentenced to prison for four months and banned for life from keeping dogs. His companion was convicted of eight charges, sentenced to one month in prison and banned from keeping dogs for ten years. A magistrate who saw evidence of the horrific injuries suffered by the terriers used for baiting, complained that the 1973 Badgers Act and its amendments were woefully inadequate to punish the offenders, as the maximum sentence was a £2,000 fine. You couldn't be gaoled for digging or baiting a wild animal, only fined, but you could be gaoled for cruelty to or baiting a domestic one. Fines for digging or baiting badgers are often small. If the offenders are out of work, it isn't realistic for the court to fine the full amount. Knowing this, those convicted of badger offences were very contemptuous of the law and carried on regardless. It may therefore be more realistic, as in this case, to charge them with cruelty to their dog, if it can be proved that it was marked by a badger. Forfeiture of the dog is an inconvenience to their owners as they are the most important tools of the trade. The League Against Cruel Sports (LACS) and the RSPCA were trying to have the law changed, however, for there was nothing to stop these men from using other dogs, even if banned from dog ownership. They could say their new dogs were owned by their mother, sisters or girlfriends (who often confirmed this), if they themselves were banned. So LACS and the RSPCA were hoping that the wording of the law could be altered to disqualify the offender from *having custody* of a dog.

It was very hard to have a successful outcome now to badger-related cases. This one was an exception. Those accused could hire the best expert witnesses and lawyers to make the most of the loopholes in the Badgers Act 1973 and its amendments, using legal aid if they were unemployed, which frequently they were.

Chapter Six

FEBRUARY ended with the most extraordinary and frightening weather. Hurricane-force winds, deluges of rain, sleet
and snow, none of which laid, for it was still very mild. North
Wales coastal villages were completely flooded and the coasts of
Surrey and Kent fared badly too. Thirteen deaths occurred in
one day. We would have brief periods of calm and sunshine,
before the winds grew to gales and chaos followed. Little Flo was
easily frightened, especially when the hail hit the metal roof with
shattering force. Some big trees came down in Ninepenny
Wood, particularly in Legget's part, where his clearing of it had
left the remaining trees more exposed. The badgers were only
briefly above ground, for they didn't like these conditions any
more than Flo.

A contact in Essex had found a sett he looked after dug out
with shovels. The Squires' blue Bedford had been seen in the
near vicinity, but nothing could be proved. He also found
something in a secluded area that sounded like a baiting pit.
Tim phoned to say that no diggers had turned up the previous
weekend, although a van hired in Lancashire appeared and
then disappeared. I mentioned the Essex contact and the
Squires' van.

The first morning of March began frosty, for it had been -2°C before first light with snow showers. Even the water bowl under the beeches in Ninepenny Wood was frozen, though not to any depth. The badgers had snuffled about in the old orchard where it was more sheltered, but went below after two hours. They were all denning at the Motorway Sett now, but were very crowded for it was so small. Would they take over the Tank Sett I wondered? I left the caravan in sunshine though the wind was still fierce. Pieces of trees and branches hung suspended, dangerously waiting for the unwary to pass beneath. The sun slanted on the beech trunks in Ninepenny Wood and a squirrel leapt upwards at my passing. It was sad to see that a large beech had splintered and fallen across the path for I was fond of these gracious trees, but except for Karen and myself there seemed no one to care.

I had missed Ashcroft Woods and, with badger-diggers very much in mind, wished to check the setts. All was quiet there apart from the wind in the trees. The elmbrush of Cliffords Bank was already in tiny leaf and the sallow catkins full open. I sat in the Yew Grove to rest, listening to the creaking and groaning of a branch on a nearby oak that was hanging all splintered high above. The wind seemed intent on torturing the twisting limb, which was like a broken arm barely connected by sinews that refused to snap. I thought this to be rather a dangerous place in the circumstances. If the wind did succeed in dislodging it, I would be well in the way. Walking home I looked at the other occupied sett, that on Colts farm, home of Mícheál, Missy, Meg and Bess. Mícheál, as dominant boar, had been marking the elder again, leaving the wood beneath the torn bark white and gleaming.

I contacted Graham who, like myself, hadn't known of the Squire brothers' blue Bedford van. He phoned back later to confirm that the same vehicle had been seen under suspicious circumstances in other areas. It wasn't registered to them, however, but to someone in the Midlands, probably the previous owner. I had assumed that one was obliged by law to re-register a vehicle in the new owner's name, but apparently not. Involuntarily I exclaimed in surprise and, appreciating how useful this must be to crooks and shady dealers, said such lack of legal obligation must cause the police many problems, not least in the length of time it might take to trace the current owner. 'A lot of vital time in road accidents too,' the rural officer commented.

That spring, there was a great upsurge of badger-digging, both locally and in other counties. Each week I would receive a newsletter from a different badger group and read the same cry. Kent diggers had been traced in Surrey, Essex, Hampshire and Middlesex, Welsh diggers in Avon, Gloucestershire and Kent. When one thinks how many attacks on setts go undetected and how few cases ever reach a court through lack of hard evidence, it is very disquieting and sad.

It was a mild, mellow night. A fine-edged silvery sickle hung in the clear sky, shining on the ghostly trees smothered in blackthorn, plum and cherry blossom. Flo and I watched the two sows digging a side entrance to the Poplar Sett. The water had retreated, though the tunnels were still wet and muddy. This new entrance went off at an angle, a sharp left. When next the rains came and flooded the sett, this new part shouldn't be affected. There was no sign of them taking down bedding, nor of cubs. A badger had also reopened an entrance of what had been the Holly Tree Sett. At 2.15 a.m. I returned to the caravan and found the sows almost on the doorstep. One moved away a short distance and appeared to be listening to – or was it scenting – something on the ground. Quickly, with those long front claws, she dug straight down through the turf, exposing a rabbit's nursery stop and eating the still-blind young. There were many insects and moths to be found in these mild nights. I had an RTA yearling sow recuperating in the large enclosure. Hearing badger sounds outside, she appeared from the darkness of the wooden hay-filled den that Steve had made inside it. Immediately the resident sows were interested, coming forward to the heavy-duty metal mesh. Unusually, one growled aggressively at this newest arrival, who backed away with head submissively lowered. Were the Ninepenny sows in oestrus and ready to mate I wondered?

The little owls were calling over the farmland, which reminded me that the resident male tawny had chosen the metal roof of my caravan as a territorial calling place. I might be sitting quietly at dusk, when a dull thud would sound above me, quite different from the squirrels' pitter-patter. Then the lovely, quavering calls would commence – a pause to listen – and repeat, before he flew off, satisfied that he had no rivals, to another spot. His mate had nested in an old oak and was incubating their eggs.

The old boar mated with both sows the following night. I was first alerted to what was happening by Flo jumping on a chair-back to look out of the window – even now she can't resist 'nosing on the neighbours'! Then his deep, throaty purring came clear as he walked with short, stiff-legged steps round Hattie, his white tail vertically raised. He mounted her dog-fashion from behind, gripping the fur at the back of her neck to keep his balance, whilst her sister ran round the two, whickering. This long-duration mating as it is called, may last up to an hour, although more usually for twenty to thirty minutes. Later he mated with the sister too. With luck, cubs would be born next year.

The days continued warm and sunny with mild, dew-laden nights: strange weather for March. The soaked grass encouraged worms to rise in pasture and meadow, luckily for the badgers. They spent the late evenings stealthily moving over the turf, taking the worms as they rose to feed on the surface. I was concerned one afternoon to find the door of the large enclosure propped open. The latest occupant had been returned to its home range so there was no fear of an unfortunate escape, but I *always* kept the door closed and bolted – how strange. A clean bowl of water stood on the paved floor and the den was filled with fresh hay ready for the next casualty. Odd, but I must be more careful in future.

It was a full moon with heavy dew and still very mild. By 5 a.m. a mist was creeping over the farmland and into the wood. It was wonderful watching the rising sun trying to pierce the mist that by now was thick and clinging. A tiny ray was quickly vanquished, then another. The world was wholly grey once more, when suddenly the sun's dazzling radiance burst through. Soon the wet ground, my hair, anorak and the badgers' fur (I was watching at the Sand Pit) were steaming in the welcome warmth. A badger appeared from between the contorted roots of a beech, its snout and paws muddied from opening up an old entrance. It stood, one paw raised, blinking in the day's first light.

Graham phoned to say he had obtained permission for us to

check for badger setts on private land near Caldwell Manor and had arranged one morning of the following week when he would be off duty. He asked if I knew of a certain man's interest in dog-fighting. I knew he had been involved with dog-fighting and holding badgers for baiting, but whether he still was I couldn't say. It appeared that the police had been tipped off about a dog-fight the man was holding in the near future, but although they had been given a definite date, the time and location were vague, especially the latter, covering as it did many miles of disused quarries. I mentioned that the same man used to run a terrier-rescue service, guaranteeing to recover any trapped terrier from any underground location. In the past, this had involved not only the wholesale destruction of occupied badger setts (he used a JCB), but also of farm banks and hedgerows on private property without prior permission or knowledge of the farmer. He was on good terms with the Squire brothers.

◊ ◊ ◊

One night, the boar had designs on a cock pheasant roosting in the wood. He tried climbing the tree, but only succeeded in disturbing the bird, which flew off with a startled 'kuttuc, kuttuc' and a whir of wings, leaving the badger to scramble down supperless. The sows looked up with mild interest from where they had been drinking at the water bowl. Badgers enjoy a good drink, but can go without water for long periods. Worms contain large amounts of moisture, as does fruit, but when these are not available and conditions are dry, adult badgers cope without liquids far longer than we could as they have kidneys ideally adapted to drought. Water is removed from their urine and recycled through their kidneys. Naturally this can't go on indefinitely and cubs are less able to cope and soon become dehydrated.

Hattie and Hazel continued to extend both the Poplar and Holly Tree Setts, digging out the crushed tunnelling and pushing out many heavy loads of soil. Exactly how much earth appeared on the spoil heaps in the following weeks was difficult to judge, but it must have been several tonnes. The boar would amble over to watch their efforts though he didn't take part. I noticed they were using goosegrass or cleavers again for bedding, but this was merely for their own comfort as neither were lactating. The boar was making a completely new home for himself well into Legget's part of the wood under a holly tree. Bluebells and clumps of goldilocks buttercups carpeted the ground in the Ellis's part of the wood; a marked contrast to the farmer's cleared area. I took the remains of my dinner one night and scarcely had time to put it under the beeches before three eager badgers appeared! Flo purred loudly at their appearance (she had already been fed) rubbing herself up against Hattie's big flanks to show her pleasure. The warm weather was still with us and we badly needed rain for already the ground was dry and cracked.

One night there was someone shooting with night-sights on Legget's land: it could have been his son Paul. Whilst I watched from the wood he shot a fox and seven rabbits. I couldn't from a distance make out whether the fox was one I knew, i.e. Foxy or Vicky, but provided he didn't bag badgers (or cats, for Flo had accompanied my badgerwatch), there was little I could do. We kept a respectful distance from one another, and since he wore a three-hole balaclava hood, he could have been anybody.

Returning one evening late from the town, I watched Mrs Ellis unbolt and prop back the door of the large enclosure and spoke to her about it. Very much on the defensive she said that she didn't like to see wild animals 'imprisoned' and her ex-husband didn't either. Whilst we both knew this was ridiculous, I took pains to explain that if a strange badger was released here, it would almost certainly be badly mauled by the resident animals, particularly if it was a boar. All badgers were returned to the areas from which they had come. This, however, triggered off another round of abuse. Obviously, I was going to have to keep the cages padlocked. A few days later, the gate from the meadow on to the drive was chained and padlocked; this was the only entrance for the man bringing propane gas cylinders to The Sett, or indeed for anyone with a vehicle. True I could scramble through or under the fence, but already I was low on gas and would need the cylinder replaced. Asking Mrs Ellis for the use of a key got me nowhere, so there was nothing for it but to buy a small camping burner and cook over that. I was conscious there was something very wrong with my land-lady's mental state; this became even more obvious when my post, which should have been in the communal letterbox, appeared torn up and strewn across the meadow. It was easy enough to have my mail redirected, though weeks later I discovered some important items had gone astray. Cooking was an inconvenience, but provided my water wasn't cut off again I could still manage to live here and care for the wild animals I took in. We lived so far from one another in the thirty-six acres that the whole affair seemed senseless, but clearly the lady wanted me out.

◊ ◊ ◊

I left home one morning at 6.30 a.m. with the sky becoming light. The blackbirds were beginning to sing, then the woodpigeon and pheasant. This pheasant sometimes called at night and sounded strange, especially when the tawny was calling too. One of the hens in his harem was nesting in a hollow scrape in the grass under the hawthorns not far from The Sett. Primroses dotted the ground and the cherry blossom was falling fast. The trees of the poplar row were in tiny leaf that smelt of incense, and from a distance appeared a haze of yellowy-green. Flo was drinking under the beeches with Vicky, who was in milk. Such a relief! She hadn't been shot, and I had seen Foxy carrying back food to the den under the Japanese knotweed, so the pair were all right.

The ladies' smock was a carpet of delicate lilac in Ashcroft Woods. There was a great deal of work needed there and first we started on clearing up the coppicers' work. Since Ray had come as warden, litter and damage to these woods were far less; he cared for the place and it showed.

That morning he cleared a gale-felled ash and I stacked the toppings, as I was shown, into a 'dead hedge'. This was preferable to burning, it gave cover to birds, insects and small mammals and in time would become overgrown and rot down. Then we went to look at The Chantry and met the farm manager checking his field. He and his men had been sowing acres of peas treated with a fungicide against rot. 'Drat the pigeons,' he said. I asked what the round, pink objects I had noticed lying on these fields were – fertiliser? 'They *are* the peas,' he laughed. Thinking how the badgers had been eating them a few nights ago, I was tempted to 'lay low and say nuthin'' in Brer Rabbit style, but confessed instead. He merely commented that the badgers were different – some could always be spared for them.

I was hearing from several quarters of a firm of solicitors who was suing people for criticising fox hunts. An acquaintance had written a letter on the subject to a local paper some years ago and was now being sued, as was the editor. The editor panicked and paid up out of court, but the friend sat tight and, it transpired, had no case to answer. Obviously, hunts should have redress if one writes anything libellous that cannot be substantiated, but from what I was hearing it seemed that the solicitor was simply trying to stop honest criticism of hunts. The threat of legal action cast a shadow over several innocent people and, though the cases never came to court, this blighted their lives for many, many months. Just as there is a thin line between libel and freedom of speech, I couldn't help feeling there is a similar line between justified legal action and intimidation.

◊ ◊ ◊

One morning I met Graham with Ellie, his dog, in the drive, and together we went to see the owner of the land near Caldwell Manor to look for badger setts, but with no success. However, there was an old, long-disused sett now taken over by rabbits and plenty of signs of badger, including fresh dung and snuffle holes. Either badgers were coming into the area from outside or there could possibly be an occupied sett in the middle of a densely overgrown copse. Now the morning was gone; I would try again another time.

On my return I was concerned to see a tractor spraying the field by the Poplar Sett. Two days earlier, a large-tyred vehicle had crushed the spoil heap and entrance that Hattie had been so busy at. I was fearful that a machine's wheels might flatten the rest of the sett. However, I stood over it and stared the driver out. Poor man, he was only trying to get on with his job – I think! Flo came and stood with me. We two don't stand any nonsense.

That afternoon I cleared the gale-blown debris in Ninepenny Wood, throwing some into the craters left by the upturned trees and making the rest into dead hedges. Then I collected all the rubbish in view, much of it blown from the motorway and caught up in trees and fences. That evening I did the same to the drive – eleven black binliners full. Everywhere looked a lot better, though I had to confess to being sick of rubbish collecting. Guess over the years I had done too much of it in Ashcroft Woods.

The last night of March was deeply frosty with the birds' water bowl frozen and ice floating on the badger's water bowl under the beeches. I left home at first light and, walking across Legget's land towards the winding lane and Ashcroft Woods, I watched the great, red disk of the sun clear the eastern horizon. It might be cold, with my breath vaporising before me, but it was lovely walking – or rather striding – weather. I checked Cliffords Bank to find at the far end entrances that hadn't been used for years dug out and fresh blades of grass taken down, some still lying where they had been dropped. It was puzzling that Crisp and the others should be taking an interest in this part of the bank and, thinking back, there had been one or two odd things about Cliffords Bank lately. Watching the rabbits grazing the frozen grass above the bank, I noticed a very young one with myxomatosis well advanced. So the virus was still about.

In the woods themselves a larch had been blown over. They are beautiful trees. The male flowers were globular and hardly noticeable amongst the fresh green needles, but the female flowers are well called 'larch roses' – like plump, pink candles. It was sad to see its demise. I sat awhile near it under a Scots pine, watching and listening to a pair of male lesser-spotted woodpeckers quarrelling above me whilst the hen woodpecker looked on.

By now the sun was shafting through the trees as I checked other setts in the woods that were still unoccupied. A green woodpecker yaffed into the morning (there were many woodpeckers of all three species in Ninepenny and Ashcroft Woods that year), and a busy treecreeper and a bright-eyed robin inspected my rucksack, left on the trunk seat in the clearing. I gave him some buttered scone crumbs, which he hopped to and fro for in his pert way. Then the mallard pair from the pond came waddling close and I threw some to them, hoping they would leave Robbie alone. The stitchwort's white flowers were like stars amongst the living green with many bluebells in bloom.

Walking home a police car passed me, then returned and stopped. I found it was the constable who had answered my call for help with the terriermen at Cliffords Bank three weeks ago.

One of the Squire brothers had reported a terrier missing in the same area, lost about the same time. We discussed badgers and their connection with dog-fighting.

I was determined to go back to the Ashcroft area that night to discover which badger was digging out on Cliffords Bank. There was a glittering crescent moon lying on its back in the sky at 9.30 p.m. so, having found the Ninepenny badgers busy foraging, I left them and Flo to find out. To my amazement I saw another badger in residence – one that I knew. It was a sow from Thrift Lane off Warby village, and she was lactating. How unexpected. Crisp was quite friendly towards her and, of course, they were related, though distantly. 'Bossie Bessie', as her rescuer called her, was picked up unconscious in November 1988 by a passing off-duty policeman from the city and brought to me. She recovered and we found the sett and returned her. The following February, most of the sett, a main one, was destroyed by the landowner, but the remaining badgers, including Bessie, survived and flourished. I sometimes went to watch them, and the family living next door to the plot of land containing the sett kept a careful eye on their welfare. Long before the motorway separating Ashcroft from Thrift Lane was built, this had been part of the original territory of Old Joe's clan. Human alteration of the landscape, however, had successfully divided them. How curious that Bessie had made her way unharmed from her home; I wondered why. She must have had her cub(s) since she moved here, I imagined, though only when I saw them would I be able to judge their age.

Walking home in the early morning light I watched squirrels nibbling off bunches of young oak leaves. They had bitten through the pale green hooded spathes of lords-and-ladies to get to the tiny flowers that grow, male above female, in dense whorls below the immature finger-like spadix inside. An ancient gean, long since dead, with its great trunk rotted down into neat red blocks, was being examined by a weasel whose russet fur blended well with the decaying wood. There were holly blue and yellow brimstone butterflies on buckthorn and alder, an orange-tip on the garlic mustard and a treecreeper working its way up an ash. I watched a chaffinch delicately taking insects from the sycamore flowers. This much-maligned tree is particularly lovely as now when the opening young leaves are shades of bronze and red. It is also a vital source of food where there are dormice, who enjoy the anthers of its flowers.

April began with the first rain for weeks, heavy and prolonged. The badgers wormed for two hours non-stop round the rabbit-cropped grass of the empty lake, three pairs of jaws working like one. The weather turned colder with sleet in the air and by nightfall of 5th we had the deepest frost of the winter (and it was already spring). This frost split the birds' water bowl in the grassy verge opposite The Sett and burnt the trees' young leaves. By 10 a.m. it was bright sunshine, however, with the grass steaming in the warmth. Within a few hours the weather had reverted to its former hot and sunny conditions and the ground moisture might never have been. I picked a sprig of holly from a tree near the poplar row that still had red berries upon it.

Tony Banks MP, backed by the League Against Cruel Sports (LACS) and other MPs, had brought his Sett Protection Bill past its second reading in the House of Commons. John Bryant of LACS had produced the actual wording of the Bill, which was no mean feat. It would now go forward to the Standing Committee and, hopefully, its third reading. The National Federation of Badger Groups (NFBG) was intending to send a brief of known and monitored setts destroyed by developers, landowners, etc., with photos where space permitted, to every MP to give greater emphasis to the need for protection. The Royal Society for Nature Conservation (RSNC) was also very interested. John Taylor of NFBG wrote to all badger groups asking for their co-operation. There was barely three weeks in which to get this information gathered in, collated and produced as a briefing document and obviously many groups would not be able to assist in time. I promised to send details and photos of some of the destroyed, active setts with which I had been involved.

◊ ◊ ◊

Wardening Ashcroft Woods the Sunday before Easter, I discovered that some youngsters had lit a fire in the hollow bole of a great beech that overlooked a steep-sided gully. This had been done before, but now the tree was rotten and riddled with fungi, though externally it appeared healthy enough. It would be difficult to put the fire out. The youths did try to help me, several giving me their full or partly full coke cans to try to douse it. The fire was way up inside the tree at a height of perhaps two and a half metres. I continued to warden, picking up litter as I did so, and caught up with a shooter who actually left on request. All that afternoon, the interior of the beech continued to smoulder and uneasily I decided to leave it until Ray came on duty the following day. The weather was still hot and summer-like; it seemed a crime to wish for rain.

When the next day we went to look at the beech, I found the warden was even more worried than me. With a stick he brought down bright, glowing embers amid clouds of smoke. Ashcroft's greatest danger is fire, particularly as it is so far from water. Together we drove over to Colts farm where we were given a five-gallon drum of water and old, well-soaked rags. Ray probed high up into the tree with the soaked rags on a stout pole trying to put out the fire as well as dousing the lower bole, in the hope that the hissing steam would cool the intense heat inside the old tree – all in vain. It was apparent that the beech was now very dangerous and a high wind on that steep slope could crack it in half to topple and crush anything or anyone passing below. By now the fire was burning merrily. The weather was so hot and the ground so dry, that sparks were setting the slope alight – mainly dry beechmast and leaves. The fire brigade was phoned and their advice asked. They said they would rather come than merely advise. Ray was uneasy in case on arrival they should be annoyed at being called to such a trivial fire – but was it trivial? Little fires can become holocausts under dry conditions, and this one had been started thirty-six hours before.

On arrival, the fire tender couldn't, of course, get in to the woods, but Ray drove the firemen with their hand gear in his landrover right to the bottom of the slope. They put the fire out and told him always to let them know, however small a wood-land fire might appear. So it was a story that had ended well, though we were all sorry to know that the great, old tree would now have to be felled.

◊ ◊ ◊

Setts in other parts of the country are always interesting and one of my favourite areas is the north of Essex where the land is very similar to that of Suffolk. In my part of Kent there is only one small stream, ironically graced with the title of river. Once it was such, but now is a few metres across at most and regularly dries up to a stony bed. My Essex friend and I walked into the copse that houses the home of her nearest badgers. Her countryside fascinates me, for you are never far from water. Streams flow here and there, chuckling, bubbling, twisting and turning through gullies edged with mosses and ferns. Droughts seem unknown and this sett has entrances opening on to the stream itself. I love it there. One part is natural marsh. In another the twisting trees bend down almost to head level, blocking the light, and fallen trunks make natural bridges that are well used by the resident badgers. There are marsh plants in abundance. One I felt I should know, but couldn't name it. I knew it to be a horsetail and took a dead stem and cone-head from last year's growth home with me to identify. It is known as Dutch rush; a native perennial that was once imported from the Netherlands for use as pot scourers. This place and its clan of badgers had no human problems, unlike the other setts I was to view later that month.

The following morning I went with Steve to another sett, this time one threatened by possible development. The city police and RSPCA had saved the day two years ago when a driveway had been mooted to cross part of the sett. The original property developers with permission to build had, fortuitously for the badgers, gone bankrupt and sold to others who were more enlightened (or perhaps more conscious of public opinion). A large, pleasant house had been built with a drive leading in, none of which affected the animals. The site of the badgers' home was a small, now disused quarry with rough ground and scrub at the top. This was leased for five years to a local man to graze horses, or so he said. The driveway was fenced off and privately owned. We wondered how he was going to get his horses up and down, and grazing above was almost non-existent. He had installed a Portacabin at the bottom of the quarry and padlocked the entrance. The sett was in a similar position to that of the Sand Pit badgers near Caldwell; these too had dug out their home beneath mature beeches. As Steve said, the whole affair seemed very suspect, but at present all was well with the badgers in the quarry. He could only interview the man, point out that badgers were protected and that the police were aware of the situation.

Easter Monday was a day of sunshine and showers. Another clan of badgers were in the way, this time of a new ring road pushing through their territory. The Department of Transport was anxious to co-operate and, with forethought and knowledge of the animals' foraging requirements, the problem could be overcome. The area was surveyed and the report duly sent by one of the Sussex badger groups which hadn't been formed so very long ago, but was already deeply committed to the area and its wildlife.

Tim and I went to look at another problem area farther down into our own county. The local council were agreeable for a development company to create a new town in 82 hectares of mature woodland. The trees would be felled to make way for the houses, eight-screen cinema, public house, restaurant, bank, shops, swimming-pool and industrial estate. The company would be prepared to landscape the area with the planting of ornamental trees and shrubs and had asked the badger group to survey for setts which were known by local people to be present. We were met by Barbara who for a number of years had successfully fended off efforts to remove parts of the wood for similar 'good causes'. She was worried, and with good reason. It was only much later that I found out why the council were so keen to lose the woodland. The development company had offered to build and equip a badly needed hospital for free.

Some of the woodland had been planted with London plane, Scots pine, rhododendron and wellontonia, but farther over there was a natural area and then chestnut coppice, including a large stretch of heather and its associated species, bilberry, growing on a slope and along both sides of the path. If this was cleared of invading birch and bracken, it could become one of the finest heather areas in Kent where this is very scarce. The three badger setts, including the main one, were directly in the way of a proposed access road into the area to serve the new town. We found signs of badgers foraging across two fields beyond and leading into a nearby Forestry Commission wood, long since neglected.

Later at Barbara's house we sat and talked. What was against us was time. I felt that the best chance we had of saving the woodland was to point out the importance of the heather area to the county trust plus, of course, all the work Barbara had done so painstakingly before, surveying her badgers and recording birds, butterflies and plants. I would write privately to the trust regarding the heath and the flora I had briefly recorded that morning and Tim would write of the badgers and the lady's work. Once the trust was interested we hoped that would stop the council from giving the go-ahead till a full and comprehensive report could be compiled. This was successful and, as far as I know, the eighty-two hectares with its resident flora and fauna are still intact. I felt very sorry for Barbara who had struggled hard and long to stop so many commercial ventures from destroying the wood she loves. It seemed that no sooner had she overcome one development, when another presented itself. Sadly, money talks, and those out to make large profits may yet have a more persuasive tone than little voices like ours.

◊ ◊ ◊

The last week of April saw thunderstorms from the heat that had built up over the past few weeks. Yellow archangel amidst the bluebells made a lovely sight under the hawthorn blossom. Hattie and Hazel were still digging out their new entrance of the Poplar Sett and it was evident from the chunks of charred wood dragged out that they were re-opening some of the original chambers over which the bonfire had been made last December. Bossie Bessie had two cubs that Crisp and her yearlings seemed content to play with and 'mother'. The greatest activity appeared at the Sand Pit with such a vast amount of excavation that the spoil heaps were enormous, spilling far down into the undergrowth below. It was on the field above that I had counted thirteen badgers at one time (cubs and adults) searching for insects and grubs in the soil. They were the most successful badgers of any I knew in the area I tried to patrol – long might they remain so. There were tiny badger pawprints in the wet soil of the Chalkpit badgers, though I didn't have the good fortune to see the cubs for some time.

I had arranged to meet a journalist and take him over Ashcroft Woods. He was really interested in the place and we sat at the Old Cherry Sett, now of course empty of badgers, talking of the different problems these animals face country-wide. He was writing an article for the *Weekend Telegraph* and promised to include a piece on Tony Banks's Protection of Badger Setts Bill due to go to Standing Committee next month. The more people that knew of its existence and took an interest the better. As we walked down Briarmead a police officer drove up. He told me that there had been two road casualty badgers and asked me to go to the station later to get the details. Though the bodies had been disposed of, there were queries on both. One had the old marks of a snare still visible round its neck though the wire was no longer there. The other had been described as 'partly skinned with the ribcage exposed'. Steve had been called to the snared one and said it was an old boar, so there was no fear of starving cubs in this instance, which is always the worry at this time of year.

Two days later, Graham called in with John, a colleague who wanted to know more about badgers generally, as well as digging and lamping. John had found the RTA described as being partly skinned, though discussing it that morning we were inclined to think it could have been dragged along underneath a vehicle.

Sitting there in the caravan talking about badgers, Graham suddenly asked me why I was using a camping gas appliance instead of Calor gas. Thus the whole sorry story of Mrs Ellis's dobermans came out – the trouble they had caused in the village over a long period of time, my returning them to Mrs Ellis and their digging out at the badger setts on Legget's land. Finally, the padlocking of the gate denying access. It had never occurred to me to tell the police. Indeed, I wasn't aware she was breaking the law, apart from her lack of control over the guard dogs of course. It appeared, however, that denying gas and vehicular access came under 'harassment of tenant' and John promised to copy out the relevant section of the 1977 Protection from Eviction Act for me. He would also meet me when he went on duty the following Friday and take me to his area to see if I could find the sett from where the dead badger had come.

Steve asked if I could take in a very young fox cub and as the cages were empty I agreed. He duly arrived the next morning with his son and daughter, complete with the tiny creature. Zoe and Clarke wanted to call it Splinter and, though their father demurred, I felt it was a welcome change from the Vickys and Foxys of former days. It is only recently talking to Steve that I found why this particular name was chosen – Splinter is a character from *Teenage Mutant Ninja Turtles*, the popular children's films from America. This newest arrival was a five-week-old dog-fox; I put him in the recovery cage.

Splinter was badly infested with fleas and mites that continually tormented him. His eyes were a misty blue and his tail more like an untidy piece of string. Every few minutes he tried to sit back on his tiny haunches and raised a hind leg to scratch. Baby-like, he would lose his balance and flop backwards, then try again. Karen helped me to bathe him in an insecticidal solution to rid him of the parasites, then she gently towelled him dry. Flo came and watched moodily for a while, then stalked off, tail held upright registering her disgust. 'All this fuss over that skinny, drowned rat' she seemed to say. Splinter hated the smelly water and stood dejectedly in the plastic bowl, head hanging to match his tail. The dark, sodden fluff that covered him clung to his thin, gawky body. He liked the towel though. Long before he was finally dry he had snuggled down into its warm security and was soon fast asleep.

Splinter's origins were a mystery. Two boys reported finding him wandering about. It was only whilst washing him that I discovered the partly healed wound running almost from ear to ear beneath his chin. He was too small and young to have been snared, nor was the injury consistent with other animals I have found caught in this way. It was as if someone had tried to slit his throat, but had gone neither deep enough nor in the right place. In spite of this and the resulting stiff-necked attitude of the cub, he should be all right if cared for properly.

Happily the fox cub could lap, so I never needed to bottle-feed nor, indeed, handle him after he was placed in the large enclosure. He wasn't weaned so I started him off with a bowl of brown bread and milk plus meat scraps. He looked lost in his new home, which was intended for much larger animals – lost and very nervous. Each time I approached to renew the bedding or feed him, I called his name softly, knowing that within a week he would associate the word with comfort and food.

At first light on the day after his bath I brought him a bowl of food and renewed his drinking water. He was nowhere to be seen, tucked away in the wooden den filled with hay. I could see him from the kitchen window though, so went indoors to watch. A small nose appeared and scented the air. Some minutes went by and a soft face was looking towards the bowl. The cub stealthily reached it and hungrily gulped the bread and milk, stopping every so often to listen. Only when it was empty did he vanish once more into the darkness and safety of his new home. Time passed and a cuckoo began calling from a tree somewhere behind the caravan. It was joined by a turtle-dove's soft cooing. Soon the trees all around were alive with birdsong, as if each were vying with the others to proclaim the new day. The cub didn't fear this for it was something he had been born into: the dawn chorus in a wood far away. Reassured, he began to explore his surroundings. His metal cage measured two and a half metres square and was one and a half metres high. Paving stones covered the floor and, slightly to one side, the wooden house or den with its tunnel entrance was placed on the paving. Two broken tree trunks sloped up to the top of the den and hay was strewn on its flat, tarpaulined roof. It was several days before Splinter found courage to scramble up, so for now the paving and ground level were cautiously explored. One paving slab rocked slightly under his timid paws and at the small movement he leapt upwards with ears fearfully held backwards and flat to his head. It was some hours, and several such leaps, before he learnt that the rocking movement would not harm him. Bushes and small trees grew round the cage and through them he could see the green caravan.

One night he found his way up a tree trunk and so on to the hay lying on the roof of his den. Foxes, like dogs and cats, enjoy a vantage point and from then on Splinter spent most of his time watching, playing and sleeping up there. He could see me at my kitchen window and sometimes glancing up I would smile to see the fox cub watching me watching him. Apples placed in the run would encourage him to play and were later eaten – all part of the process of weaning. There were endless other things to play with too: he had a large leather dog-chew, a bouncing ball and sticks to gnaw, and beetles and grasshoppers that were misguided enough to wander in rarely found their way out again. These insects were his natural food, for the first things a young fox finds himself to eat are insects, and highly nutritious food at that.

Now it was well into May, fine and warm. Everywhere was a dappling of sunlight amid the soft greens of trees unfurling their young leaves. Had Splinter still been with his natural family, the cubs would be playing outside their den in this sunshine whilst their parents hunted by day as well as night to satisfy the increasing demands of their growing family. Vicky and Foxy were doing this for their four cubs and sometimes the adult foxes would stop by the cage and look in. Splinter solicited Vicky, first barking, then howling dismally when she went on her way, but I'm sure she wouldn't have accepted him and she had four of her own to feed.

Flo tried several times to befriend him during his cub days in the cage, but each time she was rebuffed. Unlike the local foxes, he feared the cat who came to sit and communicate with him through the metal mesh. His back would arch as he hissed and a very affronted tabby took umbrage and stalked away. Karen would sit and watch them. She was always there to comfort the offended feline and Splinter would look on from a distance with interest.

◊ ◊ ◊

A nightingale sang from the low hedge between the fields and, returning at first light, I stood and watched it still singing, its beak wide open, its throat throbbing. Such a drab, brown bird; such an exquisite song! The Caldwell deer would soon have their fawns. They were browsing and relaxed in Homewood, where they kicked the dead leaves away in their quest for last year's acorns. Until I came to Caldwell at night, I imagined deer to be quiet, but like badgers at ease, deer can be noisy too. How they snorted and blew and crunched up the acorns as I sat in the bracken and watched. Fallow give off an odour like rancid butter from the glands between their hooves. Occasionally I would note it during the day, but it is very pungent on the night air.

Much later I walked over the rise to the sett in Summerhouse Knole. The badgers were nearby, snuffling for pignuts and the fat, white cockchafer larvae that feed on plant roots. Below in the valley, light reflecting on the lake seemed to beckon. A myriad insects were swarming in the warm night air and bats were taking them over the water. The large bats were probably Daubenton's with their swallow-like flight, hovering and circling above the surface, but tiny pipistrelles were present too. I noticed that unlike the Daubenton's, which can settle on water and take off immediately, the pipistrelle cannot. At least the one I watched this night that came down to drink couldn't rise again. Instead, it swam to the margins and scrambled out before flying off. The lake and the Bourne beyond resounded to the calls of moorhen, mallard and other ducks as they fed. The moorhens were particularly noisy, clambering about amongst the reeds. I followed the very edge of this shallowest of streams and saw something flick out from under a large stone. It was a lobster-like crayfish about 11 cm long. They prefer the hard, clear water of the chalk here.

I returned via the Sand Pit but was too late to see any of its occupants. Something rose out of the field ahead and I crouched down to see what it would do. Long ears with their black tips stood out like antennae above the rank grass. I had all the time in the world and was not going to leave! The antennae turned, disappeared and reappeared much nearer, swivelling as they did so. I sat, chin on knees and arms round legs trying hard not to laugh. An amber eye regarded me from the safety of the stems; they parted and a great, old hare appeared. I tried not to look directly at it for fear of frightening it away, but I need not have worried. The hare sauntered off in front of me along the track, stopping now and then to nibble at some juicy titbit and with never a backward glance.

Chapter Seven

TIM came and collected two reflector posts that had been broken in March when contractors were laying drainage pipes under the road. Their foreman insisted on stacking the heavy lengths of piping behind the little wooden posts, which had never been made to withstand such weights. In spite of several requests on my part, it had taken one by Oakley police before they finally were removed. But by then the damage was done, with two well splintered. Tim promised to paint some new ones and the stainless steel reflectors on the broken ones could be re-used. I noticed the chainlink fence between verge and road was broken down, but scrambling over to check the big sett beyond was relieved to find it unharmed. It looked as if whoever had broken the fence had wanted to gain admission to the waste ground next door, once a nursery. Drink cans and rubbish lay all around. I saw three lizards basking in the sunshine. The owner once told me that in winter lizards hibernated in his greenhouses, appearing stiff and dead. He was very interested in all wildlife, including the badgers, but I believed he no longer worked the place: it had been derelict for a long time.

◊ ◊ ◊

The days and nights continued hot. A piece of old badger pelvis lay on the dug out soil from the Poplar Sett. There were many small banded snails, which the badgers crunched up, and insects, especially moths. They were mainly finding insects, though it would take very many of these to satisfy such bulky animals so I left out moistened terrier meal by the water bowl too. It was a difficult time for them. Once August came there would be blackberries, fruits and ripened wheat. Now they turned over the manure heap looking for beetles and larvae. The ponies hadn't been put to graze in the meadow all year. The grey seemed to live in the stable yard and the bay in the paddock. The uncropped grass was a profusion of flowers with the blue of chickory, the red and lilac of the common and opium poppies and the large, white ox-eye daisies.

It was a near-full moon and too hot for a dew. I came across three hedgehogs noisily examining the undergrowth and noticed the boar had found one too. The paths of badgers and hedgehogs often cross; both like similar prey and search for them in similar situations. The boar batted his find over and over like a prickly ball, but he hadn't the knack of opening it to eat. Old Joe could do this by pushing his long claws into the join where head meets tail and pinning the unfortunate urchin to the ground. Then inserting the other clawed paw he would uncurl it like a piece of carpet. He taught his offspring by his example, but it seems not to be an inherent trait and some badgers never accomplish it.

Vicky's four fox cubs were playing near their den at the edge of the empty lake when the boar appeared. They huddled together watching his ambling progress across the grass. He inspected an entrance of the artificial sett, then swayed off down the chalk bank and on to the field below. He had moved home and now denned in a tiny outliner he had dug for himself in the hedgerow farther along the footpath. His spoil heaps at the two entrances were large sandy piles and very obvious. The two sows came to inspect Splinter, who rose spitting from inside the big cage whilst the badgers looked on, mildly interested. Vicky and her cubs visited him quite often, but, rightly, he feared badgers. By early morning the sows were mutually grooming in the dip that had once been the Holly Tree Sett. Weeks of doing this, turning, rolling and twisting, had worn the vegetation away and smoothed the walls of the hollow.

Thunderstorms and heavy day-long rain were a welcome change and in the showery night I followed the badger trails through the tall cow parsley to their setts. The undergrowth seemed to have grown since the rain, with everywhere revived, lush and green. The two sows were still sharing the Poplar Sett and a family of rabbits had taken over the holes at the side of the Holly Tree; even the smallest, a tiny creature, was out feeding. When I stood close by, they took little notice as they nibbled the grass. I saw no badgers till I returned to The Sett and there they were exploring the long grass by the door, watched uneasily from his cage by Splinter. The fox cub's face was altering, with his ears no longer at the sides, but on top of his head. Already his tail was white-tipped and beginning to look more like a brush. When he curled round on top of his den, he looked less ridiculous as, fox-like, he used it to cover his face. The red guard hairs were pushing through his puppy felting; they gave him a bristly appearance. His eyes were no longer baby blue, but golden to green/gold according to the light. Gazing at him I found it difficult to understand what pleasure civilised man can get from chasing such a beautiful creature to its death. I guess there must be something of the devil in many of us. That morning I had a phone call from a solicitor who had discussed the provisions of the Protection of Badger Setts Bill with the three MPs representing the foxhunting lobby. They had said if hunts didn't retain the legal right to put dogs down an occupied badger sett, dig into, damage or stop up an occupied badger sett, in fact everything but destroy one, they would wreck the Bill by calling 'object', which can be done with a Private Member's Bill by any MP during its course through parliament.

Two mornings later at 8.30 a.m. I went to check the setts and found the boar's outliner on fire! I could see it clearly across the field. It had started in the middle of the hedge and directly over the new entrances. The outside trees of the hedge were untouched. No one was about, but there was a strong smell of petrol. I ran to the rubbish tip farther along the path and took one of the flat wooden boards to beat the fire out. Then I stood for a long while afterwards wondering why it had been done and whether the boar below was all right. That night was a relief for he was unharmed, though he dug himself a new entrance at the side of the Holly Tree Sett and denned there. He and the sows took down bitten-off grass blades for bedding and finished at 5 a.m. amidst cuckoo, turtle-dove and pheasant, all calling from the wood.

I met John as arranged at the bottom of the drive and went to his beat some miles away. He pointed out exactly where he had found the RTA badger and went into the farm nearby to ask permission for me to check the land. This was given; the only area they didn't own was below the motorway embankment and farther along. They believed that land was still part of a large estate and belonged to a district councillor. I was welcome to check their fields and woods, however, though the dead badger on their stretch of lane was the only one they had ever seen. They would like to know if I did find a sett on their land. John said he would pick me up at the stile at one o'clock before he returned home to the village for his lunch. This gave me three and a half hours in bright sunshine.

The field banks and hedges yielded nothing apart from some possible snuffle holes, well trodden over by the farmer's cows. I followed the footpath to the first trees and found a bluebell wood with several very old cherries and magnificent beeches. Public footpaths wound through a sea of blue with very little rubbish about. One woman walking a dog and two young women on horseback were the only signs of human life. It was impossible to tell whether badgers lived here as the under-growth was so lush and unspoilt. I had no intention of crushing the plants underfoot and there were no animal trails. I slowly walked the length of the wood listening to the birdsong and came out overlooking the valley where Steve and I had searched for badgers two years earlier. It was down there that the locals had told us of the regular lamping of brockies and of the subsequently disused setts. I was too far from the sett I was looking for; the dead badger wouldn't have come from here. Now I retraced my steps and returned to the stile and the other side with the motorway high above. Here were a few distinct snuffle holes and badger hairs caught on the fence. On one side was an extended garden-cum-field containing a few sheep and a small wood tucked up right under the motorway. This was private, however, and though I knocked at the cottage no one came to the door. Thus I followed the field edge all the way round and came full circle to the lane and stile. By now nearly three hours were gone, but at least I could tell the farmer's wife that, as far as I could tell, the badger hadn't come from their land, though the wood might be more successfully checked in the autumn when the vegetation had died down.

Time was running out and I did want a sett for all John's efforts and interest. Walking up the sloping path, I looked under the scrub by the motorway bank and found a chalkpit, but it was all overgrown at the bottom with high nettles and, again, no animal trails passing through. I walked round and up the embankment to the top of the chalkpit and making to duck under the barbed wire, found myself staring at a tuft of badger hairs caught there! A tiny wood ran along the top of the pit with a lovely sett dug amongst the bluebells. There were plenty of badger trails and I scrambled over the many fallen trees to follow them. There was absolutely no sign of human walking, or dog-walking, and no rubbish at all. I followed the winding trails out and came to those sheep on the other side. Walking through their little wood and over the fence, I ran down the side of the field that earlier I had come into – with two minutes to go! There I sat for a few moments in the hedge by the stile and wrote up my notes, finishing just as the patrol car drew up alongside; very good timing all round. It was great to say that the sett had been found though it was on the mystery councillor's estate. John decided to ask the former patrol officer for the area about the owner rather than enquire locally. The sett was undisturbed so it was better to leave it that way.

He also gave me a copy of Section 1 (3) of the Protection from Eviction Act 1977 and suggested I write a friendly though firm letter to Mrs Ellis and include a copy, requesting access should be reinstated. If that had no effect, a solicitor's letter should do the trick. In actual fact I paid yearly in advance for gas, electricity and water, so these were her responsibility. However, if access were reinstated, I could have gas brought in for myself; the detail of her supplying it was immaterial to me really. My letter did nothing to ease the situation, but the solicitor's produced a key to the gate. It was marvellous after all those weeks to be able to cook a hot meal again; also to have the builder drive in with his equipment to mend the roof. The hot weather had expanded the metal roof joints and water from the thunderstorm found its way through. There were other jobs for him to do too, for the caravan had seen better days. The problem of my water going off, however, was never resolved and during that hot summer reached crisis point. Ray found me a milk churn that I kept filled when the water was briefly on and I bought a five-gallon water carrier too. Every available airtight bottle and container was carefully kept full against the nightmare of having no water, but as the waterless periods grew longer, the risk of infection and illness increased. Caring for sick badgers was a problem, for one needs to be scrupulously clean. I will always have a feeling of guilt over one cub that probably died through lack of proper hygiene due to chronic water shortage. That was a difficult summer, yet the beauty of my surroundings and my love of The Sett and the animals there, made me ignore the nagging uncertainty of how long I could successfully cope. I phoned Mr Ellis, but he was quite frank: he personally was happy that I should continue living and working there, but the land and my home were dependent on the goodwill of his ex-wife who was now in possession. He was anxious not to be involved.

◊ ◊ ◊

I was invited to meet a family who had a badger sett in the wood behind their house. This was of particular interest because their land was in the area from which Bossie Bessie and Old Joe had come. The woman kept pigs to fatten up and re-sell and the badgers seemed to get on well with them. I hadn't come across a relationship between badgers and pigs and it intrigued me since their foraging methods and food preferences have parallels. The woman and her two sons showed me round their part of the wood which went behind several properties along that lane and ended at Bessie's main sett, which had been partially bulldozed fifteen months earlier. Looking through the trees I could see the motorway with Ashcroft Woods above and, next door to this sett, the grounds of the house where Old Joe came from all those years ago. It was strange seeing all this from the other side of the valley; it brought back memories too.

◊ ◊ ◊

The Spring Bank Holiday Monday was another hot day with a breeze. Dog-roses and honeysuckle trailed in hedgerow and wood, pervading the warm air with their sweetness. Flo, as always, enjoyed accompanying me that afternoon and we stood watching the bees pushing into the tubular bells of the stately foxgloves and then, pollen-laden, backing out. She stuck her nose in after one irate bee and paid the price – big-nosed Flo! I recalled that the badgers here were taking an interest in a wild bees' nest at the base of a tree, though they hadn't attempted to dig it out yet. These nights, cat and badgers watched each other's foraging techniques intently. Flo was catching so many grasshoppers and crickets purely because they were moving and noisy. She would trap one within her retractile claws, bite it and drop the body back into the grass. Seeing Hattie sway over and retrieve it, the next one she dropped by the sow. Soon afterwards, the same badger dug down and turned up a nest of young rabbits. Her sister came over and challenged her, but growling, Hattie stood over the nest and finished the tiny creatures. Flo casually strolled over and carefully checked the area, but none had been left for her! There were many rabbits here, some quite old by rabbit standards, and no sign of myxomatosis.

◊ ◊ ◊

Splinter enjoyed lying stretched out in the sunshine or on warm nights on the roof of his den with his head dangling over. Early each morning I would cut some of the long grass of the path to spread on this roof and he would wait eagerly for it. Once heaped up in a pile, the young fox ran his long nose through it and rolled over and over in its cool lushness. He was living entirely on meat now – scraps from the village butcher, small mammal or bird road casualties and some baby rabbits caught by Flo. This last wasn't generosity on the cat's part, but unkindness displayed by Karen and me. It was common to see the cat walk carefully by with such a rabbit in her mouth. One of us would distract her with a shop-bought cat 'treat' whilst the other caused the dead prey to disappear. Obviously, we couldn't do this too often, for whatever Flo was, she certainly wasn't a fool, especially where her stomach was concerned! These small offerings were a good introduction to natural food for Splinter and he would carry them off to the darkness of his lair within the enclosure to eat.

◊ ◊ ◊

Several times when out in the Ashcroft area at night to see the badgers, I had brief glimpses of a starving, unkempt alsatian which we knew had been loose since the previous autumn. It had first been seen by the river in the Caldwell area, a local beauty spot where people from the city came to picnic, complete with children, pets and transistor radios. No one knew whether the dog had merely run off or been abandoned, but although locals, the police and a dog warden had tried to approach close enough to catch it, no one succeeded. Now it had found its way along the river and up the valley to Ashcroft Woods. Several dog-walkers in these woods had tried to entice and catch it, but hunger and suffering had taken their toll and it turned on its rescuers savagely. Now it tended to disappear whenever people were about. That morning I cleared rubbish from the pond area very early and had barely finished when I looked up and saw the gaunt creature watching from the far side of the water. I had found a long piece of baling twine amongst the rubbish and put it into my pocket with some vague idea of befriending the dog and keeping it with me till Ray arrived in his landrover. I threw pieces of my sandwiches to encourage it to follow me down to the car-park where the warden would be in an hour's time. It followed me down without too much enticement, but then came the problem: I had no more food left. So I sat on the ground with my rucksack open and pretended to be searching through it. From the corner of my eye I saw it crouched low to the ground, teeth bared in a silent growl. In the moment it launched itself into the air I had, for a second, a view of a once massive shoulder, now bare and suppurating, before I swung the rucksack at it and rolled aside. It worried at the foodless pack whilst I held the twine, still speaking gently and reassuringly at it, but in vain. It darted up out of the car-park into the thick under-growth and though I called and searched till Ray arrived, it had completely disappeared. The warden was due to take the council conservation officer round the woods, and when she arrived we all agreed that the alsatian could probably never be rehomed, but at least it should be put out of the misery it had suffered those past six months. The dog-warden was notified once more of its new whereabouts, though no one ever saw or heard of it again. That morning had been the wretched creature's last stand.

◊ ◊ ◊

I suspected that the fields on either side of Cliffords Bank were being lamped again for there had been a couple of curious incidents when moving lights had been reported and dogs and men's voices heard. A new route was laid from Briarmead Lane on to the grass ley above the sett as alternative access for a moto-cross club on to adjoining land. Unfortunately this unlocked gate was an open invitation and alternative route for night poachers too. I phoned the land agent who said that if I liked to buy a chain and padlock it was fine by him. That morning, Ray and I discussed this and agreed it was a good idea. It could also be convenient for the warden to have a spare key. In that way a fire engine would have access to the back of Ashcroft Woods in the event of a blaze. I also sent two spare keys to the land agent thanking him for his co-operation.

◊ ◊ ◊

The briefing document *The Case For The Protection Of Badger Setts* compiled by NFBG, was published by LACS and proved something of a shock for most of us I think. We all had problems with landowners and developers destroying active badger setts and terriermen attacking such setts using the excuse they were only after foxes. For a time, the 1985 amendment to the Badgers Act 1973 had helped in cases using this excuse, as it put the onus of proof on terriermen to prove they were not after badgers. Now with clever lawyers, plus dead foxes taken along on digs, most of the amendment's strength was dissipated. The aim of the new Bill was to amend the Badgers Act so as to make it an offence to 'damage, destroy, obstruct the entrances of, or otherwise interfere with any badger sett' subject to the general exceptions and licensing provisions within the Act. No briefing document such as this had ever been put together before, though most badger groups kept records of incidents in their own areas. From the three or four groups I had known some years ago, many others had sprung up out of concern for the animals' welfare and now there were fifty-five. In the short time allowed, thirty of these groups and interested individuals were able to reply to the request for information, which gave a good response across the country. Incidents involving successful prosecutions were excluded. What the survey information revealed was horrendous, with conclusive evidence of badger setts being damaged or destroyed by developers, terriermen and farmers. The largest group of people attacking setts, however, were foxhunts. This was of particular concern because three years earlier, after consultation with NFBG and other pro-badger concerns, the Master of Foxhunts Association had issued an earth-stoppers Code to all registered hunts in October 1987. This Code stipulated that hunts must:

(a) not dig into well-known badger setts
(b) not use oil drums, road cones and other such foreign objects for earth-stopping and that plastic bags only are to be employed providing they are removed after hunts
(c) soft earth should be used as the stopping method.

The Code stated 'It is stupid to attempt to dig foxes in well-known badger setts (which should be stopped anyway).' However, the abuse had continued.

The briefing document showed, for example, that of twenty-eight recorded incidents between August 1989 and April 1990 in Gloucestershire, twenty-six were directly attributable to local foxhunts. That county's badger group couldn't possibly monitor every sett – how much more abuse had gone undetected? The survey revealed that foxhunts in various parts of the country were still using all manner of objects to block setts, from fence-posts to milkchurns and even a MAFF cage-trap! They were cutting the sides and tops of sett entrances and making tunnels collapse, which led in some cases to the destruction of the sett. Terriers were being entered into active setts after foxes, even during the breeding period when badger cubs were at risk of being killed, and entrances were not unstopped after a hunt.

At the committee stage, the same points were gone over again and again by the three MPs acting for the foxhunting lobby, in an attempt to talk the Bill out. Eventually it did pass on to await its third reading, with an amendment in favour of stopping-up. It was clear, however, that the hunting fraternity were out to wreck the Bill.

◊ ◊ ◊

A woman living not far from me had found a dead RTA badger. We met at her house and together went to look for the body, but by then it had disappeared. She left me to look for it whilst she drove on to ask a neighbour. This was the lane running at the side of the copse housing the Sand Pit badgers and I found the body laid amongst the dog's mercury and fading bluebells under the trees. It was a sow that had recently been lactating; I could express no milk, so imagined her cubs were probably weaned. I thought I knew the dead animal, but close to she looked so small – not much larger than Micky my stuffed badger, which had been killed on a road when a year old.

Back home it began to rain and later I had a phone call from a man further along the lane. He had heard I was searching for the badger. Someone had put it for safety inside the wood. I promised to go out that night to see if her cubs were all right and he thanked me for my interest, saying that they tried to keep an eye on the badgers there, but it was good that someone else was alert to their welfare. It rained most of that night, but I did find the sow's two cubs and they were obviously weaned and well integrated with the dominant boar, probably their father, together with the rest of the clan at the quarry in the beech wood.

Something was happening on the far fields round Ashcroft Woods. Though the access gate was now chained and pad-locked, tyre marks had come up from the main road and dug into the wet grass of the field above Cliffords Bank. The tracks weaved back and forth erratically; no one would have got away undetected in daylight. It was too far for me to come every night in the hope of catching the lampers. Bessie now had only one cub, though both youngsters had seemed healthy enough and playing together two nights earlier. The rest of the clan were nervy and disquieted. Apart from alerting the police and com-ing as often as I could, there was nothing more I could do.

◊ ◊ ◊

Suddenly Splinter was ill. From being an alert, boisterous and energetic young fox who played on his den top and romped round the enclosure; who barked at the merest sight of me working at the kitchen window and practised rolling on his back whilst balancing objects on the pads of his paws, he lay in the dark, listless and not eating. Karen and I had our suspicions, but I would leave it for two days and warn Mrs Ellis before taking action. The previous week my landlady had put up notices on the access gate and drive, forbidding anyone to park, drive in or visit me. She had also seen Graham stop at the bottom of the drive two weeks earlier and phoned to say she would sue me if I had visitors again; she concluded by threatening to burn down the caravan. I let her know that I suspected the fox cub had been poisoned. No one was aware of the cages and animals here apart from the police, RSPCA and Mrs Ellis herself. Whilst it was obvious that the woman was no longer emotionally responsible for her actions, I was determined the foxes and badgers should not suffer. If Splinter died, she would be answering some awkward questions. To this day, I don't know whether she really did try to poison the young fox, but Splinter miraculously recovered and neither animals nor their cages were ever tampered with again. The woman was a paradox. I knew she often threw out huge quantities of food by her patio window with its flood-lighting to watch the foxes come and feed. She also let her dogs out at the same time. The resulting chaos can be imagined. I recalled her telling me in all seriousness once that she watched one of her cats 'cuddling' a squirrel. Flo and Mrs Ellis's cats had one thing in common: they certainly liked squirrels – to eat! The insistence that the cat had cradled the other in its arms cuddling and caressing it was almost as embarrassing as the idea of her four dobermans amicably feeding with foxes. The foxes merely lay low till she and the guard dogs had gone to bed and then came searching for the leftovers. In some ways she was rather a sad person.

◊ ◊ ◊

I went out at night to the Ashcroft area with lampers very much on my mind. All was well, however, and I stayed over to meet Ray. The main pond was full and the clearest I had ever known it. He had done well by removing so much debris last year. Together we checked the wildflower meadow, Little Chantry Field and walked the lower edge of Great Chantry. There are so many native species growing in this old hedge – spindle, dogwood, guelder rose, briar rose, wayfaring, hazel, gean, white-beam. Kent is still a wonderful county in spite of the twentieth century's mutilation of this Garden of England. Ray strimmed some of the verges, opening up the rides. We watched a swallow swooping low around us for insects and two spotted flycatchers taking the insects from a great sycamore tree. This led us to discuss the desire of our local trust and other conservation bodies to fell sycamores. To us, a tree is a tree whatever the species and if it has been growing for years it shouldn't be felled just because it happens to be a sycamore. Admittedly, they are invasive and it is often a good thing to remove the many seedlings that spring up, although most of these would come to nothing in any case because of lack of light. Apparently, the argument is that sycamores are not a native species (they were introduced about 500 years ago) and are poor at attracting insects. But to hack them down because of these 'crimes' seems ridiculous in the extreme. I suppose eventually those of Ash-croft will be removed, but looking at the old sycamore pollards that day, my heart grieved to think of their deliberate demise. We had lost so many fine trees in the hurricane.

Our badger group had been contacted by a Mr Murdoch regarding an albino badger and her three albino cubs seen regularly about midday round a local garage where he worked. They were fed by the mechanics and Murdoch felt they were too tame and someone could take them for taxidermy. The whole affair was rather suspect as, for instance, an albino sow mating with a normal-coloured boar doesn't produce albino cubs; the recessive gene for albinism doesn't work in that way. I phoned the man, who promised to supply me with a photo of the white badgers and would gladly come to meet myself and others of the group to show us from where the badgers actually came. Neither the photo nor Mr Murdoch materialised and somehow we felt we were being conned, but none the less a badger group should investigate any calls. The local police were advised in case strangers in the area – a small, sleepy village – might cause concern.

After talking to locals, it was discovered there was an albino, but only one. It foraged with other ordinary badgers (which is what one would expect) and although in the drought it had been seen in daylight and did come for food, people were very protective of their badgers, including the albino, so there was no cause for alarm. They knew the man who had contacted us. He was described as 'forty-ish and a bit of a romancer'. We suspected he would be given something of a rough ride when he turned up on Monday for work! Albinos are not uncommon in some counties, especially in Kent, Essex, Berkshire and Dorset. This village wasn't far from the famous Snowall described by G. Burness (1970) in *The White Badger*. It wasn't a wasted Sunday for the village knew now there was an active badger group in their area.

Splinter was his old, saucy self again, barking if I entered his enclosure without bringing food with me and prancing back and forth on top of his den. It was good to see him well once more. Flo disdained her custard, usually considered a treat, so I offered it to the young fox, who needed no second invitation. That afternoon was dull but sultry and he played and slept in the long, freshly cut grass I had laid on top of his house. Going indoors, I could watch him closely unobserved, using the binoculars. He had grown so incredibly beautiful. How could anyone wish to harm a fox?

I met Graham one afternoon as I was walking home and told him that Karen and I would soon be away on holiday. She was hiring a car and together we were driving up to Scotland and spending a few days with a friend. We would be away ten nights. Steve was coming in every day to look after Splinter and Flo. Lamping seemed quiet now in mid-June, but would the police keep an eye peeled? I mentioned the anti-visitor notices. Steve had already been accosted by someone acting on Mrs Ellis's behalf. My visitors had dropped to nil except when friends filled up the churn and drove it in for my water supply, and even they were harassed, but Steve needed to come in to see to the animals. Graham promised to have a word; again she was acting illegally. If Steve had any trouble, he should let the station know. Graham came to look at the Ninepenny setts. We could see they were well occupied. If there was an attempted badger dig when I was away, then he as our wildlife officer could state, like me, that they had been occupied shortly before. He would do his best to keep an eye on them. We discussed the disbanding of the Oakley rural office and the officer in charge who had now left. Ian, the sergeant, had worked very hard for a number of years building up the rural section to patrol and liaise in the thirteen villages around Oakley town. He regularly patrolled himself and all information came to him as their rural collator. Then a superintendent appeared, a university graduate with a minimum three years on the beat, and decided such rural sections were unnecessary. Ironically, the few men working the rural beat had received more letters of thanks from local people than the rest of Oakley station put together. New brooms sweep clean, however, money must be saved and manpower used 'to better purpose'. The superintendent went on to higher things, leaving Ian and his constables to the ruin of all they had achieved. The sergeant stayed for a time, but finally took his inspector's exam and asked for a transfer nearer home. We chanced to meet before he left. I have a sneaking suspicion this officer will become a superintendent himself before too many years have passed and though Oakley might not reap the benefit another area will.

Graham told me that only last evening he had been to see a farmer who in conversation mentioned 'the badger-diggers we had at Easter'. The officer knew nothing about the incident because he had been off-duty that Sunday. The farmer had called Oakley police and in the meantime tried to keep the diggers on his land until a patrol arrived. In vain, for the police didn't materialise for two and a half hours! The farmer took the vehicle numbers and photos of the men and their dogs. Having done this myself, I knew what a risk he was taking; wrong-doers do not like visual evidence of their actions. Three aspects of this really upset Graham – the time taken to arrive, the fact that he was never told, even though the farmland is part of his patch, and that nothing was done about the diggers or the photos. It would not have happened if the rural office existed and Ian had still been with Oakley.

Steve appeared one afternoon before Karen and I left and commented on how Splinter the Magnificent had grown. He deserved the title and it stuck. Of all the foxes I have known or looked after, he was the most beautiful. I had found a broken beech branch in Ninepenny Wood and laid it on top of his den, together with bunches of tiny, red cherries, already dropping from the wild geans. The beech husks were splitting open and the young fox carefully extracted and ate the mast. As the

RSPCA Inspector had finished his last call for that day, we walked round together and looked at the setts. Steve also offered to keep the water bowls filled.

◊ ◊ ◊

The flaxen barley was ripe and dropping its bearded heads. The Ninepenny badgers stole along the rows, scarcely moving the stalks as they picked up beetles and snails. Hazel dug up and ate a nest of wood mice. Many moths blundered by that the badgers snapped at, rising up on their hindlegs to catch them. One night I saw our resident tawny male take a pipistrelle bat in flight.

Off the old boar's sett was a rabbit burrow containing four tiny rabbits about three weeks old. I suspect the mother had already given birth to another litter; pregnant does do not use a nursery stop again the same season. They were rarely above ground at night, but surely the old badger could scent them? They were still at the age when they crouched down, rather than fleeing when danger threatened. At 8 a.m. I watched these young rabbits eating the cleavers or goosegrass round their home, washing and friskily playing. They were not at all frightened of me, provided I stood still. Each could have hidden in my cupped hand. How long would they last, I wondered? The following night that question was answered when the boar effortlessly caught two of them leaving the merest wisps of fur to tell the tale. All the badgers were gleaning the beech mast and cherries as well as the dropping barley. Legget's field around Ninepenny Wood was as dirty as last year with great stretches of wild oats and wheat 'volunteers' making it difficult to tell what was really the crop.

To my knowledge, these three badgers disposed of seven wasps' nests that year and Hattie found the bees' nest at the base of the tree. These insects are sluggish in the relative coolness of the night and an element of surprise under cover of darkness probably helped too. Undoubtedly badgers do get stung, but such nests make a wholesome and filling meal in the dry, wormless months.

We returned from Scotland about noon to find the weather in the south had remained hot and humid. Splinter was pleased to see me, after an initial dive into his den at my approach. I called 'Splinter, Splinter' softly and a sharp face with its darkly rounded, shiny button nose popped out. Later I went into his enclosure to clean it and he pranced round me working there, high stepping on those slender legs and dainty, dusky paws. His tail had bushed out underneath from 2.5 cm from the base. It was clear to see how it would soon become a brush. Each time I turned to face him, he stared into my face, his large ears upright. Two lines of black ran from the inside corners of his eyes to his muzzle; Karen called them his tear marks. If donkeys are said to bear the sign of the Saviour's cross upon their backs, then surely foxes bear the marks of sorrow for man's persecution of their kind.

The badgers eagerly ate the food I put out for them that night. I imagine they missed the soaked terrier meal when I was away. Steve had filled their water bowl and looked after Flo and the fox cub well. The cat didn't appear till that evening and acted as if we had never been away. The fine, hot days continued with Splinter lying on his den top in the sunshine. The white ox-eye daisies growing all around The Sett were nearly over, but chicory and field scabious nodded under my windows making bright splashes of blue amongst the green.

One evening Steve phoned asking if I would take in a baby bat for him. We met at the bottom of the drive and together looked into the cardboard box that a woman had left on his doorstep. The bat was less than 1.5 cm long. Its head and body with limbs clinging to the piece of material inside could fit on to the face of my watch. He said when he had first looked in, he had thought it must have escaped, so small was it. Steve left me with the box and some Lactol (dried milk) on which to feed it.

Tim was used to caring for bats and I had several times met his friend Mick Sage who had considerable knowledge of them. I duly phoned Mick and learned more about bats in that ten-minute conversation than I have ever gained from books or nature programmes! As the pipistrelle had a small amount of fur it was between one and one and a half weeks old; it had a slight chance of survival. Mick's instructions were as follows:

You will need to feed it with Lactol every one and a half to two hours. At this time of year, the mother will be leaving her roost to feed at approximately 9.30 p.m. but will return at regular intervals to suckle her infant. It will need milk for at least another week or ten days and can then be fed on mealworms and any insects that you can supply.

Place the bat on a sloping or upright situation so that it can crawl up the piece of fixed material and hang down. To feed it or exercise – place it gently in your hand and leave till it warms up and begins to move around. Offer a drop of milk near its mouth and the bat will take it. Pat its rear end gently when removing excreta, which will be messy and liquid. Bats are social creatures and like physical contact; the warmth of your hand is necessary. If the milk you offer is too rich, the stomach will quickly swell, in which case dilute to obtain the right balance. Let me know how it gets on.

Pip, as I called it, was a lovely, tiny creature. Karen stayed over that weekend to help care for it. My sight had greatly deteriorated those past few months so to offer drops of milk to the right place, i.e. its mouth, I used a magnifying glass. With Pip on my hand and a moistened finger held out with the glass in the other fingers, I managed surprisingly well, the bat raising its head with neat ears upright, each time. Its drinking was audible. If it took too much and spluttered, spitting some out, that too sounded clear. His smooth brown fur had still to finish growing as did the membrane or 'wings'. The forearms don't finish growing until a bat is five weeks old, although they are capable of short flight at three weeks. We were learning a lot about bats and enjoying this tiny creature. I didn't stay out for long that night; just enough to check the three Ninepenny badgers were fine, then back to feed Pip. We were careful not to let Flo see what we were doing. Apart from when it was fed, it was easy to conceal – a small box next to the clock on top of my filing cabinet. Certainly the easiest creature I have ever housed.

Each time he was carefully unhooked from the material, he felt cold and lifeless. A few minutes held in the warmth of clasped hands and a slight stirring could be felt, then the head would rise and he moved surprisingly fast, propelled by his forelimbs. I feared I might hold him too firmly and hurt him, or too loosely and drop him. The moment he saw my finger with a drop of milk suspended on it approaching, he emitted small squeaks of excitement and drank eagerly. Then in the early hours of one morning I had the greatest difficulty warming up the tiny body, and though he did accept a small amount of milk, it was obvious he was dying. It will sound very foolish to say that I grieved at his loss, but both of us did. We had become very fond of the tiny bat whose hold on life and struggle to survive made us feel both humble and privileged to have known him.

◊ ◊ ◊

I had been home a week from our holiday when I was told there had been men lamping on Caldwell golf course while I was away. Later, large pieces of badger fur with skin attached were collected from the rough grass area below the sett on Summer-house Knole. I phoned Graham to discover that the police had never been told – the message, complete with badger pieces, had just been left for me with a third party. It was all the more annoying for the police that the woman concerned was a parish councillor, and her husband was co-ordinator for the village Neighbourhood Watch. Graham had spoken to the husband two days earlier at a meeting and even then nothing had been said. It was this kind of thing, even more than the incident itself, that we found so very disheartening. Our police knew all about lamping and, in my experience, were quick to respond to a 'lights seen' call. I remembered the Kirsty incident of the previous year.

Kirsty had been a sister of Kate and Mícheál, Missy's yearlings from Cliffords Bank. Kate had been run over early one June morning on the quiet lane, but I had been with her sister and the other badgers when the lamping incident occurred. We were all on the cut hayfield above the bank and its sett. I lay on the grass with Crisp's three cubs using me to bounce up and down on whilst their mother busily carried hay bedding down below. The other badgers were dotted about and the moon not yet up. It was a lovely, mild night with excellent visibility. I was still lying there at about 11.20 p.m. when there was a barking, snarling and snapping, and I sat bolt upright to see dogs and two men around a badger. I grabbed up a cub under each arm and calling to Crisp, pushed them into the nursery entrance. She and the other little cub followed suit and I returned to the open field to find all the badgers gone except the one that the dogs were worrying. The two lampers were urging them on. It was only when I shouted to them to call their dogs off that they realised I was there. In anger I grasped a terrier by its scruff, swung it round and threw it as far as I could. Then did the same with another, but as a man came at me I threw the dog at his face. You can do this with terriers, but would have a job with lurchers. There were two lurchers and three terriers. The men swore and cursed and, calling to the dogs, went off into the back of Ashcroft Woods. It was Kirsty who lay on the ground, her right hindleg at a crazy angle with fur and flesh ripped off to the pad. She was bitten all round the head and an ear was covered in blood. It was a very dazed badger that lay on her side in a heap. I tried to carry her, but they are heavy animals and it was obvious that I was hurting, so I left her on the path.

It took me thirty minutes to run through the woods and phone from the farm manager's office. He had given me a key for this very purpose two years earlier. A woman answered and promised to send someone immediately. I mentioned the track through the barley at the top of Briarmead that the hay-baler had made; another easy access on and off the meadow now. Then a run back with sweat streaming into my eyes and soaking my body. I returned to see a patrol car on the field. The sergeant and a woman constable had already checked the perimeter of the area for vehicles with no success. We walked over the meadow – not only were there no lampers, but no Kirsty either. Had she gone underground? I knew she wasn't capable of moving that far. There was the spot where I left her, dark with blood and a strong musky smell hanging on the night air. A beautiful crescent moon was slowly rising and the scene looked so peaceful – how ironic! The officers were very understanding. They waited whilst I ran round calling and looking, but no, she wasn't there. I should have stayed – oh, what does one do? Get the police to drive round hoping to find a vehicle or stay, knowing that way the lampers will never be caught? What would the poachers do with her now? Keep her somewhere quiet and feed her for the weekend. A broken leg wouldn't matter, in fact, so much the better; more even chances for the dogs to bait. Oh, Kirsty, what an awful end, but at least our police knew about lamping and were more than willing to try to help.

◊ ◊ ◊

The third reading of the Protection of Badger Setts Bill on 6th July was a fiasco, with twenty-four amendments tabled by the foxhunting lobby to be discussed in the short time allowed. Had they been successful, these amendments would have neutered the Bill completely; one even excluded all landowners! But to the call of 'object' the Bill was lost. Never mind, we would live to fight another day and win – or rather, the badger would. The one thing we must *never* do is give up.

One evening about 7 p.m. Flo came marching along the path to The Sett. I was working at the sink with the window open making a meal. She turned round, sat down and looked back. There was a fox following her, a young vixen about Splinter's size, but with her brush better developed. In fact, one of Vicky's offspring. Flo and the cubs played together and this one was a particular friend. Flo yowled at the fox. She had come home because she could smell dinner cooking and her companion had smelt dinner too. However, this friendship with Flo did not include sharing! The vixen sat down, big ears turning, and looked up at me. It yawned and glanced in Splinter's direction; he watched her with interest. Then a noise of barking from the stables frightened the young vixen and she slipped away into the undergrowth.

◊ ◊ ◊

It was too hot to work now in the caravan for the sun on its metal roof made it several degrees hotter than the outside temperature, which was now more than 30°C. It was far cooler in the woods beneath the trees. The hay had been cut and baled and the harvest was over around Ashcroft Woods. The stubble was being turned under, with many lapwings at night feeding on the insects in the upturned earth. Still only July, but with the weather so hot and dry, the leaves were already shades of brown on some of the trees. Such a day was the last Sunday in the month when I wardened the woods one afternoon and evening. Before returning home, I stood in the car-park, now deserted of vehicles, and saw a kestrel drop on to a wood mouse that had been foraging on the ground. The raptor was aware of me, but not frightened, merely watchful. I lingered for several minutes admiring the barred wings and curved beak. It was worth staying till dusk to walk home in the cool of the late evening. The lanes and verges were turned to dust and for some reason unknown to me, my steps took me the long way round and through Oakley town. The streets and houses reflected the heat of the dying day. It would have been quicker and far more pleasant to have walked the fields way.

I passed the reflectors along the lane between town and village, glancing over to the darkness of the sett under the trees. Walking on I thought I heard barking and stopped a moment in my tracks, but except for the occasional car passing on the lane all was quiet. I had barely gone a few paces more before I heard the dog again coming from the direction of the holes. I returned and leaned over the fence to look more closely below. There was a dog – a large one – and it seemed to be tethered. It was a retriever, not a terrier, and it whined softly in its throat at sight of me. What on earth was it doing there? The woman with the horses who owned the land had dogs and so had the people that liveried their animals with her. Perhaps one of these people was looking at the sett and had tied up their dog whilst doing so. I didn't care to call out or go over in case I disturbed someone that shouldn't have been there. It would be best to run to the woman's house and speak to her.

Neither she nor her family knew of any dog, but they came back with me to see what was happening. Her son went the stable way round, whilst we drove up by the reflectors and went down the bank to the sett. The dog had been tied up and left. There was no sign of any disturbance to the badgers' home, nor of people at all. We took the dog back to their house and decided it had probably been abandoned. Or rather, I decided it had, for the woman is still convinced someone had been disturbed at the sett. The dog had scars and marks on it nose. Whatever had occurred, it was terribly dehydrated, to the extent that at first sight it appeared to have been starved. It had probably been tied up there on the Friday; it was now Sunday evening. Even under the shade of the trees, it must have suffered cruelly; I privately blessed whatever force had guided my footsteps to walk the long way round. There were certainly some odd incidents that summer, like the two men with Staffordshire bull terriers, who were digging a pit in a copse on isolated farmland but ran away when approached. It wasn't far from a badger sett and the general feeling was that it was either meant for dog-fighting or badger-baiting, or both.

By mid-July I saw that wild bees had taken over an entrance of the Poplar Sett, or perhaps I should say one of the tunnels that forked out from it. This was the flooded part that the badgers no longer used. They didn't seem aware of the bees in the annexe of their home though of course these insects aren't active at night. Would the badgers smell them or was the hive and its contents too far along? Recalling the baby rabbits, however, I was convinced that it would be only a matter of time.

A few nights later, the boar found the wild bees' nest and dragged out the honeycomb, grubs, torpid bees and all. It must have been some way into the tunnelling. The badger didn't go into it, but dug down to it from one and a half metres away. Three very thirsty badgers drunk the water bowl dry that early morning. I returned with fresh water and stood in the shadows watching them groom the sticky sweetness from one another. It had been a very cold night with all our breath vaporising, but the days were intensely and oppressively hot, in the low thirties. However, the nights now were often windy as well as cold. This wind was bringing the apples down which, although small, were another source of food for fox and badger alike. Blackberries were ripening too and the badgers were picking them, each berry selected one at a time.

It was first day of August that I released Splinter. I calculated he was eighteen and a half weeks old, and there was no doubt in my mind that if hungry he would return for food. I put down his dinner as usual and left the door wide open. As with former releases, it took much scenting of the air and false starts – nearly two hours in fact – before he finally had the courage to leave his confinement. Each morning and evening now, he appeared below the caravan window to be fed and each time I put down his bowl, I would put down Flo's also, a short distance away. It was interesting for me to see that he no longer feared her, though for a while, she was very much on her dignity and refused to play. For the young fox's part, he was lonely and badly wanted companionship, so I would take an apple from one of the trees and bowl it along the ground. It was thrilling to see him move. He seemed to flow along the turf in pursuit of the apple, springing over it and rolling on to his back to balance it on his paws. Even Flo was impressed and, finally, joined in. That was an idyllic summer, with two carefree animals playing beneath the hawthorns, in and out and, in Flo's case, running up a trunk and hanging there. This was something Splinter could not accomplish – his were not retractile claws. He tried it, not to be outdone by his small companion, but he could not hang! Her rounded, furry face bore a rather smug expression. Then he would nudge her with his nose as she sat there watching and she would pat him with a soft paw. She could unsheath her claws if he became too rough and he always respected her. The cat was the boss, but in those early days Flo loved to tease.

The Ninepenny badgers were searching long hours for food in spite of the soaked terrier meal and scraps I was leaving at the water bowl. At 2 a.m. one night I watched the boar return to this area under the beeches, obviously hoping more food might miraculously appear. Rather disgusted, he made to defecate – they don't seem to dig dung pits when the ground is as hard as this – and he finished up using the water bowl instead. This happened last year with the cubs, I recalled. All the short, dark hours were spent searching for food and the ground was rock-hard. The food I put out, together with the dropping cherry plums and cobnuts, was keeping the badgers here in reasonable shape. It was a pity they are foragers rather than hunters, for the resident foxes were sated with rabbits. There seemed to be a rabbit population explosion. One evening there was a confrontation when Foxy crept up for a change of diet whilst the clan were eating. Needless to say, it was the fox that beat a hasty retreat!

One night Hattie caught a pheasant. It had no tail feathers as it was well into its moult and therefore couldn't get off the ground quickly. There was a great commotion of 'kuttuc-kuttuc' and feathers everywhere. There was a fine rain that night. We all enjoyed the wet, even Flo, who had followed me. Hazel came to see what all the noise was about and a squabble started. Then the boar appeared to see what was going on – and whether it was edible! He shook himself vigorously and the water drops flew off him. Legget hadn't yet harvested his wheat and the grain was dropping out of the ears. The rain, though fine, had been continuous for some hours and now much of the field was flattened. By the next day, with the temperature still high, the rain might not have been, and by 5th August it was the hottest day on record at an unbelievable 37°C. Now the combine was on the fields and that night the full moon was a vivid orange, with the badgers gleaning the grain spilt by the hopper under a velvet sky. There were many lapwings there too, feeding on insects and larvae exposed by the combine; their mournful cries echoed all around.

Sometimes days would elapse without Splinter coming for food, which was a good sign that he was learning to hunt for himself. Sometimes he merely came to visit, as the time when Karen stayed overnight and went to leave in the morning – taking the cover off her moped she nearly stepped back on him! One evening there was Splinter, and I sat on the ground outside The Sett handing him food. He had jam butties (his favourite), some of which he cached, and dog meat which he gulped down. He returned and accepted dog biscuits out of my fingers: these he carefully cached. When there were no more, I sat on the ground and spread out my fingers, palms outwards, saying 'no more, no more'. Splinter came forward and gently took hold of my right thumb, realised his mistake and nervously licked my hand. Like a confused cat, he sat in front of me and washed himself. He became very engrossed, obviously forgetting why he had started, nibbling his front right leg and licking his body fur. Although the front of his legs were dusky and the backs a cream, a long line of russet ran through the cream; he really was so beautiful. I lay on my stomach on the ground facing him and he bent and smelt my face. When I chuckled he began to play, jumping up and bounding around me. Then a distant sound of a doberman barking made him run off down the winding path.

Chapter Eight

THE centre of a field adjoining Ninepenny Wood had been left uncut with the corn still standing amidst stubble. As I walked out one morning to check the setts, there came the sound of a combine from over the rise as a fox rushed out of the standing crop and flew downfield towards the Ellis's property, its brush streaming after like a banner. The combine bore down, but fortunately the fox had a good start, and in any case combines aren't the fastest of machines. Looking out from beneath the trees, everything was bathed in golden light: the corn, stubble, combine and fox framed round with yellowing, dying foliage under a blazing sun. The leaves were dropping fast, especially those on the elder, elm and cherry. The paths were littered with multi-coloured cherry leaves. It was 10th August and autumn already.

Three hours earlier the following morning, I saw a fox in more or less the same place; it was walking parallel to me, but in the opposite direction over the stubble of the finished field. Again it was bathed in golden light so that it could have been any grown fox. On a sudden premonition, I called 'Vicky, Vicky', and it was indeed her, as she approached within two metres of me squatting at the wood edge. She looked enquiringly at me, speaking softly almost face to face. Then off she strolled in the direction she had been going, looking at me again and again before disappearing amongst the trees. I suspected it was she who ran from the standing wheat in front of the combine yesterday, but of course I could not be sure.

Splinter hadn't appeared for three days and nights. Since the harvest there had been day and night shooting, with Legget's son amongst the shooters. Also, the dobermans were wandering about for much of the day, but like Flo Splinter feared them and unless cornered was not likely to be caught. Shooting was another matter. I had been out for most of the fourth night and was busy in The Sett at 6.55 a.m. when I heard a miaow and looked out from the kitchen window to see Splinter eagerly looking up at me. The cat came springing in as I opened the door and went straight to her food bowl. Splinter might stand patiently waiting outside my window till I happened to look out, but not my Flo! I fed both animals and then sat with Flo in my arms on the doorstep as Splinter finished his meal. She walked over to him when he had finished, rubbing herself against him and still purring. The fox looked slightly abashed at this familiarity and accepted two dog biscuits from my fingers before making off again. The ash trees' green leaflets were strewn about the paths and the birches' fine, brown seeds within their transparent membrane floated in through the caravan's windows. On all sides the haws showed a bright red amongst the turning leaves.

Later I went out to post a letter, choosing to go the field way to the village. The sun was shining in a vivid blue sky with a brisk wind racing the clouds. Some distance away sat a fox with its back to me. In the far field that rises to become a hill, a tractor was ploughing. The fox sat on the golden stubble in the golden sunshine, watching the tractor go by, turn and retrace its path. The animal's head moved slowly following the line of the plough; then its owner yawned and continued to gaze. I smiled to think that just as we humans like watching foxes, apparently foxes like watching us. All the time I was moving nearer and it's well nigh impossible to walk silently on stubble. The big, pointed ears turned and their owner saw me, looked for a moment at who was disturbing him and sauntered casually into the hedge. Those weeks of hot, glaring sun, golden harvest and foxes seemed like a Van Gogh landscape, with something of his dream-like quality. They are pictures in my mind that I will never forget.

Having posted my letter, I half expected to see the fox still watching on my return, but he was gone and, come to that, so was the tractor. I picked fallen plums off the edge of the stubble and some from the trees themselves. There were many ripe blackberries and the wind had brought down those acorns not affected by the drought; they were big and plump. How early everything was.

Splinter regularly returned now with Flo and would sit waiting under the window. The fox usually cached his food, carrying each piece or portion away to do so. By the time he returned for some more, the cat would be standing by his bowl. She didn't want or like his food, but she enjoyed teasing him. Splinter would hesitate, then cautiously approach. After some deliberation he decided to claim his bowl. Flo began to wash behind her ears – the immediate face-saving answer. A dog barked not far away and the fox melted into the shadows. I brought the rest of his food indoors, for I didn't want to encourage the dobermans to take an interest.

Some while later, Flo and fox were hunting in the dip where my water pipes and drains were laid. The covering earth had subsided after a few months and although grown over now with lush grass and ribbed and white melilot, it seemed to have become a refuge for insects, most especially grasshoppers and crickets. The two animals pounced and ate their respective prey, then hunted again. Absorbed, they bumped into one another and, caught off guard, Splinter grunted and Flo miaowed. They looked very surprised, then wandered off in different directions. I suspected they really were quite good friends!

My next Saturday to warden Ashcroft Woods was a dull, overcast morning, though still very warm. All was quiet with no one about. As I crossed the hayfield and checked Cliffords Bank it began to rain heavily. In moments, water was running across and down the field, and over my shoes. I reached the back of High Ridge, the moto-cross scramble, to find it far worse on the bare, baked and well-ridden earth. Where the hard ground was unable to absorb the sudden downpour, the water was deep and swirling halfway up my legs with debris and rubbish bumping me. Somehow I struggled across the plateau and had a shock as I tried to descend. The scree slopes had become waterfalls and below shone a fast-moving stream where the lane had been. It was a nightmare getting down and an effort struggling along the lane. A car hooted bad-temperedly as it surged up behind and resoaked me as it tore by. Farther on I tried to stand aside for a car that was coming towards me, dimly seen through the pouring rain. I didn't feel very friendly towards drivers at that moment and probably showed it. The door opened and the farm manager's voice called 'Chris, for heaven's sake. I'll give you a lift.' Drivers could be friendly after all!

Karen was with me that evening and talking together we happened to look out of The Sett. There was Splinter with Flo next to him, both sitting bolt upright and looking our way. 'When *is* dinner?' was the question on both their faces. As Karen so rightly said, 'It's a good job not all the animals you've looked after come back to be fed, Mum'. I filled each bowl and, inevitably, the cat finished hers first and went to inspect the young fox's. At least she intended to, but she saw Splinter watching her closely and in some confusion began to wash. After all, he didn't move away as he used to and he was a great deal taller than her now. Karen walked up the path and sat down with both animals. The fox was very skittish and wanted a game, but with human company the tabby was on her dignity and jumped into Karen's lap instead.

Much later, well after dark, I went to walk round. It had long ago ceased raining and everywhere smelt wonderful and refreshed. I walked through the meadow and turned the corner as something flashed by me and hid behind the fence. It was the typical Flo action when she is looking for attention, but I knew she was indoors, curled up on an easy chair next to Karen. And Flo does not have a white tip to her tail. I called 'Splinter, Splinter, you idiot', and sure enough he came sauntering up, barked and ran round a tree. I continued to the empty lake and, again like the cat, he allowed me to get ahead then rushed up and past me. Sometimes he tired of this and simply trotted by my side, occasionally looking up at me. I had such joy from this young fox. His tail was a real brush now, wide and cylindrical with a thick, white, cotton-wool tip. The fur of brush, shoulders and flanks was a rich russet brown. He was still very long legged, which made him look thin, but he was merely rangy as a healthy

147

fox should be. Back at The Sett I found him a shortcake biscuit which Flo came to inspect, to make sure she didn't want one too. She didn't! The two animals sat outside whilst we sat inside talking. Looking out, we saw the fox lying dog-like with head on paws, the cat sitting all humped up in her going-to-sleep position. Eventually Splinter rose, stretched and gave his companion a nudge with his nose. She opened her eyes, yawned and, following the fox, wandered down the path into the night.

It was whilst watching the Ninepenny badgers that I found I had company; not Flo, but Splinter was by my side. However, badgers and foxes don't mix well and the boar made a short rush at him so that Splinter ran off. The Bank Holiday weekend culminated in a series of thunderstorms and rain that was steady, easing the drought conditions far more than the last. But there were still no worms to be had: it would take much cooler, long-term rain before they reappeared near the surface. The badgers didn't emerge till the thunder eased, but did well on the apples, pears and plums that the storm brought down, as well as taking the dropped grain. There was still a great heap of the latter, where the combine's hopper had missed the lorry. In those heavily misty nights, slugs and snails abounded. Flo accompanied me and played with the sows, but Splinter didn't try badgerwatching again.

Yet another wasps' nest was unearthed by Hazel, this time at the side of the meadow. The entrance was in a disused mousehole by the bramble bushes, but as always the badger dug down a short distance away, exposing the nest and grubs. Looking that morning there was not much left: pieces of grey papery nest, a few dead wasps and two survivors crawling amongst the ruins.

I had been saving every drop of washing water for my garden and the wildflowers I had brought there. Standing by the recovery cage watering the plants, I smelt fox so strongly that I looked round expecting Splinter to be standing there. He wasn't however. I stepped back and trod right on the poor creature who must have been waiting patiently for my attention directly behind me! He yelped and ran off a short distance and looked back at my call of 'Oh, Splinter, I am sorry lad'. The tone of my voice must have reassured him, for he came right up again, big brush waving and almost dancing on his toes, the way they do when pleased or asking for a game. I made him a big jam butty as an apology.

As Flo sat on the path in front of the caravan waiting for Splinter that evening, a green woodpecker ran along the ground towards her, calling. She jumped indoors, somewhat confused, but it recalled for me the days before I had a cat when such a bird (could it have been the same one?) would fly on to the doormat and sun itself there. Splinter never appeared. Later I heard sounds of a dog fighting and a woman's voice calling. It crossed my mind it might be the fox getting the worst of a good hiding. He did love going round the stables as the young lodger living at the Big House would throw him pony nuts. The sounds ceased and I thought no more of it.

The following evening Splinter came limping out of the bushes to be fed. He had an injury to his right eye from which pus was oozing, a bite out of his right flank and both front legs badly bitten. He was very nervous as he fed, continually looking round; a sound disturbed him and he staggered off. How had he come by his injuries? Fighting with other foxes, though the extent of his injuries made that seem unlikely, or with a dog? Could last night's sounds have involved him?

No Splinter. I hadn't seen him at night or by day though I walked round calling several times. It was almost dusk on the third day when a limping figure appeared along the winding path to The Sett. Poor fox, he was so much worse. His front legs seemed scarcely to support his light weight and the eye had discharged an evil-looking fluid. He ate ravenously, all the while looking this way and that, starting at the slightest sound. When I made to go indoors, he staggered away and crouched staring at me through the long grass. I came back down on the ground near the food bowl and he crept near again. I seemed to be some sort of protection: it surely must have been a dog. I spoke gently to him, noting with sadness the cruelly injured legs and filmy eye. Four days ago he had left me so healthy, beautiful and full of life; now he looked a maimed reject.

I had been days without water and all the containers were now empty. When I heard someone working in the stable yard I took a bucket and walked round meaning to ask if I could take some from one of the ponies' baths. It was the friend of Mrs Ellis who was also her lodger, a young woman of nineteen who, for once, quite happily allowed me to take a pail of water. She would even keep the tap on for me at the caravan when she had finished. From this I suspected that Mrs Ellis was away. Both pony baths were full and the hose lying on the ground gushed water over the cement floor, presumably cleaning the yard. A whining made me turn; and shut in an empty stable was one of the dobermans. On impulse I asked if it was this dog, a bitch called Lucky, who had injured the fox that evening. Rather taken aback she named another doberman as the culprit, and mumbled that Mrs Ellis was fed up with foxes and the dogs helped keep them away. Why encourage them with handouts outside the patio window or pony nuts at the stables, I was tempted to ask, but with the pail now full of water that seemed somewhat unwise. I merely remarked that perhaps it was for the best. The fox had always mistrusted dogs, but now the terror of what had happened would remain forever with him. He had learnt a bitter lesson. She replied, 'I didn't mean it to happen; Bonnie cornered it in the stable where I had put down the nuts for it', and I don't suppose for a moment that she did. At least I knew the truth now, and Splinter would never forget that dogs meant pain.

I bought antibiotic capsules for the fox from the vet. The difficulty with the eye was that I never touched him, so no way could I bathe or administer ointment to him now. The capsules hidden in food should help his general condition and I hoped the eye would improve too. He was appearing regularly again to be fed. One morning I offered him a hen's egg, which he gently took from my fingers, then walked a short distance with it in his jaws and lay down on the grass in the sunshine. I saw him nose it a little, before grooming himself stiffly. Much later I renewed the water bowl and found the hen's egg intact – not even a crack. He had raw eggs now over his dinner, but I had never before actually given him one still in its shell. Next time I would let him see me break it into his bowl. That night I heard barking outside The Sett and saw the lodger stumbling about in the dark with all four dogs running loose. They streamed off under the trees on the scent of something and she said they were chasing rabbits for exercise. She and Mrs Ellis were certainly a strange couple!

Splinter spent most of his time watching, playing and sleeping on his grass-covered den-top.

Cage door open and freedom beyond, but it's a big world out there.

Splinter in his den-top,
watching me at the
kitchen window.

Ashcroft Woods.

◊ ◊ ◊

I was asked to contact a farmer who had badgers on his land, and on doing so found myself talking to the same man who had photographed the badger-diggers that Easter. He offered to show me the setts he knew of the following weekend and told me I was welcome to come at any time after that to check the rest of his fields. Splinter was still returning and the antibiotics seemed to be improving his infected eye.

Now were nights of heavy dews that soaked the grass and laced the many spiders' webs adorning bush and briar. It was also the time when Mr Legget decided to have his poplars sawn down to half their height, including those over the Poplar Sett. I imagine this was to make them bush out and form a better windbreak. Not very consistent though, for some were left intact and two dead ones still standing at the motorway edge remained untouched to fall in the next high winds. I spent three hours dragging a huge branch clear of the badgers' entrances. The high-pitched whining of the saw working had been heard from the lane some distance away. Luckily the badgers were unharmed, though uneasy and nervous. This was scarcely sur-prising, however, for the noise and vibration over their home must have been tremendous.

Just for good measure, the dobermans had taken to digging out the setts again. Sometimes I felt these badgers were doomed. Yet their tenacity and perseverance against every obstacle shamed me into being less bitter on their behalf. However often they were dug out by man or dog, however often flooded, buried or crushed, the remaining animals re-dug their homes and rebuilt their lives. When these same sows had wandered calling over the flattened sett containing the bodies of their cubs, it had angered me that educated and otherwise intelligent people refuse to attribute feelings or emotions to animals less than themselves. Yet others know differently from personal experience. The Leicestershire Badger Group printed an article in their newsletter entitled 'Faithful Attachment', which I quote here.

A lady informed the group of a dead badger near the M69. It was found at 11.30 a.m. and had its mate with it who was reluctant to leave. It eventually sidled away when people approached closely. This faithful attachment in the badger is not unusual. Many years ago, a sow badger was reluctant to leave her three dead cubs, which had been run down by a bulk milk carrier, early one morning. The sow did not leave until the cubs were removed.

The newsletter continued with the most infamous record of such a happening recorded in *History of the Earth and Animated Nature* by Oliver Goldsmith. The following was related by a gentleman who resided at the Chateau de Vernours, France.

Two persons on a journey, having occasion to pass through a hollow way, accompanied by a dog, he started a badger, and persued it till it took shelter in a burrow under a tree, and from which it was at length hunted and killed. As they were only a few miles from Chapellatiere, they agreed to drag the badger thither, so that they might receive the reward offered by the commune for every one which was killed, and besides, to sell its skin to the manufacturer of badger-hair brushes.

Having no ropes, they twisted some twigs, and drew the animal along in turns. They had not proceeded on their way very long, when they heard the cry of an animal apparently in distress. They stopped to listen from whence it proceeded, when another badger approached them slowly. They at first threw stones at it, but this did not deter it from approaching its dead companion, which it no sooner reached than it began to lick, and made a mournful cry. The men observing this, desisted from offering it any farther offence, and continued to draw the dead body along as before. The faithful animal continued to follow the dead one, and lying down on it, took it gently by the ear, and in this manner was actually dragged into the village; and even amid the crowd of boys and dogs which were soon collected around, it could not be induced to quit its situation, and, to their shame be it said, they had the inhumanity to kill this affectionate creature, and afterwards burn it, declaring that it could be no more than a witch.

Oliver Goldsmith, in the paragraph immediately preceding this article, when speaking of badger persecution, wrote: 'Although the Almighty gave man dominion over the beasts of the field, it could never be expected he would exercise such unrelenting cruelty to one of the most harmless of creatures.' Our attitude towards animals seems to have improved very little in two hundred years. Even today, it is sometimes deeply religious people, quoting from the Bible, who have the genuine belief that animals were created merely for man's use. St. Francis was surely a man born out of his time.

Splinter was well again and catching much of his own food, merely coming back to me for companionship or a game. One evening I laid out some dog biscuits in the grass and, with Flo at my side, sat in the caravan's doorway. It was the end of yet another hot day and a pleasant breeze had sprung up. Diplomatically, I offered Flo a dog biscuit and she nearly broke her teeth before abandoning it. Splinter sauntered out of the bushes, sniffed at his biscuits, then sat back on his haunches to have a hearty scratch. He didn't really need feeding now, my offering was merely a token of our friendship, so he commenced to do what all of his kind do to surplus food – he cached it. The first biscuit was carried over to the base of my gas cylinder. A hole was dug and the food dropped in. Then grass and dirt were tupped back in place over it with his nose. He returned for another biscuit and took it beneath a hawthorn to repeat the procedure. Flo was bored. She wasn't hungry, it wasn't cool enough to play and she had time on her paws. Waiting until the fox's back was towards her as he busily tupped over his third biscuit, she crept stealthily over to the gas cylinder and retrieved his first cache and put it with the rest of the pile. Then casually she licked a paw and began washing her face. Splinter returned to the pile and stopped short, carefully sniffing. 'Now I could have sworn I hid that one' his bemused expression seemed to say, and smelling Flo's scent upon it he looked her way thoughtfully. The tabby sat busily washing, however, the perfect picture of feline innocence; always a bad sign where Splinter was concerned. Again he took the same biscuit and returned it to the base of the cylinder, then another he took round the back of the caravan. Flo removed the cylinder biscuit, returned it to the pile and continued with her toilet. The fox reappeared, sniffed his biscuits and sat back on his haunches, regarding the cat with a jaundiced eye. You would have thought she was the dirtiest cat in the world, so energetically washing was she. He picked up the biscuit for the third time and trotted purposefully to the cylinder. Carefully he re-cached it, then backed oh so briefly on to the place before returning for the next. Safely out of the way again, Flo's washing halted and she padded quickly up to the cylinder and bent her face close – ugh! the fox had scent-marked his stores, and foxes are very pungent. So Splinter was left in peace to hide his surplus supper whilst Flo came indoors to torment me instead.

◊ ◊ ◊

Checking the setts one evening, I found a piece of fresh sweet-paper at the Holly Tree Sett that hadn't been there before. One of the trees nearby had been marked three times with a knife and a piece of smelly rag was tied tightly around it as if to mark the sett. Was it children playing in the wood or terriermen with an interest in these animals? The first didn't matter, but the second possibility was worrying.

Gulls had joined the lapwings feeding on the upturned earth at night. The Ninepenny badgers were foraging there also, with an occasional rush at a seagull who approached too close. Both birds and badgers were after the same larvae and insects so there was considerable competition. Seagulls will frighten lapwings into dropping their prey, but badgers don't scare easily even when dive-bombed. The old boar seemed unwell. He stood shaking his head slowly from side to side and eating appeared to hurt him. He was old, though I had no idea of his real age. Just as hard and stressful lives can age us, so can they age animals, and certainly his struggle to survive against the odds in this countryside had been enormous. Did he have infected teeth or an abscess? This can be a killer if it leads to septicaemia. His condition worried me and the vet who had successfully provided Splinter's capsules suggested penicillin in the same form would be the only practical answer. We both agreed that to attempt to cage-trap and tranquillise such an old fellow would be a mistake. The problem would be to get the boar to take the antibiotic without the sows having some too. I laced a jam sandwich and cut it into small pieces, waiting till I had the sick animal on his own. No success, however, for he was hardly eating anything. The others were shunning him. Scarcely surprising, for he had become so irritable and aggressive. Oddly enough, he appeared at The Sett door after I had come in just before first light. I went out again and offered the food, breaking it into tiny pieces as I did so. This was the first time he actually approached and ate from my hands; all the pieces, with the penicillin enclosed in one. Slowly and with difficulty it was true, for one side of his face was becoming terribly swollen. Do animals realise you are trying to help I wonder? I mixed powdered glucose with some of the Lactol left from Pip's stay and, again with some effort, he drank. Sitting on the step with Flo on my lap, I watched him in pity; even she seemed subdued as if knowing something was very wrong. The first birds were singing as he slowly moved off down the path to the wood. I would have given everything I had to ease his pain; I felt so appallingly inadequate.

Now it was easy to find the boar alone. He was becoming shrunken in upon himself, an outcast amongst his own kind. Sometimes he would accept the food and penicillin, but often not, though he might take some of the glucosed milk. His small, purblind eyes were rimy and he seemed near his end.

◊ ◊ ◊

It was the weekend of the annual NFBG Convention, for the first time hosted by the Mammal Society as well as a badger group, which this year was the Herts and Middlesex Group. The speakers came from Great Britain, the Republic of Ireland and Holland.

Dr Paddy Sleeman from the Republic of Ireland spoke on the Irish badger. There are six million cattle in Ireland: many more cattle than humans. He confirmed that badgers and cattle rarely come face to face. He has found that sows may move as much as six kilometres (3.7 miles) – UK studies have indicated that they are much more sedentary. He felt that in low-density areas of Britain badgers may move considerable distances too; UK zoologists tend to study in high-density areas. Privately, I agreed. Paddy felt that vaccination was probably the only solution to the huge economic problem of bovine TB in the Republic of Ireland.

Jaap Dirkmaat from Holland said his country has very low

badger density levels. Badger clans will move forty miles and young badgers have been seen to move this far to find other setts. How do groups of young badgers know there are vacant setts forty miles away, he asked. Holland's 1,200 badgers have slowly increased to 1,500. He was sorry he had encouraged us to use badger reflectors as it had now been decided they were of no use in preventing road casualties. Initially badgers will approach them with caution, but they soon become accustomed to them, as they do with other flashing lights, whether from torches, cameras or cars. 'In the early 1980s reflectors were placed on a 1.5 kilometre stretch of road in the area of Grave, but all were demolished by road maintenance after four years. The incontestable fact is that the number of badger road victims did not decrease during the four years, proving conclusively that reflectors serve no purpose whatsoever.'

Again privately, I could from personal experience disagree with this. Flashing lights from torches, cameras or cars are very different from lights reflected successively from a series of reflectors. Even though my local reflectors couldn't be ideally situated, there had been no further badger deaths there in the four years since their erection. This wasn't due to a decline in badger numbers, as I knew the badgers there had increased to the extent that some had moved away to recolonise other areas. Whilst I would agree that reflectors are limited in their use, as they are not practical under certain types of lighting or with fast-moving traffic, etc., I could not condemn them out of hand.

Les Stoker talked about his wildlife hospital and had some very interesting comments to make on snares. These can cause horrendous injuries that are not always apparent at the time of release. For example, a fox found in a snare seemed unharmed but was kept just to make sure; two days later a wound erupted on the site of the snare. Moral – keep snared animals in captivity for a few days. The hospital rears badger cubs on goats' milk, making sure to wean them as soon as possible. They are never handled except to toilet (stroke anal glands) and feed. Badgers can contract parvo virus from dogs and black-leg from cows.

Guy James, solicitor for NFBG, spoke of the mutilation of the 1973 Badgers Act, which only became law after certain clauses were removed. The most glaring loophole was the landowner's exemption, i.e. a landowner could have badgers dug out and removed from his land, so they were only protected on common land or that under public ownership. This loophole was closed with the 1981 Wildlife and Countryside Act. Another clause protecting the badger's home, its sett, had also been removed from the Badgers Act. Tony Banks's Bill to protect badger setts had failed, as we all knew, but it was hoped that another attempt to provide protection would be made. He paid tribute to John Bryant of LACS who had started the ball rolling and worded the original Bill for sett protection.

I stayed overnight at the college in Hertfordshire where the Convention was held. Karen was in charge at The Sett. Unused to being indoors all night, by 2.30 a.m. that Sunday morning I was watching several badgers foraging on the football pitch and not a football amongst them! There were muntjac deer and squirrels too in the park-like grounds. I wasn't the only visitor by any means to see the college's badgers that weekend.

Dr Tim Roper talked on badgers as 'food specialists' rather than omnivores. He summed up by saying that availability of food is the key to understanding the feeding habits of badgers. Therefore badgers do not specialise. Jaap Dirkmaat came in here saying that he took the skull of a five-year-old badger to a dentist, who said that its teeth were so worn down that it was evident it wasn't intended to eat such food as earthworms. The sand and earth particles present in this prey were wearing down the badger's teeth too fast. Did this mean that earthworms had been turned to out of necessity, rather than being their natural diet?

Dr Jim Barry for the Republic of Ireland spoke of the meat and milk economy in his country, which has a very high farming population. Farms are tiny by our standards, on average a mere ninety acres per farmer, of which only forty-five acres are viable by EEC standards. Farmers' incomes had dropped by 10 per cent the previous year. Encouraged by their government and the farming press, farmers were convinced that the eradication of the badger would solve their bovine TB problem. Jim felt it was too late to turn back the clock on bovine TB in southern Ireland. There were 1,000 cases of human TB in the country who were a potential source of infection. West Germany was virtually free of bovine TB, but three outbreaks in the past ten years had been traced to human TB, caused by man's age-old practice of urinating in cowsheds. He referred to micro-bacteria in the soil, saying we did not know what strains of TB were there.

John Bryant had spent twenty years in animal welfare. LACS has an average of fifty calls a year from farmers or landowners asking for help against hunts. These were not necessarily animal welfare campaigners. Many hunts were arrogant and indifferent to the damage and trouble they caused. It was because of the foxhunting lobby that the committee stage of the Protection of Badger Setts Bill had continued for nine hours over three consecutive Wednesday mornings, rather than the usual one morning. In the end, as we knew, it was they who had destroyed the Bill. It would be introduced by another MP next session. There was also to be another Bill introduced next session disqualifying convicted badger-diggers from having custody of dogs, and the government were agreed on it. LACS was continuing its undercover work and had followed up an advertisement offering terriers for sale that stated the dogs would face any quarry. If it had meant fox, why did it not say so? LACS rightly felt that badgers were implied. The badger-diggers' group was so successfully infiltrated that the terriermen allowed their activities to be recorded on video. Such videos, which need no processing, are often made and are big business in such circles. This work successfully culminated in the conviction of the diggers who were filmed in a sequence that showed three badgers being tortured and a dog losing teeth and suffering other horrendous injuries. The men were convicted, but the sentence had been delayed. John said they would probably go to gaol, not for the offences to the badgers, which merely carry fines, but for leaving the dog's injuries untreated. And he was right.

It was David Clarke MP who successfully brought the amendment through parliament in 1985 that placed the onus on those digging at badger setts to prove they were not after badgers. He was currently conducting a survey amongst police forces on how this was working. We knew there were successful convictions for the three following years, but 1989 figures were low because diggers were employing more skilful lawyers, as well as taking dead foxes along with them on badger digs.

Tony Crittenden, a Chief Superintendent for the RSPCA, discussed his organisation, which had just under 300 Inspectors to cover England and Wales. He listed a variety of Acts that can often be used in badger-related cases, apart from the obvious Badgers Act and its amendments. Where pesticides had been put into setts, for instance, the Control of Pesticides Regulations could be evoked. A pesticide can only be used for the purpose stated by the manufacturer. Where dogs had been brought to or taken from the scene of the dig under bad conditions, the Transit of Animals (General) Order could be used. Likewise, the Abandonment of Animals Act might be applicable if diggers rushed away when disturbed, leaving their terriers below ground. There were Forestry Commission and Local Authority byelaws that might be useful in badger-digging cases too.

The RSPCA publication *Problems with Badgers?* would be available in its second and amended edition that autumn. As one humorist remarked, perhaps it should more accurately be called *Problems with People?*

◊ ◊ ◊

Walking home from Oakley station through the village, I seemed to have been away far longer than a weekend. Taking the winding path to the caravan, there was Splinter sitting in the sunshine as if waiting for me. At The Sett was Karen with Flo in her arms; she had been sitting on the step talking to both animals. 'I knew you were coming,' she said. 'Splinter heard you from a long way, but he didn't run. Just his ears kept turning as he looked in your direction.'

That night I couldn't find the old boar, though the two sows were in good health, if chasing seagulls was anything to go by! Had he gone below ground to die? How strange. In the morning I heard Flo repeatedly miaowing under my office end of the caravan, and crawling to where she stood I found the old badger curled round as if in sleep. Had I been right to try to help him, or had the penicillin merely prolonged his life and his agony? I knelt beside the huddled body I had taken from beneath the caravan, remembering. When his daughters had approached to groom him, he had sprung at them growling, then stood alone under the beeches, head drooping from his once massive shoulders. The pain had been too great for company or mutual grooming. Carefully examining him, I found very old snare scars round his neck. His mouth was tight-closed in death, but the smell from it was horrible. He died an outcast, curled up beneath The Sett; even I had deserted him that night. I buried him very near to the wild service tree. His passing left me depressed; of the entire clan, only two sows were left. Would they move that autumn in search of a mate, or might they stay and perhaps have his cubs? It was possible that at least one of them would, for both had mated that year.

Again I was out of water and had just finished the very last drop in the churn. It was a good opportunity to wipe it out with a damp cloth, especially as a white sediment tended to appear on the metal inside. Splinter and Flo were two interested spectators who till then had been lying together sun-worshipping. Splinter crept closer whilst his feline friend sat washing a short way off. Twice I nearly stepped back on the fox, so I picked up a windfall apple and bowled it along the wide, grassy path for him. Oh joy – what fun as he rushed after it, leaping over the glossy ball and turning round to catch it. Then, apple in mouth, he ran in and out the long grass under the hawthorns inviting me to chase him. I left him to his apple and busily scraped the sediment away. The late sunshine streaming across the path lightly touched me and bathed all in a rosy glow.

By now Flo was sitting in the doorway above me; her favourite vantage point. A movement behind me and the apple rolled past. I turned and bowled it back along the path with Splinter racing after like a golden whippet. He was so excited that he leapt on and off it, then rolled on to his back with the apple balanced on his forepaws. It fell into the grass by his face and he turned over and lay there, touching it with his nose, the picture of beauty, youth and playfulness – was ever a creature more lovely? He rolled on to his front and saw me approaching laughing along the path. Ears forward, head on ground and nose on apple he watched, his great brush waving. Then down the path he rushed at me, leapt up with paws lightly touching my chest, then round and round my standing figure. He was asking me to throw the apple again in the only way he knew. I sent it bowling back towards The Sett as Flo jumped down to meet it. Too late, Splinter leapt and landed, not on the apple, but on the tabby! A spitting tornado rushed under the caravan and a surprised fox hit the churn with a hollow boom! The apple lay serenely in the sunshine. I returned and offered it to the fox, and holding it gently in his mouth, with head high, he walked gracefully into the tall grass which closed behind him.

◊ ◊ ◊

Tim called and we discussed the Convention. That year had been a busy one for him and the group, who had surveyed for setts and helped with problems. They had made and sited badger gates, liaised with MAFF and BR over a goods-line where badgers had to be deterred from living in a railway bank. At the Convention we had spoken to a group from South Yorkshire who had successfully repaired thirty-two setts badly damaged by diggers and had rendered them impossible to dig in future, with off-cuts of metal mesh that are used to reinforce cement. There was so much to do, but this pooling of information and experience was vital; Tim hoped soon to be taking on sett reinforcement too.

   Probably as a result of David Clarke's survey on how the 1985 Amendment to the Badgers Act was working, Tim had been asked to take a group of magistrates to a badger sett to see the typical signs left by the animal, as well as those made by its persecutors. This was part of a course on countryside offences and I was delighted. One of the problems in badger cases can be to get a magistrate out of the courtroom and to the scene of the offence. If you have never seen a sett and never encountered the sight of crowning-down holes and similar destruction, how can you possibly begin to understand? Photos are no substitute for the real experience. This showed that Tim and the group had some standing in the community. I was pleased, for he had worked so hard and long for badgers, despite personal tragedy. However many knocks life gave him, he merely picked himself up and continued his work. I was as pleased for Tim as for the brockies themselves.

◊ ◊ ◊

At Ashcroft Woods, the badgers were digging out after a period of coolness and rain. At last the agony of the drought seemed at an end. My untidy friend Crisp was clearing long-disused entrances of the Old Cherry Sett in the woods, helped by Meg,

161

her companion when last she denned there. The two sows whickered around me with Meg allowing the other a prior claim to my attention – Meg was a wise animal indeed! I sat watching the early morning light filter gently through the dying foliage with the calls of a tawny owl disturbing the small birds.

The strong winds and heavy showers were sending the last conkers earthwards to lie with the autumn leaves. At The Sett, our resident tawny still called from a nearby tree each evening through rain and even thunder. Going out to see the Ninepenny badgers, I invited Flo to come too. She yawned from the depths of the armchair, stretched out a paw and went back to sleep. She had come a long way from roughing it in a stable and no mistake! I had been concerned that the contract ploughmen might have gone over the Poplar Sett entrances. The place was so damaged by the dobermans now, they could easily be forgiven for thinking it abandoned. I was relieved to see they had burnt the sawn-off poplar branches well out into the field, before rolling and re-sowing the fields.

I saw Splinter once more before he disappeared for a while. On my return home one morning, there he was waiting under the hawthorns all dappled with sunshine, but I didn't have time to play. His tin bowl I placed outside with several dog biscuits in it and left the door open whilst I got on with some jobs. Later I glanced out to find the bowl gone. Splinter was there busily scratching, but where was the container? I knelt down by him and spoke questioningly, which was a mistake. He knew full well what I wanted and bounded round me, big ears forward and mischief in his every move. I sighed, told him he was a nuisance and went in search. I thought I saw something in the grass under the hawthorns, but to get through to it I needed to crawl on hands and knees to avoid the spiteful branches. Next thing I knew, there was a gleeful fox beside me – 'You aren't much bigger than me now,' he seemed to say as he waltzed around me. It was a great game by fox standards and I had to laugh – my next mistake!

The 'something' in the grass turned out to be a cloth he had run off with when I had cleaned out the churn. As I picked it up and turned to crawl back, Splinter came by dancing on tip-toe; in his mouth was the tin. By the time I returned and could stand upright, fox and bowl were lying side by side near The

Sett. I approached slowly; he picked it up jauntily and returned under the hawthorn. I had no intention of repeating my crawl, and instead went indoors to get on with my work, but still leaving the door open. Much later, with both fox and bowl forgotten, I made to go out and found the tin sitting neatly on my step. Splinter had become bored with no one to chase him and wandered off to more interesting things.

Chapter Nine

A vermilion-streaked dawn stole through the last of the trembling aspen leaves – promise of the rain to come. I found some old pieces of wood dumped at the side of the drive and laid them across the top of the Poplar Sett, then I put flints on top and covered the whole in earth. This was no sooner completed when the rain began and continued all day. That night the sows were busily carrying down the fresh hay I gave them; the wood had held and, provided the dogs dug out no more, it shouldn't flood. At least there were plenty of worms for them now; it was good to see them catch and eat their spaghetti-like meals again. The following night brought a deep frost that continued well into daylight hours. The earlier wetness caused the hoar to stand out like glittering crystals. That evening Flo appeared with Hattie and Hazel, and the three came up to the caravan door. The tawny regularly called his boundaries each evening from The Sett's roof, and amongst the many pheasants the big old male still seemed to be the boss. In the fields, corn was already sprouting, giving the bare earth a fresh touch of green.

Three weeks after his last visit, Splinter returned. I was walking round the back of the caravan to check the hay in the dull, damp morning light when he danced up to me. I said his name in delight and stood a moment talking to him before continuing round the back. However, he chased after and jumping up behind me caught hold of the end of my jersey as if to say 'Well, wait then!' Later I stood watching as he ate and noticed he had a piece of fur missing, making a raw area on his right flank. It was not bothering him and was clean – probably a fox fight. I wondered how the other fox had fared! Splinter was full of joy after his meal, dancing round me and touching me with his nose.

I sat on the step and he smelt my hands, so I spread the fingers out palms upwards. He gently took each finger in turn, holding it a moment in his teeth before taking up the next. I laughed and he gazed intently into my face, put his forepaws on to my knees and reached up to sniff my hair, then bent down and touched my nose with his. When I chuckled, his brush began to wave and he did his silly act, rolling over and over on the ground.

I went indoors and perhaps an hour elapsed, the rising sun beyond the trees touching the caravan with prying fingers. I went out again, this time to clean and refill the water bowl in the verge. There was Splinter leaning backwards against the gas cylinder, four legs splayed out, chest and belly exposed and head held upwards with eyes closed, though they opened briefly to regard me. He was sunbathing. The warmth of the sun on the metal cylinder was drying off his thick coat and the rest of him was bathed in sunlight – clever fox!

Some days later, I found Lucky and Bruno digging out the sows again. The pieces of wood had been pushed aside and Lucky had so greatly enlarged her entrance that she disappeared down it. Only by grasping her hind-quarters could I make her desist and, inevitably, I was bitten. Once they had gone I surveyed the damage. One had only to look at the size of the entrances with claw marks at the *top* of the holes to know it was due to dogs. I felt very downhearted. By 10.30 p.m. that evening, the two sows appeared to be moving away. I followed them south-eastwards out of their territory, then returned to wait at the Poplar Sett, but they never came back.

The following evening I went to see the Sand Pit badgers and discovered that as I had suspected my two sows were amongst them. They would have been related to this clan and didn't appear to have been molested. It was a relief in a sense; their nearest human neighbours, together with the farmer who rented the land, all kept a watchful eye on the sett here. As I returned in the early morning along the poplar row, there was a movement below in the great hole left by the dobermans. Standing there, a handsome head came into view and there was Splinter examining the wreckage. I suspected he knew the badgers had left, for I didn't imagine he would dare explore otherwise. As he came out to greet me, I recalled Steve's description – Splinter the Magnificent – it suited him.

◊ ◊ ◊

The blackthorns at The Sett had lost their yellowy leaves, but for the rest all was a symphony of reds, golds and burnished browns. The wild service was on fire, competing with the field maples' showers of fluttering gold. I had a great clump of primroses in bloom by the caravan. Even Flo was beguiled, pushing her snub nose in amongst their pale flowers and sneezing. Hayfever in October? – surely not!

I saw a crow attacking a kestrel in mid-air on Colts farm. It was joined, rather half-heartedly, by two more. The three crows soon flew raggedly off across a vivid blue sky and the kestrel continued with his hunting. I met the farm manager and thanked him for cutting the grass of Little Chantry Field; it was really beginning to resemble a wildflower meadow now. Badgers had dug out at the long disused setts in Ashcroft Woods and rabbits were opening what had once been Old Joe's home in the Chantry. It was a good idea on the contractors' part to bury the root balls and fill them over with earth. One day the badgers would return again to this place overlooking the valley. Already the seeds of beech, oak, holly and hornbeam had sprouted. There was the mullein Aaron's rod growing amongst the willowherb. Would the birdsnest and early-purple orchids return also? One day this would be beautiful again.

Crisp and Meg had not returned to live at the Old Cherry Sett. It was still too exposed after the coppicing, and school parties taken round these woods invariably sat to eat their sandwiches and chatter there, using the sawn stumps as seats. And holes are useful for dumping your cans and litter when teacher isn't looking.

That morning I had just met Ray in the car-park when a police car drove up and Graham got out. He had come to see a stolen van that had been driven into the woods the previous night, smashed through the padlocked gate and burnt out amongst the trees. Fortunately, it hadn't set the wood alight. Graham had his December duty rota and gave us the dates when he would be available in the days preceding Christmas, in case we had trouble again with people taking holly and yew trees.

One of Legget's men had found the dobermans digging at the Poplar Sett a few days earlier. The man didn't approach too closely because their ferocity was well known, but he had contacted the police. Graham knew from me that it wasn't badger-occupied now and, in any case, such digging by dogs isn't an offence. He could only point out to Mrs Ellis that her dogs were causing damage on private land. She replied that a taxi driver had come to the house and left the gates open. As there was only part of a fence in place and they went where they wished, that was almost amusing. She also told Graham she was trying to rehome one of her dobermans that 'led the others astray'. Apart from warning her to keep the dogs under control, there was little he could do.

When Graham left, we walked about the rides collecting litter and discussing how long it would be before a new gate could be fixed into place. The greatest danger to a wood is from fire and Ashcroft had once been a favourite site for burning out vehicles until Ray's arrival as warden. We passed the dormouse nest in the holly tree, now abandoned and falling to pieces. It was Ray who discovered it much earlier in the year when we came this way. I had mentioned photographing the naturally leaning holly years ago, because of the way its long, hanging foliage swept down over the path, hiding the bole of the tree. That day we had ducked underneath to see what birds might have built their nests in the flowing canopy; hollies are popular with a wide variety of nest builders. Almost immediately, Ray had spotted a nest, the like of which we had never seen before. It wasn't made by a bird, neither was it built by any of the mammals we knew. Could it be that of a dormouse? Some years earlier I had watched dormice feeding at night in another part of this wood, though I had never found one of their nests. We looked around the holly tree and there was another canopy, this time of honeysuckle. There were plenty of hazel trees in the near vicinity too and this was an area which had not been coppiced for many years and was well overgrown: ideal dormouse habitat.

We discussed a talk we had both attended on these delightful creatures. Dormice spend half their lives hibernating, from October to April. Cold is the best thing for hibernation, but the worst weather for such creatures is that of our recent winters – not cold enough to hibernate, but too cold to stop using up their fat reserves. They emerge at dusk to feed and return to their nests again before dawn, but if it is very wet or cold they will not venture out and may become torpid, well deserving their nick-name of 'sleepmouse'. I would watch them hold on to a stem with their hind feet when feeding, leaving the front paws free to grasp food. The tail is used only to balance, not to grip. They build summer nests, such as this one, of woven honeysuckle bark covered in leaves. Pregnant females prefer to build breeding nests round the wood edges where it is several degrees warmer than in the wood itself. They eat caterpillars, insects, catkins and blossoms, or rather parts of these flowers. A good indication that dormice are present is sycamore flowers devoid of their anthers lying beneath the trees. Conservationists please note, even the hated sycamore has its uses! Dormice eat the lower end of honeysuckle petal tubes where they join the stem. They leave a smooth, round hole in hazelnut shells from which they extract the kernels piece by piece; the shells' outer surface will have tell-tale teeth marks radiating outwards. Berries of the wayfaring tree will be taken, though the seed inside will be dropped if it is too hard. They don't usually consume the bulky part of flowers and seeds, probably because they cannot digest such cellulose.

Throughout their normally active period from May to September (twenty-eight weeks) they exploit hazel, buckthorn, blackberry, ash, hawthorn, sycamore, wayfaring, elder, dogwood, yew and honeysuckle. Yet midsummer may see the dormouse die of starvation between two peaks of food supply – the spring with its blossom and catkins and the autumn with its nuts and berries. They need to eat well in early autumn to store up enough fat for their hibernation, for on emergence they will have lost almost half their body weight. I recalled the first time I saw a dormouse and my surprise at its tiny size: an adult's average weight is only fifteen grams.

They are completely nocturnal and totally adapted to a life in the trees. Their feet, claws and ankles are well suited to searching from twenty to sixty metres up in the tree canopy. They never normally come down on to the ground and will avoid doing so at almost any cost. Only once – and that was an accident – did I see one on the ground and it appeared deformed in its walk as it moved with paws outwards, almost hobbling. The moment it reached a tree, however, it was a different creature. They only travel about fifty metres from their nests at most. Coppiced woodland is ideal habitat once it is grown, but the high canopy is needed as well as low-growing shrubs. They can't jump far so need an arboreal network formed by a multi-layered tangle of shrub and mature trees, so they are more likely now to be found in overgrown coppice or ancient hedgerow. Such old, untouched hedgerows become wildlife highways from one isolated copse or wood to another – not just for dormice of course. Thus the present practice of woodland conservation, coppicing large areas and making wide rides to encourage butterflies and birds, increases dormouse vulnerability to extinction. This has probably happened in Ashcroft Woods, for two areas where I once watched them had been coppiced; I hadn't seen them there since. Perhaps the answer would be either to coppice very small areas at a time, or to leave a line of shrubs and mature trees in larger coppiced areas, to provide arboreal paths for them. At the talk, the speaker had told us that in the past dormice have only come to light when coppicing has taken place in the winter. By then their tree canopy is destroyed, and they are too: either they are disturbed from hibernation or killed. Dormice are now found mainly south of the Thames and a few places along the borders of Wales. An indication of the decline of dormice in this country is provided by the fact that they are now absent from seven counties where they used to occur. I found it interesting that an acre of woodland will support only two or three dormice, as opposed to, say, ten woodmice. This explains why I never saw more than three dormice at any one time.

They have only one family of three to five young each year and often skip years. Their babies are born naked and blind. Adults normally go out all night to forage, but a mother with young will stay close to them for six to eight weeks – far longer than do mice. This is probably the constraint on their number of litters. There is a 50 per cent dormouse mortality rate in their first winter, though they can live for several years. The birth of their young often correlates with the ripening of nuts and berries after weaning. Looking at the old abandoned nest that day, we were cheered to think there were probably still some tiny, orange-furred sleepmice in this overgrown part of Ashcroft Woods.

Returning home that afternoon, the skies grew dark and threatening with a powerful wind blowing. I had still some miles to go when thunder sounded and it began to hail. In a few moments I was soaked and the wind buffeted so that walking was slow. By the time I reached the poplar row the sun was out again and my hair and clothes were steaming. Rounding a bend in the path, I had a great surprise. There, standing gazing at my green door, were two dry figures – Splinter the Magnificent and green-eyed Flo. There was also another character quite as splendid – the grand old pheasant, looking at fox and cat looking at the door. I said hello and opened the door as Flo leapt inside miaowing to be fed. Splinter, always the gentleman, sat down and waited. The pheasant strutted up and down in no way put out by the fox. Indeed, Splinter seemed to find the large bird rather overwhelming. I quickly found a packet of minced dog food and emptied it into Splinter's bowl, then crumbled a tired scone and threw it to the bird. Flo ate what she wanted and came up to me for a fuss. Splinter ate what he could manage and began to tup over the remains. Only the pheasant seemed dissatisfied with his scone. The moment Splinter went off to do his tupping, said gaudy gentleman nipped over to the bowl of soft dried mince and quickly began to peck it up. What amused me was Splinter himself who sat down to watch him. It was as if the fox knew he wasn't yet mature enough to catch the wily old bird and the pheasant knew it too.

At 4.30 p.m. a full moon rode high in the sky outside my kitchen window sending shafts of white light to touch each trunk and twig. Many birds were still busy searching for a last meal amongst the berried branches. Later that evening I went out to post some letters and found I had both Flo and Splinter for company. They ran along, one each side of me. I would be allowed to walk ahead as they played boxing and pouncing, sometimes at nothing, sometimes with each other. How fey and graceful were feline and vulpine in the moonlight. Once well ahead, I would suddenly be overtaken as two swift bodies rushed by each side of me. A broad path wound through the meadow, but being no longer grazed, the surrounding grass was very high. I could hear it crackle as they bounced through the frozen stems, and when they disappeared little puffs of vapour rose above the dead seed heads to dissolve into the clear, still air. I clapped my hands and Splinter jumped high to see me as he galloped back. Short-legged tabby ran round the clumps so that both reached me together; their antics made me laugh. At that, both stopped to look as if surprised, then ran round and round me in circles till I at least was giddy from watching. Just as suddenly, they were gone. Remembering what I was supposed to be doing, I continued downfield and saw by now the pair were hunting together on the plant-covered heaps of china clay once intended to puddle the bed of the still unfinished lake.

I duly posted my letters and, returning along the lane, went to walk in at the drive. To my surprise and concern, Flo was sitting on the low wall there; she sprang down to greet me. I picked her up and carried her under the fencing and so back into the meadow. I had never known cat or fox to come so near to 'civilisation' and felt rather concerned. The lane with its sharp bends is a nasty one at any time, but by night it is worst of all. Walking upfield, Flo sprang out of my arms and there was Splinter ready for another game. I stood surrounded by deeply frosted grass, gazing at the moonshine on the great wellontonias and walnut trees. My companions grew bored with such inactivity. The tabby miaowed, at which the fox barked. Then he sat back on his haunches, still barking, and suddenly he was howling! I had never heard him do that before. I fancy he liked the sound of his own voice, but neither Flo nor I were enthusiastic so close at hand. We left him to it; a silver fox in a silver field calling to a silvery moon.

The pair of resident jays were burying acorns in Ninepenny Wood. Last autumn I watched this and was later amazed to find how many they retrieved between them. It couldn't merely be luck. This autumn they were tucking them in amongst the empty mast husks around the big beech tree by the water bowl. Some, I was sure, the badgers would find when they foraged, if they were to return of course; I felt they would.

Badgerwatching at the sett by the reflectors, I noticed how nervous the animals were of the fireworks continually going off. Though gardens were some distance away, they sounded unpleasantly loud none the less. Added to this were youths using the stretch of road to let off bangers and rockets. One or two nights for 5th November would be of little concern, but Guy Fawkes now seemed to continue for several weeks.

One night I found that Hattie had returned to the Poplar Sett and by 2.15 a.m. had dug out a new, short tunnel and taken down bitten-off grass blades for bedding. The following night Hazel also returned to den at the Motorway Sett. It was great to have the sisters back, for I had missed them. That morning I met the rural policeman and told him of Hattie's return. I mentioned the possibility of repairing the sett entrances, as one of our badger group had offered to help.

My turn to warden again and approaching Ashcroft Woods I was surprised to note how leafy the trees were. They still had a yellowy-gold sheen when viewed from a distance and within the woods themselves were plenty of green lower leaves, especially on the sweet chestnut. Could this be because the lower, more sheltered foliage hadn't had the continuous heat of the sun during the summer months compared with those above? Walking beneath the trees, prickly chestnut cases were rather painful as they hit me rather than the ground. There was a constant sound of them dropping. The yew berries were already gone, but those of the hollies were splendid: so vividly red and numerous amongst their glossy, evergreen background.

Ray had mentioned a problem with these woods. When it rained heavily, water had always tended to pour down the path leading to the car-park and so on to the farmland until it reached the lane. Now that the trees in that part of the woods were coppiced, and the place much more open, this had escalated. The hot summer had killed off much of the ground vegetation and baked the earth; the sudden surge of water had nothing to hold it now and so give it the opportunity to sink in. Once out on the farmland, it had dug a deep gully, at the same time bringing down debris from the slopes now covered in stumps. Ray had tentatively suggested a pond might be dug at the foot of the slope to take the volume of water; he was somewhat uneasy that his idea might not work, for water doesn't always oblige by draining in the required way. No one had any better ideas, however, so his was to be adopted in the winter months.

I sat at the wood edge above the Old Cherry Sett slope writing my notes when a stoat appeared about a metre from my feet, quite unaware of me. Looking at the ground I noticed a small area of fresh, sandy earth, nearly covered with very old dead chestnut leaves; no way could such decaying leaves have landed on fresh earth. I pushed them away with my foot and found the earth concealed a plastic bag containing five newly made snares and a length of wire. That accounted for the cigarette ends and lager cans I picked up when first I came there that morning. It appeared that someone had also sat there making the snares for future use.

Although the sett below me was unoccupied, the recently dug out entrances could lead someone to believe badgers were in residence. In the past, snares had been fixed over these holes and the occupants caught. Was it merely a coincidence the snare owner had made and hidden them here? Snaring is so much easier than digging or lamping for badgers. It is a great time-saver and no dogs or equipment are required. One man can position the snares at dusk and return to collect the contents at first light.

I gathered up the nooses and wire with the litter and continued on to look at Cliffords Bank. This was well badger-used with fresh digging out, hairs in the sandy earth and dung pits, the typical signs of brockie activity in the autumn months. I returned to the woods and still picking up litter, found a small, torn plastic bag containing airgun pellets. How wrong we were to think that snaring and shooting here were things of the past!

Homeward bound, I saw Steve's van parked outside the village and we talked as he gave me a lift to the drive. We agreed not to approach Legget with a view to reinforcing the sett on his land. If he knew beforehand he might find an excuse not to have it done, but once repaired he could scarcely demand it undone and still maintain he liked badgers. We also agreed that no way would we ever relocate badgers on his land or anywhere bordering his farm in future. I mentioned the snares found hidden above the badger sett. Oakley and the surrounding villages had been free of snaring for a period; we hoped this would not mark a new era of the 'sport'.

The county council were proposing to build a gypsy site on the wet meadow below the Sand Pit badger sett. I had quite forgotten it was they who owned the land. For the first time I met Val, who with her husband had looked after the sett since they first moved to their house nearby in 1974. There was a certain irony in the fact that we had never met in all that time but should now do so under such worrying circumstances. Any development nearby would herald a blight and gradual decline to these badgers, but a gypsy site sandwiched between the sett and the lane would be fatal. There was no doubt that the gypsies needed a site, in fact many sites. Originally, it had been left to the district council to find suitable ones. Gypsies generally are not popular neighbours; as each site was mooted, protests were registered and their desirability brought into question. Finally, the matter was placed in the county council's hands and it was decided to use abandoned and derelict land that they owned. Unfortunately, one person's derelict land is another's wet meadow with its water-loving plants attracting particular species of birds and butterflies. What the county council viewed as a tangled wilderness, local people saw as a wildlife sanctuary. There was also the large, thriving badger sett which owed its successful survival to the alertness of its human neighbours who kept very quiet about the brockies that came foraging in their gardens and the adjoining farmland. No one wanted meetings and petitions to stay the county council's hand. Could they get through to the authority without going public on the badgers? It was a sensitive issue.

We stood on site that day discussing the situation. A resident and a parish councillor doubted the feasibility of the place for such a site. Apart from the sloping nature of the land and its wetness, the meadow was bounded by a narrow lane and was near the junction of a larger road that led to Caldwell golf course. Gypsy sites must be financially viable and should not exceed a stated budget, which was determined according to how many pitches could be created in such a small space. Could an architect be privately engaged to draw up plans and do a costing to hand to the county council? The county trust would be asked to do a flora survey; a tree survey of the entire parish had been made some years earlier by the present parish chairman and voluntary helpers from the village. I would map the other setts belonging to this clan of badgers, together with the neighbouring clans, with the help of the local farmers and residents. All of us were very uneasy. The lack of gypsy sites in our county had been an ongoing issue for years and had eventually been taken to the ombudsman. It was only right that people should have somewhere permanent to live and the county council must now find these sites.

I had never met our local county councillor, although she had once helped enormously over a remnant of ancient woodland that had been earmarked for the same purpose. Those fifteen acres had survived the worst of the 1987 hurricane – a natural disaster – only to be threatened by a more permanent man-made one. However, this councillor had influenced her colleagues and saved the wood. I phoned and found her very sympathetic. She would ask if her fellow councillors realised the wildlife the area contained and suggest that a meeting be arranged between them, the nearest residents and the parish council. She fully understood the principle of not publicising the fact that badgers were present. She asked that I send her a copy of the setts belonging to the respective badger clans and told me not to worry. I trusted her, but had little faith in the rest of the council, and after all she was just one amongst many. I recalled too a certain lake with its surrounding trees, wild-flowers and aquatic plants. Even as I negotiated with the council for its survival, the machines and equipment had come in one afternoon and destroyed everything. Then I thought of Val and her neighbours; it was reassuring to know there were other people anxious to save the badgers too.

It rained steadily for two days and nights. We needed the rain badly, but inevitably the Poplar Sett was flooded and a very bedraggled Hattie left her newly renovated home to live with her sister by the motorway. It seemed such a pity they hadn't recolonised the artificial Tank Sett, but having once been frightened off from there by the dogs, they had never returned. It was, after all, in Mrs Ellis's grounds, so to her there was no reason at all why her dobermans shouldn't worry at the entrances. I thought of Mr Ellis and his enthusiasm when he made this sett, working at it for several weekends under a blistering August sun. He told me that as a boy he played truant from school to go out into the countryside with a friend; the memory of those excursions had remained with him all his life. When he left school, his headmaster remarked that although he had little aptitude for lessons, he undoubtedly had a considerable knowledge of natural history. 'It was the greatest compliment he could have paid me,' laughed the businessman, and that compliment had fostered the ambition one day to have a nature reserve of his own. It was tragic to see how things had turned out.

That weekend I started on the sett survey. One of the farmers met me and we went to view his land. There had been an active main sett at the side of nearby woods, but now it was empty. The lane running alongside had once been quiet and peaceful, but increasing traffic, especially when Caldwell golf course was opened, had sealed the badgers' fate. I had been called out to three dead badgers here in recent months, but the nature of the winding lane made it unsuitable for reflectors. It had saddened me at the time of examining the last animal, its position on the tarmac and the entrance above. It appeared to have returned that night, dug out an entrance in an otherwise derelict sett and then jumped down the bank. No motorist could possibly have seen the sow in time. I had laid her by the old entrances barely six weeks ago. Now there was merely a small heap of grey fur with the jaw and a section of spine protruding. Picking up the jawbone, I found I had the complete skull and lower mandible. She hadn't been a young animal for the teeth were very worn down and three empty sockets showed where she had lost some. Rough hairs lay on it and a tiny piece of skin still clung to the forehead. But for these, it was very clean for such a short space of time.

We slowly checked all around the wood. A badger had dug out not so very long ago (could it have been that sow?) under an old pile of flints cleared from the surrounding fields. Someone called out and came running towards us. It was a neighbouring farmer who knew of a 'big old sett in these woods, but not used now'. We went and looked and sure enough there had once been a large sett under these autumn leaves; it was now given over to rabbits. It was so disheartening. The two men believed this was due to the activities of the Forestry Commission some years earlier. Contractors had moved in with heavy machinery and worked 'for weeks and weeks over this sett, clearing between their rows of trees; the disturbance was awful' the farmers said. Certainly the once chalky spoil heaps were flattened and the only holes visible now were those dug out by the rabbits. We thanked the farmer's friend and he went off, whilst we crossed the field to check out another place he had suggested. Nothing but rabbits. Each hedgerow was checked, then back to the woods for a last look. Certainly there were no badgers now in this area, but we stood to admire a great and wonderful old yew tree that the farmer had known and loved all his life.

Returning, we were met by another farmer – my guide had circulated the news that I was mapping their setts – but by this time I knew all but one of those he described. These men recalled more badgers in bygone days; now only the Sand Pit colony was still flourishing. They all kept an eye on the animals there, passing the lane below the sett several times in the course of their working day. Technically they were probably smallholders rather than farmers, working long hours, weekends and employing little, if any, labour. All their land was rented from the county council. Most of it was beyond the Oakley police area, which was why I didn't know the farther fields and woods. It was encouraging to meet so many new faces during that and the following days. What transpired from this survey gave strength to our desire to preserve the site earmarked for the gypsies. The Sand Pit badgers were flourishing due mostly, I felt, to human vigilance against the activities of badger-diggers, plus the lack of concealed parking space for a vehicle. But the neighbouring badgers were not. If any badgers still survived of those in the Forestry Commission area, they were very few, and of their other neighbours – the Ellis/Legget badgers – only Hattie and Hazel remained. Yet I had seen thirteen cubs and adults at one time on the field above the Sand Pit and there were probably more. Occasionally, these badgers too suffered a road casualty, but not so often as to endanger the survival of the clan.

It had been a deeply frosted night with an orange moon waning in a clear sky. That morning there were blue and great tits feeding amongst the hawthorns, pecking at the haws. Fieldfares and redwings were taking these berries too. The trees all

177

around The Sett were alive with avian movement, from the tiny wren feeding on the honeysuckle close by my office window to the clamorous magpies and jays. Walking through the poplar row at 8 a.m. I noticed a great many tiny fragments of brown, rotten heart wood lying by the side of a poplar and the path. This tree was broken off at about five metres, and perhaps two metres up from ground level was a new, neatly rounded woodpecker's hole. Even as I watched, a great-spotted's head peered briefly out and was gone again. It is surely unusual to make a nest in November, or do they do this for a refuge against the cold? It was certainly fresh, not just freshly cleaned out, and hadn't been there on the previous day.

Going out to the Ashcroft badgers that evening I met Splinter, who wanted a game. He still returned from time to time, but unless I gave him something really special to eat he merely hid it and returned with an old apple to be thrown for him. Now he was running ahead, then returning to leap gracefully from one side of my path to the other. At first I slowed down, apprehensive that we might collide, but soon realised he could well judge my progress. At the end of the path where the Dutch barn blows in ruins, I sternly told him to go home. His ears went back and he knew I meant it. Splinter returned the way we had come and I walked on. That night I watched Crisp with her three yearlings, Pip, Squeak and Wilfrid, digging out many entrances both at the sett in Cliffords Bank and at those in the woods. All along my route, the tawnies had been very vocal re-establishing their territories against newcomers; it was the same story as I returned before first light. I found Hattie, Hazel and Flo still foraging in the old orchard, the badgers eating decaying apples whilst the cat prowled about in search of voles and mice. Rotting fruit has the advantage of containing worms, slugs and insects, which the badgers also enjoy. At an earlier state of decay, when apples are at the 'cider' stage, badgers and sheep may become drunk on a surfeit of such fruit. Once sheep grazing below orchard trees were a common sight in the neighbourhood, but they were always removed before the apples dropped. Watching the fieldfares, blackbirds, thrushes and redwings quarrelling that morning over the rotting apples, it occurred to me that birds should be capable of getting drunk too.

A new Bill to protect badger setts had been drafted. The

NFBG arranged a meeting with representatives of the British Sports Society and the Master of Foxhounds Association to see if they could agree on the new wording, which took into account the legitimate activities and interests of farmers, developers and landowners. There was no point taking a new Bill to parliament if the sporting lobby would not agree on its content. There were also meetings with the World Wildlife Fund (WWF) and the other conservation bodies involved in the First Bill. By now, all these organisations working together had become known as the Badger Coalition. The RSNC favoured the Labour MP Roy Hughes to re-introduce it as a private member's bill.

◊ ◊ ◊

It was at 10.30 p.m. one evening when I heard a fox screaming behind The Sett and discovered Lucky and Bruno pulling the creature apart with the other two dobermans trying to get a tooth-hold. They snapped and snarled at me when I tried to make them let go, but by now the fox was silent and must have been dead. I couldn't bear to see it mauled about though and finally managed to take it from them. It was one of Vicky's sons; what a vile end. The next day was a Sunday and sometimes Mrs Ellis took visitors to walk around her property. I laid the fox remains by the little clearing near the empty lake. It was obvious what had happened and although it was useless and unwise of me to say anything, the two-piece carcass might shame the woman into being more careful of her dogs in future – or was this wishful thinking? That evening I found the fox had gone, with two small tufts of blood-soaked fur to show where it had laid. I hoped it was Mrs Ellis rather than her dogs that had carried it away and that, perhaps, her conscience troubled her.

At the meeting of residents, parish and county councillors, the feasibility of the gypsy site was questioned. That the meadow was prone to flooding was no problem, we were told; proper concrete foundations would be laid and the water channelled. The councillors were shown the badger sett, which was photographed. The field above the Sand Pit was also being considered, but pylons crossed it and, owing to the undulating nature of the land, were rather low. We were assured that this could be rectified. We returned to stand in the wet meadow facing the badgers' home and continued talking as it grew dark and a near-full moon rose on high. Commuter traffic hooted in the narrow lane behind us. Someone asked what mode of transport were the gypsies likely to bring with them; a car and lorry were expected with each pitch we were told. Although we had spoken by phone, I met our county councillor that day for the first time ever, and instinctively I liked her. If anyone could save the badgers, I felt it would be her.

◊ ◊ ◊

It was at the end of November that the city police called me out to a RTA badger. The two men had laid the body on the verge, thinking it was dead. The young sow was covered in blood which, as it happens, is rather unusual. I walked along the hedgerow somewhat puzzled whilst the policemen waited, understandably impatient to get the unconscious animal to a vet. There under the bushes was a large, fresh, dead boar, also very bloodied. We placed both in the back of the patrol car and drove off.

The vet put the sow down. Standing looking at the bodies I commented that they were rather unusual for road casualties. The vet looked at me sharply and nodded 'I was thinking that myself. I can't do two autopsies for free, but I'll clean them up and take some X-rays, then let you know the results.' We thanked him and the policemen drove me home. Later the vet phoned to say both badgers had been attacked by at least three dogs, but probably more, judging by the jaw-size of the bites each animal had sustained. The boar had died from five stab wounds to his neck, back and belly. Had an earlier passerby found the body and lain him in the verge? Baiters often leave the carcasses on roads in the hope that they will be mistaken for traffic casualties.

◊ ◊ ◊

Each Monday evening I would carry the weekly rubbish across the meadow to put in front of the first houses in the village, where it would be collected the next day. One such night there came a thudding of small feet and a striped body hurtled by me; Flo had decided to be my escort. She loved this type of progress and would stand watching as I caught up and passed her, before repeating the performance. Once the path disappeared into the long grass, however, her behaviour altered. Now she was a jungle cat, body winding in and out as she stalked an imaginary prey. Splinter was a-courting and had more serious matters on his mind. I ducked down under the fence, whispering to my tiger to stay till I returned. The curving lane with its occasional fast car still worried me, but it need not have done so, for Flo feared it too.

I put the black binliner with those at the third house and stood talking for a few minutes to the lady there, before returning along the lane. A small tabby sat waiting on the low wall and I carried her, purring into my face, back to the meadow. We stood together far below the great lime, beech and horse-chestnut trees, listening to the tawnies serenading. The sky had cleared to reveal a glorious half moon and the temperature was dropping fast to allow a frost to stiffen the plant stems and freeze the water of all but the bowl under the beeches in Ninepenny Wood. The next day was bright, sunny and very cold with a bitter wind. Cleaning the reflectors that morning it seemed impossible to think it would be Christmas Day in three weeks time.

◊ ◊ ◊

On the 5th of that month, Roy Hughes's Badgers Bill was given its first reading. The Bill's long title had been set down as 'to make provision for the protection of badger setts and connected purposes'. It was due for its second reading in the Commons on Friday 15th February 1991. The advantage this Bill had over the earlier ten-minute rule Bill brought by Tony Banks was that Roy Hughes drew position No. 5 in the annual parliamentary lottery for private members' bills, which meant it had guaranteed time allotted to it. Neither could it be killed by a single objection, but it was, however, vulnerable to wrecking tactics and could be filibustered or talked out of time. To prevent that happening, the bill needed the support of at least 100 MPs on the day of the reading. At best, Fridays are bad attendance days in parliament; many MPs live at a distance from their constituencies and return home early for the weekend. All badger group members were asked to write personally to their MPs asking them to be present on that day and many were drawing up petitions of local signatures to be sent to their parliamentary representatives. We all felt that if this Bill didn't get through it would be a very long day for the badger before another could be attempted. Tony Banks's Bill may have failed, but it had made people aware as never before that badger setts were not protected and why certain MPs had killed it.

◊ ◊ ◊

Another deeply frosted morning with mist in the distance, but the sun was rising when I went out again at 8.30 a.m. to put fresh water under the beeches. At the Poplar Sett, the view across the white fields with the trees' twiggy fingers starkly pointing above my head was a Rowland Hilder portrait of my beloved Kent. A white-backed house stood distantly on the skyline – Val's cottage – and that cluster of trees nearby were the great beeches, home of the Sand Pit badgers. A sudden scurrying amongst the crackling dead leaves at my feet made me wake from my reverie of torpid brockies snug and warm in their earthbound fastness; a woodmouse had found my right boot, which he carefully explored. Returning through Ninepenny Wood, my shadow led the way, its legs grotesquely elongated against the verdant green butcher's broom and bramble. Where the sun had yet to penetrate, ghostly heads of long-seeded grasses still stood to frozen attention. Yesterday had been mild and overcast, one of those dark, dank, December days. Today was bright and cold, a glowing contrast.

Dave, one of our badger group, phoned that afternoon to say he had been given some plastic pipe offcuts by the gas board which would be suitable for the Poplar Sett; no dog could ever dig through these. He would let me know when he could deliver them. Dave looked after the area adjoining mine and already knew about the Sand Pit badgers and the proposed gypsy site. I mentioned that the parish council secretary had advised me of the HM Land Registry Explanatory Leaflet No. 15 entitled 'The Open Register; a guide to information held by the Land Registry and how to obtain it'. As from 3rd December 1990 anybody can obtain information which is held on the register. Prior to that date, only registered owners themselves or persons with the owner's consent could inspect the register. It can be so difficult to find who owns land sometimes when surveying for badger setts and I do hate trespassing. This could be very useful to all badger groups.

I might be busy outside the caravan and then look up to see Splinter close by.

Splinter waiting for Flo outside The Sett.

Ninepenny Woods.

Splinter waiting below the
kitchen window.

A badger pawprint in soft earth.

A sett entrance between tree roots.

Badger claw marks on
sandstone.

Splinter soliciting a game
from Flo . . .

When it's deeply frosty or merely very cold, many adult badgers won't venture above ground and can stay below living off their fat for long periods, though they don't hibernate. The youngsters – this year's cubs and the yearlings – however, will be back and forth looking for odd titbits, exploring or playing. Crisp's three yearlings, Pip, Squeak and Wilfrid, discovered snow that night; quite a difference from the few flakes of the previous year. It was falling in heavy flurries, blown on the wind, then stopping for a time. Squeak, who was rather a tearaway, thought it great fun and went cross-eyed when a large, fluffy flake landed on her snout. She sneezed, tried to eat it as it dropped, then ran round and round in circles head-butting the others. She also head-butted me in the general excitement and the fronts of my legs felt as if they had been bulldozed; badgers tend to have hard heads! The three rushed in and out of the trees, falling over themselves on the steep slope of the sett. Crisp came out very briefly, probably to see what all the excitement was about, sniffed the freezing air in disgust and beat a hasty retreat back to her nice warm bedding. Badgers often sleep together for warmth, although the bedding they collect earlier on in the autumn is good insulation. They dig vent holes which go straight down into the maze of tunnelling below; these air the sett and stop bedding going mouldy. On very cold days – and nights come to that – you can actually see vapour rising from them; a sure sign of animals below. It is something that badger-diggers look for too.

It snowed again the following night and part of the day with a bitter wind. However, we in the south-east fared better than most. The midlands and north were at a standstill, whilst some people died stranded in their vehicles. I walked out that afternoon and noticed the male pheasant running under the hawthorns. Whenever he saw me, he would stretch out his neck and hurry off with long leaps. If, however, he got too far ahead, he would stop and look round. He reminded me that I hadn't seen Splinter except at a distance for some time. By that evening most of the snow had gone, and out of the wind it was mild.

Dave came with the promised piping the following morning. It was 2 cm thick and beautifully strong. We walked out to view the Poplar Sett with a bitter wind blowing across field. I would collect flints to pack round the sides of the pipe and we would need somehow to roof over the area beyond them. The dobermans had made such enormous holes that where the entrance branched off into further tunnelling, that was open too. We wouldn't put the pipes too far down or the other tunnels would be cut off. I say we, but it was Dave's hard work that saved the badger sett. Walking back, he commented what a nice little shaw it was and I said how I would love to clear some of the brambles and debris from successive gales away to give the next year's wildflowers more of a chance. It was a shame to see the wildflower meadow too. It used to be cut twice a year which not only gave the flowers more room, but also kept the hawthorns at bay. Now the latter were recolonising the grass and soon it would be a meadow no longer. We agreed that it was strange how people thought that if you left everything it grew into a beautiful wood or wildflower meadow when, of course, the opposite is true. Dave promised to come at 11 a.m. the next Saturday to try to repair the sett. Stubborn as ever where her home was concerned, Hattie had returned; I had the strangest conviction that she would have cubs in the New Year.

Each Saturday morning, early, I did a short phone-in for Radio 5, talking about badgers for a few minutes. That morning I mentioned that Dave and I would try to repair a sett dug out by dogs and that badger setts were not protected by law. This led on naturally to Roy Hughes's Bill (though accidental digging out by dogs would not be covered in it) and Jon Briggs, the presenter, asked listeners to write to their MPs requesting them to be present in the House on 15th February. Jon's enthusiasm helped to get the message to many people who would never normally think twice about badgers.

Phone-in over, I got on with some work when at 7.50 a.m. I heard the lodger calling Lucky and Bruno from the stables. With a horrible premonition I ran through the wood to the Poplar Sett. The tip of Lucky's tail (unlike the other dobermans, hers had never been docked), protruded from an exposed inside entrance and I could hear sounds of growling. Bruno was running up and down excitedly barking; he wanted to be down there too, but there wasn't room! Even as I tugged hard on her tail, Lucky backed out followed by a *very* angry Hattie. This, unfortunately, didn't put off either doberman, who clearly thought it was great fun. Lucky dodged, ran in and feinted in front of the sow with Bruno biting her from the back. I grasped Lucky's collar and shouted at Bruno who lowered his head when he realised he was in disgrace. Why, oh why wouldn't Mrs Ellis care for her dogs; it wasn't their fault, but her neglect. To my vast relief, Hattie turned and trundled back down the ruined sett still grumbling to herself. I didn't want her or the dogs badly injured; badgers can inflict the most appalling damage when roused. I took the dogs back to the house and knocked and knocked on the door and called out, but no answer, although her big BMW car was parked nearby so Mrs Ellis wasn't out. Finally I shut the dogs in the back courtyard.

Before Dave was due to arrive, I phoned the police explaining what we were going to do that morning. If we should be seen from the footpath, we were not badger-diggers, merely trying to repair the sett. I also mentioned the dogs that morning and the officer groaned. It had been the seventeenth time since keeping a record that I or others had seen the dobermans at that sett! He promised to put the repair on record and tell the patrols. Waiting for Dave's car that morning ready to unpadlock the gate into the meadow, I saw Mrs Ellis in her car go out farther down the drive. The same two dogs were loose again, though fortunately they didn't bother us working at the sett.

The worst part to repair was the gaping hole. We could only put the pipe so far down or it would close the tunnel branching off to the left. Having done that, there was a large gap between pipe and the top of the soil. We had no wood wide enough to cover it and metal sheeting would be dangerous to the badgers themselves. In the end we compromised by laying branches across, then packing over them all with dead cleavers, grass and vegetation before covering the whole with earth. Dave carefully dug this from farther away and carried it in a bucket back to the damaged sett. I fetched some of the flints I had collected a few days before and packed them round the pipe and in the spaces between it and the tunnelling. Gradually Dave continued piling the earth over and flattening it down; I took some photos. Soon only the edge of the yellow pipe showed. He had done a good job. At one time as he worked, Dave heard noises underground; was Hattie still grumbling to herself? The second dug out entrance was easier, for it was not in such a bad state. Again there was a tunnel branching off, this time to the right and again we couldn't lay the pipe too far into the sett. Branches were laid over the space and the same procedure followed. Both looked grand after just an hour and a half's work.

I promised to have the photos developed as soon as possible, so that Dave could show before-and-after pictures to the gas-board men who had given him the pipes. Much later and nearly dark at 4.15 p.m. I walked into Oakley via the village and found the dobermans still running loose and now in the traffic. Coward-like, I left them to it and continued on my way.

Chapter Ten

HATTIE had not come above ground that night, which didn't surprise me after all the disturbance she had been put through the previous day by dogs and us. Badger group members monitoring setts have reported that interference to them by foxhunts inhibits badgers from emerging for several nights, so it would be interesting to see when Hattie came out again. I could easily tell from the soft soil round the pipes and their present clean interior.

The rubbish we collected in the Poplar Sett area when repairing Hattie's home filled three black binliners. These old pieces of tin and barbed wire had once been piled on the fire made over the original sett entrances when Legget cleared his wood a year ago. I carried the bags down to the house in the village and returned again through the meadow. Coming along the winding path to The Sett, there was something lying there. Though dark, visibility was good. It was part of a rabbit; touching it, I found it still warm. A movement against the bushes and Flo came towards me – followed by Splinter. A sprightly, brush-waving Splinter, the long, fluffy white tag of his tail like purest cotton-wool. But who was that a short distance behind him, standing timidly by the undergrowth? Another fox! Flo didn't touch the rabbit, but, purring, rubbed round my legs, clearly meaning 'Look who I have brought to see you.' I whispered his name in delight and Splinter danced up on the tips of his toes, mouth open, tongue lolling. I picked up the rabbit and gave it him; he turned and offered it to the vixen who coyly looked away. I could see she wasn't that coy though, merely playing hard to get and slightly uneasy at my presence, though only slightly. Could she be – yes, I think she was – one of Vicky's daughters? So I was not all that much of a stranger to her. I walked happily down the path with Flo and turned before the corner to see Splinter paying court to his lady.

Four nights after the sett repair and still Hattie had not emerged. Her sister at the Motorway Sett had been out and about; she scent-marked round the Poplar Sett's entrances, but with no response. These nights hadn't been cold, but now the temperature was falling fast. The radio forecasted snow flurries, but said none would lie; they should have come here, where a white canopy soon covered the landscape and the snow still fell.

Tim phoned that morning; he was due to repair the reflectors again as two had been vandalised. He would come the following day if possible and would also bring a sett alarm system for the Sand Pit badgers. Val and her family had watched a TV programme in which Tim had shown one of these alarms he had made and explained their placing and use. He promised that her badger neighbours should have one. The snow continued. Snug and warm inside The Sett, I looked out on a beautiful frozen white landscape. Winter had come and the trees stood, bare arms outstretched as if forever crucified.

The snow ceased that night. I met Flo as I was following certain small pawprints. They reached the twiggy Y-trail of a bird; there were signs of a scuffle and a few minute feathers lay there. Farther on lay a tiny mammal stomach. Obviously, the tabby had eaten. Snow lay in wondrous symmetry on every branch; not a breath stirred to mar its perfection. Flo followed daintily in my footsteps, jumping lightly over the intervening snow till we reached Ninpenny Wood. No sound, no sight under the beeches, only distantly the tawnies calling and an occasional drop as of something falling. At the Poplar Sett, Flo rubbed her chin on a piece of protruding piping, then paused to miaow stridently down it. Inside, it was as clean and unmarked as when

Dave placed it there. Flo paused and called again, then stole softly into and down the short length. I was wondering unhappily how Hattie might react to the cat disturbing her, when first Flo and then the big sow emerged. The badger looked hard at me and shook herself vigorously sending up light puffs of snow as she did so. Now she sat back on her haunches and began raking her long claws through her fur, sometimes biting at a tangled bit, sometimes having a scratch. Badgers seem to positively enjoy a good scratch, setting to with noisy gusto. She shook herself again, sniffed the piping, perhaps smelling Flo's scent upon it, then trundled below. Silence. The cat had gone off hunting into the wood; so much for relationships!

By the end of that night, the temperature rose and a thaw set in. Tim mended the reflectors and came on to show me his alarm. I was amazed to see how small the components were: they fitted into a large margarine tub which would protect the contents when hidden under the ground. The circuit of wire leading from it could be as long or short as required. A broken circuit activated the alarm, which would be heard at a considerable distance. There are several different types of alarm suitable for bugging setts, but this was a deterrent that would send the diggers rushing off in a hurry before any real damage was done to the sett or its occupants. Val wasn't at home, so Tim demonstrated it to the parish councillor living nearby who had first notified me that the site was earmarked for gypsies. Tim promised to form a working party from members of his group on the third Sunday in January to install the alarm system.

That night there were lampers on Caldwell golf course. A local farmer spotted their parked vehicle and approached as they were leaving. The poachers said they had only been after rabbits, which the council allowed them to take; I knew no hunting was permitted there. However, the farmer had been unsure of his ground, though he gave their vehicle number to Oakley police. If their night activities had included a badger, it was too late now to find out, but it reminded me to warn residents to be on their guard during the Christmas and New Year celebrations. Badger-lamping and digging are popular holiday sports and, traditionally, Boxing Day (or night) is the most favoured time. I mentioned this to Jon Briggs of Radio 5 and again he was most supportive. During the brief phone-in that Saturday morning before Christmas, we discussed how lampers plied their trade and how listeners' vigilance on bright lights at night as well as digging by day could save badgers if only the police were directed to the scene quickly. Far better and safer not to approach as the farmer had; leave it for the police to decide whether the diggers or lampers have permission to be there and what they are really after.

In the run up to Christmas there were few problems with people taking young yew trees or holly for decoration, so no one needed to bother Graham after all. It would seem that most visitors to Ashcroft Woods had finally come to accept that you don't help yourself to whatever takes your fancy in a nature reserve, although for some years it had been an uphill struggle. The last few days were mild and damp in contrast to the earlier snow. I spoke to the farm manager as I left the woods. A friend had permission to graze sheep on his meadow and the shepherd remarked that there seemed to be lots of badgers in the area, judging from the many pawprints in the snow. The manager replied that there were not many and in any case, they did no harm to sheep. The man agreed, but said that sometimes they go straight through electric fencing and dislodge the parts, although sheep apparently will do this too. I recalled seeing a badger touch such a fence with his wet snout. He leapt up into the air like a jack-in-the-box from the shock, and, fur on end, raced madly off. I imagine it depends on the stability of the fence and the circumstances. Neither man was bothered; we were lucky in our farmers and managers.

Returning from wardening along the poplar row that Sunday, I heard a plaintive miaowing and looked up to see a pitiful Flo high in the crook of a tree. Did I rush to get her down? I certainly did not. Moments later, as I walked through the poplars, a small figure shot past me and sat waiting on the fallen tree at the end. Her endangered species act might not work, but she was certainly a trier! Both of us met Hattie and Hazel worming together along the field edge that night. A fine crescent moon showed occasionally through thin clouds. The tawny pair were very vocal in the early evening and before first light. They roosted together by day amongst the thick ivy creeping over the acacia's deeply furrowed bark. Months earlier, Steve had nailed a nest box just above; might they use it later in the New Year?

Christmas Eve morning, and three of the dobermans attacked the Poplar Sett. Fortunately, the big pipes held. The great, old, ponderous dog Butch was amongst them; his was a sad story. Once he and I had been great friends and although he had bitten others badly, I had never feared him. He had always been the businessman's dog, devoted to his master. When the Ellis's split up, the ex-wife had kept the dog because of its great size and formidable aspect, but she had no love for it – indeed, she feared the creature, as did her lodger friend. The old dog aged greatly after his master left; there were times when he appeared senile. Occasionally, he seemed still to know me. I might be sitting in the caravan's doorway or walking home from the village and suddenly he would be there, pushing his head into my hand to be caressed. Other times on meeting he would stare, then growl ominously. Speaking quietly and reassuringly would usually calm him; I was sure, too, he was going blind. Last time the builder came to make some repairs to the caravan, it was only quick intervention that stopped Butch and Lucky badly mauling the man. Now at the Poplar Sett I looked round for a stout stick, then spoke angrily to the three dobermans. Young Bruno backed off without too much insistence on my part, but Lucky growled threateningly and Butch stood, head raised and teeth bared. I took a deep breath and summoned all the anger and aggression I could muster, remembering how successful this had been when the builder was threatened. I shouted, threshed the stick in the air, then rushed straight at the great dog. For a horrible moment, still snarling, he held his ground; the next, he was blundering through the undergrowth with Lucky and Bruno ahead. Pack-dog like, they had waited for the leader's reaction; if he attacked, so would they. Long after the dobermans disappeared, I sat on the ground feeling rather sick. Normally I like dogs and don't fear the odd bite or two. That morning I had to confess I was badly frightened.

By 1 a.m. Christmas morning a wind was rising and two hours later we were in the midst of a gale. By daylight, it was buffeting The Sett with a great roaring as the rain beat down on the metal roof. Well, the badgers would be snug enough and warm underground; I hoped the tawny pair were safe in their tree hideaway. Flo, wise cat, had stayed in all night. Throughout the day, the wind still raged and many homes were reported to be without electricity. So far we were all right and the caravan was still here, although the roof sounded sinister when the strong gusts blew beneath it. By Boxing Day morning the winds had eased slightly. Between rain showers, I walked round The Sett, cutting to ground level those ash saplings and briars that were trying to push their way under my home. Snip, snip went the cutters and a small, furry, bewhiskered face popped out. I laughed and continued to move round still cutting. Snip, snip, and a larger, longer, bewhiskered face appeared! I was disturbing that terrible twosome, Splinter and Flo, from their rest. Soon the rain returned in force and the gusts became stronger. The forecast warned of gusts approaching 90 mph in the south. Please let the caravan remain intact. Flo came indoors and Splinter disappeared to his den deep in Ninepenny Wood. He was probably the safest.

Dusk came early at 3.43 p.m. The wind screamed through the roof and bent low the trees in its path. Above the torrent of darkness came the lone call of a tawny close by me as I stood outside my little home. A small, dark shape perched in a tossing ash, back and forth, back and forth, but still he called and peered at me below. At 10 p.m. again I went out into the rushing that filled the air as twigs, leaves and pieces of branch flew by. The trees of Ninepenny Wood agonised as the wind, bending the trunks, twisted and contorted them. These, the greatest of growing things, like man's buildings are but straw in the face of the gale. The smallest earth-bound creatures are the safest, tucked away beneath grass and hidden in hole and crevice. Man is brought face to face with His truth; for all our civilisation, earth, air, fire and water are not ours to control. The elements are wonderful levellers. Man may destroy, but the earth will destroy him and, in time, renew itself when he is gone.

The day dawned dry and bright with a gentle, if blustery, wind. I was called out by the city police to a RTA badger which we took to the vet who had tended Iffy. It was hurt internally. The vet would phone later and let me know. Flo made much of me on my return; the welcome sun was warm as she basked outside The Sett. But for the branches and debris strewn about, the gale might not have been. The vet phoned about 4 p.m. to say the badger had a shattered pelvis, amongst other injuries. Keeping it in captivity for the necessary six weeks would not have been a problem for it is now known that even after such a period, a badger will be accepted back by its clan. The vet however, doubted that the pelvis would knit properly so we agreed he should put this boar down.

We discussed keeping badgers for a length of time after surgery and I mentioned those I had heard of with a leg amputated and returned to the wild. Whilst I respect vets who do this and appreciate their motives, such returns bother me. I have spent many hours watching badgers mate, dig for food, climb, dig out their setts, drag the excavated earth up from the depths to kick on to their spoil heaps and collect bedding to drag backwards and down into their homes. I have sat watching such operations and tried to imagine the same animals coping with these activities with only three legs. It is good that we humans are capable of compassion; we do so much evil, wittingly and unknowingly, that it redresses some of the bad and gives hope for mankind. But whatever decision I have to make over badgers or foxes, I always ask myself 'Will this be best for the animal? What quality of life will it have?' There are enough pressures on our wildlife in twentieth-century Britain without the trauma of a missing limb; a trauma that will probably end in lingering death.

The repaired Poplar Sett was in good trim in spite of the gales that had recently blown across the fields. I had replaced the soil dug away by the dogs and planted cleavers, nettles and couch grass in the moist earth. I walked over to the Motorway Sett and discovered a neat ball of dried grass lying a short distance down one entrance: rather a surprise for December, but the weather was mild. The end of the month was pleasant with showers and excellent visibility at night thanks to a near-full moon behind clouds. Hattie and Hazel foraged in Ninepenny Wood finding grubs, snails, worms and beetles under the dead leaves. Rooting about in a rotting tree stump, Hazel turned up something that looked, at a glance, like old pieces of grey cable tangled together – but it wasn't. It was a group of hibernating slow worms. I was curious to see how the badgers reacted to the stiff, apparently lifeless, lizards. Nosing them over, some came loose and Hattie had a few to examine too. Both badgers began to eat, at first hesitantly, then with enthusiasm, even having a grumble at each other as they nosed around in the leafmould for pieces. Badgers haven't a great turn of speed like the fox. If they do meet a slow worm or grass snake in the warmer months, they will pounce upon it, pick it up in their jaws, shake and throw, then come at it again. Chances are, however, the reptile will have flashed away into thicker cover before they pounce. They seem to do this to anything that might bite. A dead but still warm squirrel, for instance, will be treated this way.

Flo had been indoors for several hours and shortly before my phone-in that morning I decided to put her out. She did so enjoy fighting the telephone cable when I was on the phone and she was already in an aggravating mood! It was still dark as I opened the door. Splinter was walking past. He looked back at me and hesitated, then glanced down to see Flo running towards him; I could almost hear him groan. He trotted off with Flo still running after, but at length took pity on his determined companion and waited for her to catch him up. It wasn't just me the little tabby liked to torment!

That last Sunday of the year was a glorious, sunny day; what a change from gales, grey skies and rain. Splinter was waiting as I left the caravan. He looked a royal mini king of beasts standing there: erect ears, long, slender body turned to fire by the rising sun and that wonderous brush. We parted at the field edge and I walked on to warden. There were couples hiking through Ashcroft Woods and families enjoying the place; my favourite type of day with no problems. I checked the setts to find all was well. A gentle wind blew the lissom birch and overgrown chestnut coppicing, both bare except for the tiny unopened birch catkins. Light dappled the Scots pines' plates of flaky bark; their needled tops stood out like high green foreheads. At the Old Cherry Sett, the great dead tree from which its name derived was hidden by woodsage and bramble as it settled more surely into its earthy bed. Nearby, downy seedcases on their tall spikes of Aaron's rod were growing amongst the spiny teasels.

By 3 p.m. it had clouded over and the walkers gone home. On Colts Farm I noticed one of the sheep was out. There was a three-strand electric fence on plastic posts that the enterprising animal had worked through without too much difficulty. I approached the ewe and immediately she tried to get back. She tucked her head between the two lowest strands and in jumping through knocked out the post. Now nearly five metres of wire fence lay on the ground. A whole flock of sheep could pass over that – and I thought I was helping! I re-erected the post, but on picking up the wire received a shock, of course. I tried again, but it was no use, and walking up to the farm manager's house I met him just as he was coming out. He had seen the performance from his window and laughed, saying 'It's usually only one sheep that gets out and that encourages the others; was there only one today?' That ewe could end up being a Sunday roast if she wasn't careful!

The winds returned on the last day of the old year and by evening had become gale force. The thumping, roaring sound it made under the metal sections of the roof terrified Flo, who rushed out into the night. Indeed, she was probably safer outside. She could either creep underneath into the hay-filled, upturned packing case or go into the old summerhouse where the hay bales were stored. Or into the Tank Sett of course. Karen had come to see the New Year in with me. What would we be doing and where would we be this time next year?

◊ ◊ ◊

1991 began with gale-force winds and lowering skies, although it continued very mild. I spent many happy hours clearing the wildflower patch I had planted two years earlier at the end of the poplar row and building a stock-proof fence around it. The long, trailing cuttings from hawthorn, briar and bramble invasively encrouching on the area made a formidable barrier when woven across. The orange and dark mulleins and viper's bugloss had done wonderfully in the last hot summer and some of the seed collected from them could be sown in other places. These were localised or rare species in Kent and I was anxious that nothing should disturb their growth. Years ago I had been given the seed by an elderly friend whose property had been under compulsory purchase for development. It is unfashionable to plant in the wild, but fortunately such seed will keep almost indefinitely, if stored under dry, cool conditions. When I was invited to make my home at the caravan, Mr Ellis had been happy for me to plant them in his nature reserve. The viper's bugloss once grew freely round the field edges above the Bourne valley, but alas no more. Strangely, that year it appeared in Ashcroft Woods in an area coppiced last winter. It had never been recorded there before; this brilliantly handsome plant is a lover of dry soils and grassy areas. Near The Sett it grew with the pretty yellow and orange flowers of toadfax, but of course I merely happened to plant it there and it seemed to thrive.

◊ ◊ ◊

A farmer contacted me through a mutual acquaintance. A young man who had worked for him since the previous summer chased off terriermen from holes in a hedgerow and told his boss it was a badger sett. The farmer had no knowledge of badgers on his land, however, and didn't wish to contact the police in case, as he said, he should 'look a fool'. Would I come and see what I thought? It seemed incredible that the man had lived all his life on this land, and his father before him, without either knowing this magnificent sett was indeed badger. True there was a warren at the end of the bank and foxes were present too, but in the middle section well under the trees were the typically large, semi-circular entrances with their great spoil heaps, dung pits and a well-scratched elder. The good side of this was that I had a very interested and concerned farmer and his employee. The badgers would be safer now, though from the crowning-down hole that left a bedding chamber exposed and tufts of badger fur lying there, it was probable at least one animal had been attacked. The farmhand was certain the terriermen had taken no badger with them and we discussed the gaping hole that left the sett open to flooding. Boards were found from a pile in the barn and a good repair job effected, with earth hiding the damage. I mentioned the possibility of cubs and why badger-digging at this time of year is so popular. The two men promised to be vigilant and we shook hands on it.

I arrived home to find Karen waiting. Contracts had been signed and exchanged on the house she was buying in Yorkshire; for the first time she would have a place of her own. She had found something in an area that she could afford and where there was work; properties in the south-east were far too expensive. I was delighted for her sake, though I would miss my daughter. Laughingly, I asked did she realise she was going to the worst county in Britain for badger-abuse and what would Flo and Splinter do without her frequent visits? The tabby miaowed loudly on hearing her name; the previous night's gale had left her very nervous. Gusts struck the caravan sideways on with frightening force, trying as always to pry their way under the roofing. Poor Flo had clung to my lap with closed eyes and body pressed into mine. I could sympathise with her. That weekend nearly thirty people were killed and a couple strolling along a Sussex beach were swept out to sea and drowned by a freak wave. Miraculously, The Sett had withstood the elements and our part of Kent was no worse affected than by other gales.

The 12th January was the first day and night that month without a gale-force wind. The war of the Titans was over – the ensuing quietness, a peace and a blessing. It turned colder with a frost by night. As I sat on Cliffords Bank, Crisp appeared and climbed into my lap. Putting my arms around her, I could feel her unborn young beneath the taut skin. The sow wouldn't allow any others to approach me, so I still didn't know whether Missy was pregnant too. In Ashcroft, a soft breeze touched the branches; truly the sighing woods. Walking home that morning I met Graham patrolling, and he asked if I knew of the proposed gypsy site by the Sand Pit badgers. Residents had written to the head of Oakley police station about the likely traffic congestion on an already busy lane if the plan was agreed. I mentioned the letter I had written to the county council after consulting with the NFBG's solicitor. If the gypsy site went ahead with all these badgers *in situ*, there was a strong risk that the authority would be evoking the 'cruelly ill-treating' clause of the 1973 Badgers Act. Graham asked for a copy of the letter for his Inspector and I promised to take one into the station, together with the survey of all the marked setts, both within and outside Oakley's area.

The coldest night so far of that winter was -5°C with a deep, deep frost. Crisp only came out very briefly to greet me – and she was lactating. None of the other badgers were above ground, and who could blame them, sensible creatures! I didn't stay long and returned across the farmland to find Hattie gathering dead grass from deep within Ninepenny Wood. The frost hadn't penetrated there so it was dry enough for bedding. As usual, she carried it along backwards and, coming to the Poplar Sett, I had a surprise. When Dave reinforced the sett, we had wondered whether the pipes would be too slippery, but it appeared they had a certain advantage that we could never have foreseen. I watched as Hattie backed on to the pipe, sat down comfortably, her striped face peering above the bundle of dry grass, and then slid gracefully backwards down her ground-floor-to-basement lift!

Wednesday 16th January was a day few in Britain would easily forget. That morning war was declared on Iraq. It was difficult to credit we were really at war, and even now it was declared there seemed an aura of unreality about the whole affair. Perhaps Saddam Hussein would withdraw his troops; perhaps he would realise the USA and the allied Forces were serious. Before daylight the next morning, I tuned my radio to the BBC World Service and found we were bombing Baghdad; the war had begun and there was no turning back.

I was due to help Ray in Ashcroft Woods. I would go early via the village and buy a newspaper as I passed. I had time to spare so could go the longer lane way and check the Chalkpit Sett at the same time. The bombing had been too late for the early editions, but outside the newsagents a friend told me of it. Three others joined us as we stood talking; the possibilities were frightening. I left them still talking, to walk along the lane that wound through the farmland, the morning sky all colours of red, pink and mauve. The Chalkpit Sett lay so peacefully under the trees, that I sat for a while on a fallen log, looking about me. On some nights before the recent gales, I had heard the heavy drone of engines overhead, quite unlike the usual passenger planes and light aircraft. They brought back forgotten memories of childhood and another war. Thoughts crowded in on themselves, of Ashcroft Woods and its old bomb craters. The beauty of this small place hurt with a physical ache as the rising sun sent shafts of coloured sky between the trunks. I wasn't to know it then, but this was also the morning that sealed my fate at The Sett. As I neared the motorway, whom should I find but Lucky and Bruno causing havoc in the rush-hour traffic. This time I did stop — and caught them for the police who also appeared. I was bitten, but more importantly for Mrs Ellis, so was the officer who took them to the station for her to collect. Two days later, the electricity to the caravan was disconnected and never restored.

◊ ◊ ◊

Hattie was a comic badger; she really liked her gas-pipe home! To see her trundle backwards towards the entrance with her carefully gathered bedding and gracefully slide out of view was very funny. Flo sniffed at the pipe after she had gone and looked my way, but wisely didn't follow. She did, however, go down the other tunnel and pottered about in there before returning. It reminded me of how she took over the Tank Sett last year; what an odd cat!

Tim and his working party were due to alarm the Sand Pit Sett. Members from the East Kent group and some from Essex had asked to help too; they were meeting at Val's house. I told Graham what they would be doing that day. Workload allowing, he would try to call on site to meet them. He warned me to be on my guard against what my landlady might do. He was worried by her past threats of arson, saying that until she actually set light to the caravan, there was nothing the police could do. 'It will be poor consolation to you after the event, especially if you go up with it!' He urged me to find somewhere else to live, even offering to make enquiries for lodgings on his beat, though we both knew he was unlikely to find any. It was a pity the final dog incident had happened, but the clock could not be put back. For a year I had continued to live there quietly, hoping Mrs Ellis would mellow, but nothing had changed – with the water more often off than on and now no electricity. If the police were concerned for my safety, then it was indeed time to move. I decided to accept a friend's invitation to live with her in Scotland. It would take some time to wind up my affairs here, however. I also wanted to see if Splinter and his mate would produce cubs before I left; it would mean a great deal to me if they did.

◊ ◊ ◊

There was a meeting of the NFBG in Warwickshire. The first talk was given by a MAFF employee on badger problems. Their Wildlife and Storage Biology Department gives free advice and assistance to the public on nuisance situations. They avoid destroying protected species where possible and are the licensing body in cases where damage by badgers is occurring. In cases where damage is not occurring, for example new roads or development where there are badger setts, the statutory bodies to contact are English Nature for England, the Countryside Council for Wales and the NCC for Scotland.

I imagine this talk was of as much interest to other badger group members present as it was to me. One of the things you take into account when dealing with badgers is the problems they cause to their human neighbours. There is the genuine problem, which can often be resolved to everyone's satisfaction without too much difficulty; then there is the antagonistic person who will only tolerate wildlife if it is on their television screen. The speaker discussed electric fencing and queried how humane it was. He said there was no such thing as a badger-proof electric fence. With a fair amount of successful experience in this field myself, I couldn't honestly have agreed, and surely whatever voltage is considered humane for livestock would be equally humane for badgers. Renardine can be used to deter dogs and cats in gardens, but it cannot legally be used against badgers. As we already knew from the RSPCA, there is no effective substance one can legally use now to deter badgers. MAFF will investigate any unusual badger deaths if they feel the circumstances warrant it.

The gassing of foxes by non-governmental persons is banned, but something I learnt that day was that MAFF doesn't approve of the gassing of foxes. That was interesting as I knew this was still popular. I had contacted the rep of a chemical distributors when I was trying to find out how easy it was to obtain such poisonous gases as Cymag or Phostoxin. Legally, one can now only use chemicals for the purposes they are intended, so if the label states rats and rabbits it shouldn't be used against foxes. (This also applies to such substances as creosote and diesel oil, which have been used as deterrents in the past. Again, they can only legally be used now for the purpose intended.) The rep mentioned that Cymag and Phostoxin have the batch number imprinted on the container so, up to a point, can be traced, if the container is left in the sett or den. I had asked how careful one needed to be when opening up such a poisoned sett and the answer was *very* careful. A special respirator is needed – an ordinary facemask is not sufficient. With Cymag, the gas is released when in contact with moisture, so canisters are either opened and dropped into tunnels or the powder is spooned in. The powder must never come into contact with the skin, which is naturally moist. If the canister is dropped into the tunnels and some powder still remains, when the sett is dug out and opened, gas could be given off.

Other speakers were equally interesting. The numbers of badger groups had grown from the original five that existed ten years ago at the first Convention, to seventy-five groups countrywide *and* more groups were being started. A survey was commencing that autumn on a sample of at least 200 setts in each area covered by a group. Some would be large areas (where badgers are scarce) and some fairly small. Badger numbers had decreased in some counties and the reasons were not always apparent. For example, years ago a survey had been done in Essex by R.A.D. Cowlin, and twenty years later, 36 per cent of those setts had disappeared. The mean actual Essex clan size had been six adult badgers; now it was two. This county has been the target of badger-diggers for many years. It has been the scene of much land re-use and development too. The speaker believed the decrease was also due to contamination by sprays and spray drift. Sub-lethal doses of organochlorine insecticides affect thyroid activity, reducing reproductive success and inducing changes in the behaviour patterns of various mammals. These insecticides are very persistent and badger carcasses still contain measurable levels of these and other pollutants, twelve years after their banned use. Moreover, the use of approved insecticides, fungicides, etc., on intensively farmed areas inhabited by badgers is largely unknown.

The second reading of the Badgers Bill was due in three weeks time. All discussions with the Coalition and other interested parties had ended in agreement, except those with field sports and foxhunting interests. Public support for the badger had never been higher; it was doubtful whether the hunting lobby would kill it this time. They were more likely to insist on amendments to accommodate their sporting interests. Unfortunately, these could create loopholes for illegal activities, so effectively neutering the Bill's potential. In the event, we underestimated the field sports lobby who had learnt a hard lesson on popularity when Tony Banks's Bill had failed. Sir Nicholas

Bonsor, chairman of the British Field Sports Society, was hoping to submit his own Sett Protection Bill, which would cause considerable legal ambiguity if it reached the statute books. That day, however, ignorance was bliss.

The weather continued dull, damp and miserable. Apart from having no way to spin-dry or iron clothes and no light, Calor-gas heating soon causes condensation. I didn't use the electric fire much normally, but it had been useful to dry stored clothes that became wet through condensation. I had always kept them in plastic bags to minimise this, but even so things quickly became damp. Cold didn't bother me over much, but the caravan walls always ran with moisture in the winter months and needed drying down every day in this weather. Now arthritis was beginning to plague me. I had been out for two hours and returning at 4.30 a.m. met Splinter and his shy little mate. I called her Fran; somehow it suited her. Fran stood looking on as Splinter pranced up to me, brush waving. Near The Sett, I found they had gone as silently as they came. As I boiled water in a saucepan for a mug of coffee, the dog-fox was there again outside my window; was he hungry? By the time a tin of dog meat was opened and placed in his old dish, he was gone, but I left it outside.

An hour later I was trying to sleep, but in spite of the pills the pain wouldn't leave me. A movement directly below me beneath the thin floor made me forget humdrum miseries – Splinter was still near. How could he ever know the joy he gave me? A soft double bark, pause and another. I struggled painfully to my feet and peered out of the tiny office widow. There he was looking back as he gave the soft double bark again. Had he found the food, or was he hungry? I hobbled back into the kitchen, found the key and fumbled to get it into the lock. He wasn't there, but the dog meat had been scattered a little and left. Why did I always feel he returned for food? Was it my mother's instinct to fuss and fret now my own were grown and gone? A movement on the path and they were there once more. Leading the way, he walked off through the trees, his vixen following. 'Goodbye Splinter,' I called softly. He turned, looking back directly at me, and she drew to his side. They touched noses; she gently snuffled his muzzle. There was a quietness, a oneness in the act. I have seen so many foxes mate – seen their actions and attitudes before and after. These two had surely mated. Struggling back to my sleeping bag in the damp little room, a great joy filled me. In the fullness of time, Splinter would bring their cubs back; and I would stay long enough to see them.

It continued damp and dull. Hattie came out briefly one early morning. She sat up to wash herself and I saw she was lactating! After all the bother with the dobermans and the repairing of the sett she still produced cubs, probably because implantation and growth of the foetuses would already have begun. Hazel had taken over the other entrance, which rather surprised me. Flo came to sniff at Hattie, obviously noticing her milky smell. One night that cat would get its ears cuffed! I thought of all the dry bedding the sow had collected. Her newborn cubs would be pink, blind and helpless with thin coats of silvery hair through which the skin would show. Young as they were, faint black stripes would be visible on their faces. The nursery was filled with the insulating bedding Hattie had patiently collected and her cubs would be warmly hidden away inside it.

The last day of January was overcast with snow flurries. I was glad to be helping in Ashcroft Woods where Ray was pollarding the old crack willow near the cottage site. At least it was a way of keeping warm. A builder had dumped hardcore, roofing felt, battens and cardboard in the car-park overnight, so at least we could use all but the hardcore to get a really good fire going. Willow toppings don't burn easily, and when green are even more difficult, so for once the dumped rubbish actually helped us. We worked hard all day. The pollarding itself didn't take too long – perhaps two hours – but piling up the logs and gathering the toppings and debris to burn all took time. We discovered woodspurge and grey iris struggling to survive under gale-felled trees and gradually cleared the whole area. There could be some lovely wildflowers there in the spring. Pussy willow buds were opening in the woods. At The Sett, my primroses were still blooming from last autumn. The snow showers continued.

Returning home that afternoon over Legget's land, I found someone had positioned a stick across the nursery entrance of the Poplar Sett. When I removed it, I found it had been firmly pushed in. It is the old, old way to find if an animal is going in or out, although it doesn't tell you what animal. At such a time, when she was nursing her cubs, this could bother Hattie. I felt it was someone from the village or maybe the farmer himself. Terriers would immediately scent the badgers below; badger-diggers don't need sticks!

Val's husband and I attended County Hall to hear the council debate the advice of the committee with regard to gypsy sites. Although it had been recommended that the Sand Pit site be deleted from their list, we felt there was no real guarantee that it would be. We met our councillor again who seemed quietly confident that we had nothing further to worry about, and she was right. Happily the recommendations were accepted. The debate continued over other sites. Our councillor came out into the hall as we left and assured us that the Sand Pit site and another one that had worried me were secured.

Driving home we spoke of the bugging of the sett that previous Sunday. It appeared that my lack of basic amenities and decision to move had been discussed. I was offered the use of a generator, but talking it over we realised that access to the Big House would be necessary. Since Mrs Ellis persistently refused the electricity board access to restore the 'fault' she would scarcely allow anyone else access to set up a generator! However, it was good to know others cared. In a sense it was rather ironic that I had so much friendship and backup here and it was all coming to an end. Never mind. I felt those two and a half years had been an interlude. In spite of the miseries Mrs Ellis was inflicting, I had experienced the joy of tending sick and orphaned badgers and foxes and rehabilitating them back to the wild. If in some small way I had been able to help badgers like those at the Sand Pit, then that was reason enough to be grateful for my time at The Sett. The only regret I really had was leaving so many good friends in the south. The Sand Pit badgers' human neighbours were thinking of asking the county council if they could buy the land housing the sett, together with the immediately adjoining fields. With the nature surveys already carried out and the formation of a trust over the area, it would be an added protection for the animals there.

I had copies of our badger group's petition calling on local people to support the Badgers Bill. Our nearest pet shop and library had willingly taken a batch each for people to sign and I photocopied some more to take round to friends in Oakley. I was determined to devote that weekend to asking people to sign. The forms would be sent to our local MP asking that he attend parliament to vote the Bill through. I had written to him earlier, but his reply had been vague and noncommittal. Several friends not only signed, but asked for an empty sheet to get signatures themselves. There would not be time to return home for a meal that day, so I walked into the shopping precinct to buy something. I met a couple I knew by sight and seeing my board and biro, they asked to know what it was about. By the time they signed, others passing by noticed the badger motif heading of our group and asked to sign as well. Many already knew one Bill had failed last year, but everybody was interested and really enthusiastic that this one should succeed. Several congratulated me for standing in the cold, which made me feel a humbug – after all, I had merely come to buy a bar of chocolate! When eventually the shoppers became less (and I had sixteen filled sheets) I gradually worked through the estate where I used to live and knocked on past neighbours' doors. People were so pleased to see me that I hadn't the heart to say I would soon be moving far away.

Now the day was over and, fortified with cups of tea and coffee, I walked out of Oakley to some of the farmers and managers, for I knew they and their families would sign. I returned home to Karen and Flo at the candle-lit Sett at 9.30 p.m. having been out twelve and a half hours and completed thirty forms, not including those I would later collect from friends. Before I went in I heard sounds of fighting and there was Splinter seeing off another dog-fox by the empty lake. I was far warmer than Karen, poor lass. The Sett was always several degrees colder than the outside temperature in winter – and hotter in summer.

Chapter Eleven

IT was a fiercely frozen landscape with the path painful to walk upon, so hard was it. Such a beautiful night; everything breathlessly still. No tawny called, no fox barked in the bright lunar landscape. Oh, to take a photograph and keep it forever at hand. There was a movement by the Poplar Sett; Hattie emerged and used a dung pit a few metres off, then returned underground. It was solid dung as one would expect, but I wondered what she had eaten. Their metabolism slows down in the winter and they often eat very little, thereby defecating infrequently too. This could be the result of feeding, say, five nights ago; also keeping the nursery clean by eating the cubs' faeces.

The temperature had dropped to -10°C, the coldest night of the winter so far. Such a wonderful fairytale world and yes, Splinter appeared at midday by the caravan with his lovely lady standing silently nearby. (Flo was fast asleep in the armchair!) Frost didn't go from the branches till 11.30 a.m. and ice that had formed from the condensation from yesterday's cooking began to melt and drip. One large drop fell on a certain tabby's head; she shook herself in disgust, miaowed plaintively and asked to go out. I had fed the birds by then and they had drunk their fill of fresh water, so I could safely let her ladyship out.

That week the temperature dropped even lower. The water pipes froze and where my sleeping bag touched the filing cabinet and wall, it was frozen to them – rather chilly! Never mind, thank heavens for Calor gas. Flo was tightly curled up on the armchair under a pile of covers. She came stretching into the kitchen to be fed whilst I made some tea. Breakfast over, she sat unhappily on the doormat. I knew she badly wanted to relieve herself, having been in all night, but she hated the cold. I opened the little door, but she backed away, so picking her up firmly I tried to put her out. However, she did her old trick of spreading her legs so wide that I couldn't push her through the narrow space. I walked out with her and determinedly placed the tabby on the frozen ground. Inside now, with closed door, I saw her rush under the trees opposite, crouch down awhile and then meander off over the snow-like frost. What a cat!

Walking to Ashcroft Woods that afternoon, the sunshine was lovely and very welcome. The hazel catkins were pollen-laden and the long, speckled alder catkins were opening. Ray and his friend had dug out the pond to take the surplus water; they had made a fine job of it. Now it was snowing and very cold. Kent had been forecast 15 cm of snow by the weekend. These past freezing nights there had been little badger activity at all above ground and even the foxes were hunting by day. This evening before dusk, I met Splinter and Fran and they returned to The Sett with me. I put out dog food and scraps, some of which they took. Two hours later there came the sound of angry exchanges and Flo looked up from the depths of her armchair with faint interest. Two other foxes were quarrelling over the remainder. And still the snow fell.

That night the weather report said that Kent was a degree colder than Moscow. I was really in no position to argue as the caravan door was frozen shut and I couldn't get out. Years ago, both back and front doors of our Oakley house were frozen tight and I couldn't get *in*, so things could have been worse. I was snug and warm, however, sleeping fully dressed with a quilted anorak lying over the blankets and sleeping bag. My arthritis was so much better; I could cope with anything now. This background pain was bearable, but when it was bad I found it difficult to take problems in my stride. The taps were still frozen and would remain so. A mug I had rinsed and left upturned on the draining-board the previous evening was firmly stuck down. I wasn't going to risk breaking it, so it would have to remain there. I had already broken one; half-filled and left by my side when I lay down in the office to sleep for a while, it froze and burst. I wouldn't be doing that again in a hurry!

The water in the churn outside had frozen nights ago as had the bottles of emergency water stored in the cupboard above the draining-board. But the five-gallon water carrier under the table was fine. The biggest joke was the water and milk in the tiny fridge; with no electricity and positioned in the middle of the caravan, they were fine. Terry terrapin was snug in a hay filled box. He could live out of water for long periods.

At 7 a.m. the morning was made lighter by the snow outside. A heavy grey sky with the wind blowing great clouds of fluffy white past the caravan windows. Flo heard me moving and came to investigate her food and milk bowls. I dragged the Calor-gas fire out into the kitchen area in an effort (unsuccessful as it happened) to unfreeze the taps. Flo jumped on to its warm flat-topped surface complaining bitterly. What was wrong with the cat, I thought impatiently? Glancing more closely at her bowls, I noticed last evening's Whiskas was covered with white, and picking it up, saw it was not only frozen, but appeared to be frosted too. Needless to say, her milk was solid, so I poured her some more from that in the fridge and shook out some dried food into a clean bowl. The gas fire was causing the ceiling to drip. The condensation from last evening's cooking had created long icicles decoratively hanging above my head. I carefully snapped them off (the longest was 24 cm) and fed them into the water heating in a saucepan for a mug of tea. It was like cooking spaghetti; sad there weren't more. Flo regarded my activities with disgust, especially as wet patches on the thawing ceiling were dripping all around. She jumped down to floor level and asked to go out. This time the door did open, after a gigantic push, and the cat gazed in unconcealed horror. All that white stuff; where was the path? The hawthorns seemed little more than bushes. Water bowls, grass and the tall stems of last year's flowers were hidden under the white mantle. When it first snowed, I had seen her playing with the drifting snowflakes – jumping, patting and then running through the winding trees before leaping out to the attack once more. A few fluffy snow-flakes are one thing, but a blizzard was clearly something else!

Flo teetered uncertainly on the metal step with its glassy covering of ice, kept her balance for a moment before dropping on to her feet in the snow. Paws, legs and striped body disappeared. I leaned out, fumbled in the disturbed area and hauled her back. Whilst she sat washing on the doormat, I walked slowly through the snow, dragging boot-clad feet carefully along to make a path. By the time I reached the poplar row I was panting, but carefully returning in my own drag marks, I improved upon the route. At The Sett I watched Flo struggle along the relative safety of her new path. Karen phoned and talking to her I said how the cutting off of the electricity had at first seemed a minor disaster, but that it soon became merely an inconvenience. The water freezing and the deep snow making access difficult was happening to many people, not just to me. In a sense, it was a challenge. When the last of the water had been used there would still be snow to melt; we would survive. As Karen remarked 'It's worse for other people; you have already come to terms with functioning on so little.' Whether Flo felt the same as she plodded homeward was another matter!

Returning later myself from buying milk and bread, I found my snow-clad hair was frozen solid. Only my bare face was cold and looking at passing villagers with their glowing, reddened faces, I suspected they felt the same. The warmest daytime temperature that day in Kent proved to be -7°C . We were apparently still colder than Moscow!

In spite of carrying the shopping back from Oakley through the village (rucksack on my back being the most practical way), I enjoyed the walk through the snow. Bread was difficult to get; there was little in the shops, but everyone was very cheery, from the three postmen joking with a stranded milkman in Oakley, to the people in the village shops. Broken-down cars littered the route, with passengers pushing in an effort to get them out of the way or started again. The wind twisted the whirling flakes; wild dervishes dancing in the bitter air. Someone mentioned the heavy planes they had heard overhead that night; engine after laboured engine, recalling another war. The Gulf War and the blizzard gave us camaraderie. Beneath the smiles and patience was the knowledge that more countries could be dragged into the conflict; the Middle East was not so very far away.

Later that day I walked under the beeches of Ninepenny Wood. The still-falling snow hid earlier trails and prints. It was a virgin world, incredibly precious – this England. Thoughts came of the Persian Gulf, now polluted beyond hope with countless tons of oil. Newspapers showed pictures of black waves gurgling against black beaches with bird and beast unrecognisable in their oily shrouds; streams of starving refugees told to return and get exit visas, left without food or water on the borders of their devastated land. Whatever this war might be about, whatever the rights or wrongs, ordinary people are always the greatest sufferers. Saddam Hussein had pronounced this the Mother of Battles, a Holy War. How many wars down the ages, have been fought in the name of God? I walked on through the unmarked snow, ashamed that my steps were sullying it, if only for a while. Man does that to everything – despoiler and despot.

I came to the badger sows' home with its yellow piping and smelt a strong scent of musk at the right-hand hole. There were recent slide marks too in the tunnel, now lightly covered with wind-blown flakes. Looking out across the pale expanse of farmland, there was a white cottage on the horizon seeming to keep vigil over the nearby snow-covered trees of the Sand Pit Sett. There was comfort in the thought that some things remain stable in a changing world. A movement through the trees and Flo came bounding over the snow in my tracks. She went to look into Hattie's entrance, smelt the musking and backed away. 'You're a wise cat', I whispered, 'That's Keep Out to everyone; she's protecting her cubs.' Flo turned her head as if listening and I strained my ears too, though I didn't expect to hear anything. There was a purring, but not of a cat and an answering chirruping, warbling; Hattie was nursing her young. I cradled Flo in my arms as together we wandered the homeward path – she gazing skywards as a flurry of descending flakes indicated the presence of squirrels above; I feeling the cat's warmth and thinking of the sow and her cubs.

By dusk, snow was piled high on every branch; perhaps the caravan would be warmer with its own thick layer. The windows, beautifully patinated with frost that morning, had disappeared in snow where the wind had blown it against them. I was keeping warm and cheerful, collecting snow in washing-up bowl and pails. A large pail of snow made only 5 cm of water when melted down, but if boiled it could be drunk. Water made like this had a smell rather like wet material, but I soon was used to the different taste. Truthfully, it must be purer than tap water with its additives. The problem would come when the snow stopped falling and that lying became dirty, but at present it was fine, free and virtually unlimited.

The snow continued throughout the night and by daylight was half a metre deep, going over the tops of my boots as I floundered through to the lane; 450 metres of rough path and meadow was quite a feat! The night temperature of -13°C seemed bearable too inside The Sett with its covering of snow. At least another five days of snow and intense cold were expected. All the country was affected, though the south-west only slightly. The south-east and particularly Kent were the worst. My friend in Scotland phoned to say it was quite pleasant there. Eight centimetres of snow had fallen a few days earlier, but no more. The pipes never froze in their stone-built house.

Walking out that night it was still snowing though the wind had dropped. It really seemed quite mild compared with two days earlier when the wind was so bitter. I wandered the length of the wood and the farmland beyond, for the joy of being out alone in this wonderful world of white. The trees at the Sand Pit seemed smaller, crouched under their grave clothes of snow. The gnarled trunks and buttressed boles stood solid and sturdy against the elements. Everywhere the white gave a brilliant visibility, quite unlike daylight – snow gives a unique quality of light. A faint sound disturbed the absolute stillness – snow dropping from above released a laden bough that swung back up, relieved of its weight. The loose snow dropped successively lower, each branch copying the first and the tree was hidden in a white haze.

Now a striped face appeared fleetingly beneath the tree roots and was gone. Moments passed and it was there again, then a badger scampered out in a flurry of snow, another was out and another. One sat on its haunches and raised a hindleg to scratch vigorously. Another dug into the snow, backed on to it for a pause, then began to groom. The third reappeared along the trail precariously winding from entrance to entrance below the top of the Sand Pit. It was a sow and she carried a stick perhaps 35 cm long in her mouth. It caught on a protruding root, but she tugged it free and drew level with the others. She tried to go headfirst into an entrance with it, spent some frustrating moments unsuccessfully taking it down and growled angrily as it jammed in the earthy walls. Now she backed down holding on to one end and I wondered what would happen when she reached a bend. This was an adult animal and she wasn't playing with it. Sticks have been found in badger bedding, and sometimes I find them myself dragged out amongst discarded or soiled bedding. Various reasons have been suggested for badgers taking sticks into their setts. To aerate the mass of material is a popular one, but it is doubtful whether they would do this. To chew up below ground is another, but if so, why? It certainly isn't an easy feat to take sticks so far below ground and the ones I have found discarded, haven't been chewed. Soon the other badgers had gone to earth too and I wandered homewards.

All the neighbourhood's dominant foxes had mated now and in these bitter nights, were holed up snug and safe from the worst of the weather. Hunting by day was more likely to be successful with rabbits and small mammals, besides the birds, also foraging in the warmer daytime temperatures. The caravan door had iced up again and didn't yield to me pulling it. After some effort, and not a few well-chosen words, it opened to reveal Flo, impatiently waiting to go out. She didn't travel any distance, however, but merely dropped on to the step and dived beneath the caravan where it was dry and snow-free. The surrounding snow completely encased the grassy ground beneath The Sett, with one or two runs made through it by various small mammals. I collected the pails and bowl, pushing snow into them and went indoors thankfully to make a drink. Feeding snow into a saucepan over the burner warmed my numbed hands, the brightness of the little flame, the only light. Something dripped on to my face; the icicles adorning my anorak hood were melting along with the snow. It was a painfully slow way of making a hot drink, but at least there was plenty of it – and it couldn't be turned off!

I snuggled down into the sleeping bag, hands warming round the hot mug as a shrill scream sounded from below the floor on which I lay. It stopped abruptly and I imagined Flo had found herself a breakfast in spite of the untouched, now frozen, food in her bowl. I guess I mustn't criticise; after all, she was acting no differently from Splinter and Fran, or indeed the badgers.

The following Sunday was much milder, although the snow still lay as thick. That morning the Calor-gas fire had broken down, so it was a relief that it wasn't so cold. Both taps over the sink thawed; I now had water. Karen was with me and I was cooking a roast dinner. We could hear the water tank filling behind the wall. I was uneasy, however, for the tank continued to fill *and* the gas jets of the water-heater were fully burning, although no water was being run off. It began to overheat (there was obviously a leak somewhere), so I had to turn the gas off at the cylinder outside. The leak soon made its presence felt. One of the pipes under the sink had burst and water was gushing out over the floor. The jet of water, high up on the pipe, poured over seats, carpet and table. Karen tried to stem the flow by wrapping cloths round the break, whilst I struggled over the untrodden snow to the Big House. There was no way of turning off the water at the caravan; only Mrs Ellis herself could do that. Instead, she refused, claiming she didn't know how to! No plumbers were available either, which wasn't surprising: the sub-zero conditions had caused many people to be in the same situation and it was also a Sunday. Meanwhile, Karen was terribly cold and wet, so I suggested she left whilst she could still manage the long, miserable trail through meadow and village to Oakley. Even if we hadn't been snowbound, no buses ran on a Sunday. She had lifted as many things off the floor and away from the kitchen area as she could, but the water was spreading and there is a limit to where you can put things up high in a caravan.

When she had gone, I thought of the builder from Oakley. He wasn't a plumber, but would he help? Yes, he would start out now and get as near as he could in his car, but would I try and persuade my landlady to turn the water off? That was a forlorn hope, but I waited at the bottom of the drive for his car to appear driving carefully over the icy lane and together we tramped through the snow. The water was still gushing forth over floor and belongings. He said he could mend it in spite of it not being turned off; only it would cause even more mess when he cut out the damaged pipe to replace it with a new piece. Fortunately, the floor had several holes that normally I covered with underlay against draughts and cold. This I had removed when I first discovered the leak, though the water gushed too fast for it to run away freely. It had, however, taken the pressure off the floor. The builder successfully fixed a new piece of pipe, but not without soaking himself. It struck me as ironic how I had longed to have tap water again and now I had!

Dusk comes early in winter. I worked against time, trying to mop up the worst of the water before it froze. I attempted to close down the water heater, so that I could use the gas stove. The extreme cold of the past few days had made the control button brittle and it snapped off, but I seemed to have done it at last. I turned the gas on outside with fingers that didn't seem to belong to me, then stumbled inside, closing the door. I continued to mop up the water, which seemed never ending. It had worked its way into the cupboards and the foam-cushioned seating was heavy with water as was the carpet. By now it was freezing and I was so cold and shivering that I decided to light the oven and leave its door open to get warm. With ice-cold, fumbling fingers I lit a match. There was a tremendous explosion that threw me into the office and against the metal filing cabinet. Obviously I hadn't closed the heater down properly and it had been allowing gas to escape all the time. I staggered up to find The Sett door swinging open and crockery from the overhead cupboards smashed on the frozen floor. Unsteadily I scrambled outdoors into the snow again and shakily turned off the gas once more. Inside, I heard a plaintive mewing and found the cat under the kitchen table where she had been thrown. Poor Flo! There was nowhere dry for her to stand and no fire for either of us to warm ourselves by. I fetched a clean towel and wrapped her in that, then sat in the armchair with my arms round her, trying not to shiver. Gradually she brightened, even poking her head out of the covers. I might have no form of heating or lighting, and no oven now, but I still had the camping gas burner with its little butane canister. I warmed her some milk, which she drank eagerly, then I heated some water in the saucepan and stood a tin of her favourite Whiskas in it to warm. By now it was night, but the snow outside gave a good light and the cat seemed more her old, perky self. I began to clear up the

. . . and the game in full spate!

The enclosure half hidden in the snow.

February 1991.

Flo coming home to be
fed.

broken china that littered the frozen floor and she watched me from the depths of the armchair and my old sleeping bag. 'Good cats are scarce' I told her and she purred agreement.

Now the temperature was dropping fast; it was to be -13°C again that night. Flo asked to go out, which rather worried me, but thinking about it, she had a choice of accommodation outside The Sett which was at least drier, and therefore, warmer, than my own home. I said goodbye and watched her careful progress down the well-trodden way towards the poplar row and the wood. The snow each side of the narrow path was a metre high in places, quite dwarfing the small, tabby figure till it was lost to sight. It was bitterly cold in the caravan. Although I couldn't blame her, I did miss the company – and warmth – of a certain little feline! I sat fully dressed with bodywarmer and anorak on in a sleeping bag and listened to the radio until the voices petered out. It was too cold for the batteries again. I hadn't been able to understand why my clock and radio had both ceased to function some days ago and taken them in to be repaired, only to be told there was nothing wrong with them. 'Batteries don't like it too cold' the man had commented. 'Try warming them, but not too near the fire mind, and both will work fine.' He had to be joking!

I had no intention of going out that night. The explosion had left me feeling very dazed and light-headed and it seemed foolish to do so. I was desperately tired and cold and longed to stop shivering and sleep.

I didn't wake up till the following afternoon and the first thing I saw was a patch of grey sky from the window which wasn't quite covered with snow. I felt grey and cold too. Had I gone out at night or had I dreamt it? The next thing I noticed was the snow on the frozen carpet. It hadn't been there last evening, and whenever I came in I was careful to remove any snow from my boots or myself out of doors. It was strange. I made a hot drink – how marvellous to have water on tap – then heated some more to wash. I must change my clothes too. I might sleep fully dressed, but I didn't go about by day in the same ones. Those I had washed and hung up indoors – how many days ago? – had stopped dripping, probably because they were frozen stiff. No point in trying to wash more for there was nowhere to hang them except outside, where they would also freeze. I felt fine really, but still oddly light-headed and shivery.

I decided to go for a walk to get warm, and followed the path to the poplar row. Sometime in the night it had snowed again, covering the bird tracks and Flo's pawprints of last evening. I was interested to see what must have been my own bootprints, leading *towards* The Sett intermingled with those of a fox. They were all sharp and clear; when had the snow stopped? I back-tracked them to the snowbound meadow and saw I had appar-ently wandered off the path. How on earth could I have done that? Once off the route that my frequent walking had kept lower than the surrounding snow, the way became very deep. Here I had floundered, my prints were haywire for some paces, then I had fallen again. All around were fox prints – and the dream of the night; had it been reality? What had I thought I was doing out in the snow? There could be no doubt it was me; the same bootprints with their chain impression. Thoughtfully I walked back to The Sett and, rounding the band, there were Splinter and his mate standing looking my way. He approached quietly, not his usual prancing, and stood staring up. 'Oh, Splinter, what a fool I was,' and he reared upon hindlegs, forepaws at my waist to touch noses. What had he made of my lying in the snow? As his cold nose touched my face, the memory of the night returned. His nose had pushed against me and his paws dug at my body as he whined. Now Fran stood by the little green door as her mate went round the back of the caravan. I could hear sounds of water and going round myself found him drinking from another pipe that had burst; fortunately, it was outside this time. Both foxes carefully drank from the gushing water and I left them to go indoors.

It snowed again that day, adding a little more height to that already lying. I walked out several times to keep warm and also to keep the path open. Where had Flo gone? I re-opened the path to the Poplar Sett and bent down to look inside the piping. To my surprise – should I have been? – cat prints were visible on the wind-blown snow in Hattie's entrance. It looked as if the badgers had taken her in!

I had forgotten how dangerous sweating is in very cold conditions. Years ago, I followed foxes in the Ashcroft area during January and February, especially to observe them mating. You need to run steadily over long distances for that and inevitably you sweat. That is no problem, till you stop; quickly the sweat cools and you begin to shiver. Then I had a warm house to return to and a hot bath if necessary. Now I had a caravan as cold inside as out and no bath or shower. It was lovely to go out walking in the snow, especially to get warm, but I must remember not to walk so quickly as to begin to sweat. When I first returned to The Sett it was great; I was glowing with warmth, but quickly that turned to chill and cold. Well, at least I was learning the art of self-preservation.

That evening I sat by the window looking out at the brilliant landscape, marvelling at the beauty of the snow. As I looked, a small striped tabby came into view followed by first Hattie and then Hazel. I opened the door and she left her friends to jump inside and be fed. Badgers have a thick layer of fat to live on during snowy nights, but I couldn't forsake them. What had I that was suitable? Wholemeal bread didn't seem very interesting, but spread with salmon paste, perhaps, and cut up? A bowl of fresh water might be worth offering too. The outside bowls had long since disappeared under the snow, though the birds had a small plastic one up high that I thawed each day for them. (Each time the water froze in it, it rose up to a point in the middle and looked so odd that I took a photo.) The badgers made very short work of their improvised meal and snuffled about in the doorway for more. All I could think of was my breakfast cereal – six Weetabix disappeared without trace! It was good to have their company as they whickered and snuffled and grumbled noisily on my step. I found an apple and, cutting it in half, offered a piece to each. Two crunches and it was gone. Flo sat washing herself just above them; as Hazel reached up, so the cat gave her face a quick wash too. Now the badgers moved off back the way they had come along my path and Flo followed. 'Deserter!' I said to her retreating back with its jauntily upright tail, 'It's rats, not cats that desert sinking ships, you and your friends,' but I was pleased really. Flo, like Iffy, was a natural survivor.

The cat continued to live with the badgers, returning with them each evening to be fed. The milk in the fridge had long since frozen, so she, like them, had to make do with water. The village butcher gave me scraps and bones and I treated the sows to a large bag of peanuts, a highly nutritious food that badgers adore. I believe Flo would have stayed indefinitely with the sows, but for the arrival of my next patient.

One day I had a phone call from the city police; an RTA badger had been seen near the common – could I come? Armed with cage and grasper, we found him on the verge. He was barely conscious and had a small cut above his left eye. I lifted him by the tail and the scruff of his neck – not the loose skin on his rump, for this was badly scarred. He made no attempt to bite. The police had another call out by this time and dropped me and badger at the vet's surgery; they would be back. The vet chatted as he examined the boar. He took X-rays which showed that no bones were broken and stitched the cut. We looked at the scars above his tail – some old and two very recent. These were not scars caused by baiting, but by badger fighting badger. A surplus of boars often ends in this fashion; either the dominant animal keeps the subdominant well down the pecking-order or causes it to wander in search of fresh territory. This searching usually involves crossing unknown roads, which could be the reason why this badger came to be injured.

By now our boar was coming to, though it made no attempt to rise. Together we carefully laid it back in the carrying-cage; its jaws had been bandaged shut all this while. Safely in, the vet untied the binding and fastened the door. It was suggested that I keep him for a few days in the warm and see how he progressed. Warm? I explained my circumstances. I could have him in the sitting room with sleeping bags tied round either the cage itself or the large packing case. That would be fine. Now one of the officers returned and together we drove back to the village. We discussed the badger's scars and how he had come by them. He was a fully grown boar, but undersized and something of a runt, although till his accident it seems he had been fairly healthy. The policeman knew about Hattie and Hazel and suggested I relocated the badger with them. This rather worried me, not least because Steve and I had agreed never to do so again in Legget's vicinity. It wasn't just that though – one doesn't just take a badger from A and put it in B; badger life is far more complicated than that. There was also the legal side, of course, although this relocation would have been but a few miles, rather than from one county to another. In the end I compromised,

agreeing that should this badger turn up again in similar circumstances, perhaps we would. By now we had reached the
drive. The policeman carried the cage over the snow to The
Sett, but looked rather horrified when he saw where I lived. He
was even more shocked when on entering he hit his head on the
icicles that had formed once more on the kitchen ceiling. I
assured him it wasn't nearly as bad as it looked and the badger
would really be all right. 'It wasn't the badger I was thinking
about' he retorted, which made me laugh. I promised to let him
know when the patient could safely be returned and left him to
retrace his way in the deep snow, whilst I made the badger
comfortable.

I'm not sure when Flo put in an appearance and sat on the
armchair to watch the proceedings. I laid black binliners on the
floor, then arranged plenty of newspaper on it and stood the
packing case on this. It was full of hay (and badger), and by now,
sported red and blue sleeping bags tied around it. I nearly gave
him the luxury duvet that my daughter had loaned her poor old
mum to keep out the cold, but Karen was coming back and forth
to check I was still in the land of the living and would have been
very annoyed had she seen it. Flo really didn't approve –
badgers should be outdoors, not in. Perhaps she felt the boar
had taken her place; she certainly regarded the sleeping bags
thoughtfully. Blissfully unaware of a certain feline's feelings,
the patient slumbered on.

The badger improved, as did the weather. Flo continued to
live at the Poplar Sett, returning home with her friends to be fed
and occasionally dropping in to see me – or was it to see the
recuperating boar? For his part, he seemed content to doze the
hours away and, although often awake when I went to inspect
him, seemed the most unaggressive badger road casualty I had
encountered for a long time. Gradually the nights grew warmer:
a mere -5°C in fact. Lack of heating was no longer such a
problem and the best way to warm chilblained hands was round
a hot mug of tea. The camping burner boiled a saucepan and at
least I had water now from a tap – two taps to be precise. No
more early morning forays to gather snow and melt it before I
could wash or drink: such a time- and energy-consuming occupation. Those earlier days I had seemed to spend all my time
merely surviving, but at least I appreciated basics such as water

when I had them. Flo hadn't cared overmuch for melted snow either!

There was the badger to see to. He seemed to have little desire to eat, but eagerly drunk the warm glucosed milk I offered. Flo had some too. The old piece of nailed-down carpet in the kitchen area was no longer frozen and would have to dry itself out gradually. With things piled high on every available surface out of the wet, there was nowhere to dry it even had it been unnailed. I kept myself physically busy rather than sitting writing as I would have preferred, and in this way kept warm. One afternoon proved to be sunny and although it made no difference to the snow I did my washing and hung it out to drip. A shepherd's pie that I had made with the roast dinner that fateful Sunday, and subsequently frozen in the arctic conditions, was hacked into portions and put in the saucepan to warm through. Flo and I enjoyed ours. I offered some to the badger and had to wrest the spoon back off him – really, manners. The cat looked on with some interest and sniffed the spoon, which was now bent double from its encounter. She came and sat by the badger with a certain respect in her manner and made her little, crooning purr. They touched noses through the barred opening – his big snout, I noticed with pleasure, now slightly moist and Flo's tiny snub one almost lost amongst her furry cheeks.

I longed to photograph Flo in the snow. Unlike Splinter, however, the cat hated cameras. Although friends heard my tales of the fox, he never appeared when they were visiting me. Only the many photos Karen and I took of him were proof of his existence; all other humans he distrusted. He was quite happy to be photographed and the instamatic's noisy wind-on mechanism never bothered him. Flo, however, disappeared in haste if she as much as saw the empty case. Anything directed her way or pointed at her was to be feared and I wondered if she had ever been shot at, so frightened was she. I could creep up on Flo indoors as she was sleeping and take a photo as she awoke with a jerk. If Karen held her, she might permit me to quickly take one without a struggle, but outside in the open she fled as if from some terrible danger, so pictures of her and Splinter together were few and far between. Now I walked slowly through my snow path to the poplar row, trying to encourage the cat to follow. I held the camera under my coat and tried to take photos without her seeing me. The sun still shone and she looked comic sniffing the snow with disdain. However, she saw what I intended and ran back to The Sett. Perhaps one or two would come out.

The next day the temperature plummeted again and it began to snow. I went out that afternoon when it eased to post some letters and to put one in Val's door. At least it was a way of keeping warm once I was out of the wind in the sunken lane. To my surprise and pleasure, there was Val just finishing clearing the snow away from her drive. It was good to sit in the warm and talk. Later, at home, I phoned the vet and reported on the patient's progress. He suggested it was time the badger was put outside for a couple of nights ready for a return home. I cleared a path to the large enclosure and pushed plenty of fresh hay inside its den. The thick snow on top of the cage was best left, for it gave good insulation and unless we had a sudden thaw, seemed likely to remain there for some days. Walking back in the grey light, I finished the reel of film in the camera. For all the cold, it was such a beautiful, delicate landscape.

By 5 p.m. it was dusk and too cold to type any more in spite of the large mug of tea I kept holding. My ears were itching and I found there were chilblains on their edges. I supposed the real art of self-preservation was to grow a fur coat and hibernate! I gave the badger his last meal indoors. Flo had hers too. She sat next to the wire of the case and communicated to her brocky who 'hhhhhhmmmmed' back. I was rather worried about their relationship. He might have been looking for a mate when he was run over, but how could I tell him cats only have kittens? Once the boar was put into the outside enclosure, he quickly disappeared to the hay-filled den and Flo returned to her friends at the Poplar Sett.

That night I heard badger noises nearby and opened the door expecting the sows to be waiting for peanuts and scraps. Not so, however. Very excited, they were standing on hind legs, bodies pressed against the enclosure's metal mesh. February is the peak of badgers' sexual activity and not only for recuperating boars! Sows with cubs but a few days old will be receptive too. A very frustrated boar was pacing stiff-legged back and forth on his

side of the cage with two seductive sows on the other. Poor Flo –
she was forgotten by all!

A friend phoned the next morning. Jean, her husband and
the owner of a four-wheel drive Rangerover would bring a
portable gas fire and bottle to the caravan. It was bright sunshine, but still very cold and well below freezing. I plodded on
my pathway through the snow and began to clear the build-up at
the gate leading from the drive into the meadow. It was slow
work, but certainly kept me warm. Soon Jean, her husband and
friend arrived. More snow clearing, but it was decided against
driving over the depth of snow. Jean trotted ahead with the
empty gas fire on a home-made sledge. Peter tied a cord on the
bottle and began to drag it. The gas fire suddenly bounced off
into the snow and Jean forged ahead at twice the speed. Chok-
ing with laughter, her unkind friends fell about hysterically. 'It's
a shame to tell her,' remarked her husband, 'she's getting on so
well.' Sensing no one was following, she turned and saw the
empty sledge – and the three of us! Poor Jean – still wheezing
from a bad chest infection, she couldn't help but laugh herself.

The gas fire and bottle duly travelled to my caravan and were
installed inside. Coffee all round with Jean and I sitting talking
whilst the others walked round to the back of The Sett to try to
stem the gush of water. It appeared that a section of pipe had
slipped from its couplings in the cold; it was not broken. They
both tried to push it back into place and reclip it, but the
constant pressure of escaping water prevented this. The water
would have to be turned off or it couldn't be done. However,
they had managed to reduce the volume pouring into the
ground. All too soon it was time for them to go. It had been good
to have visitors after so long. It was heaven to have a fire again
and to be really warm. Sitting in the gloaming that evening with
Flo on my lap, I thought of those living in Cardboard City; those
homeless in London with perhaps a few blankets and boxes to
keep them warm. 'We're incredibly lucky,' I told her as she
stretched up a soft, lazy paw and purred.

Chapter Twelve

IT was a grey, misty day and the rain was causing a thaw. It was also the day of the second reading of the Badger Bill in the House of Commons.

My RTA badger in the outside enclosure seemed fit and well, if his interest in Hattie's and Hazel's visits was anything to go by. I made arrangements with the constable who brought him; he was off duty and would come that evening. He asked if I could mark the boar in some way so that the police would recognise him as the same animal if found wandering. With cochineal and a pastry brush, I made a curving red line in the white fur of his face above the eyes. It resembled the bridge of a pair of spectacles and made him look highly intelligent. I was only able to do this with ease because he seemed besotted with Flo (in the absence of the sows) and totally unaware of me when she was nearby. I obtained the consent of my local NCC office to do this, as under the 1973 Badgers Act the marking of badgers is illegal except under licence. I agreed with the police and vet that if he did turn up again, and had been bitten, we would release him here. Hattie and Hazel would love to have him, though there would be some competition from Flo! It was difficult to know what to do for the best. I hoped I was mistaken in thinking he was being pushed out of his own clan and that he would not be found again. In a couple of months the dye would wear off, but certainly we would know him again till the spring.

Ken, the policeman, came off-duty to collect the badger and me at about 8 p.m. He found the boar's new look highly amusing; he thought him not so much intellectual as soulful, and promptly christened him the Dean! The badger took all this in his stride, treating his driver to a stony stare. There was only one sett in the area apart from an outliner two-entrance one in the bank, and both were on the same side of the road. The Dean had no intention of leaving his cage; on opening it we found him curled round with his rump presented to us. We waited patiently for some minutes in the damp, misty air. The thaw was well under way; grass and bushes appearing, together with green wild arum leaves. Another few minutes that kept us shivering whilst the Dean's flanks gently rose and fell. He was either sleeping or putting on a good act. There was nothing for it but to tip the cage, at first gently, then more firmly, and the boar slowly dropped out. He scented the air and ambled slowly over to the first outliner entrance, but didn't go in. We watched him disappear along the hedgerow in the direction of the larger sett. Ken and I were rather uneasy; we cruised slowly up and down the road for an hour, half expecting to see our badger again. Finally, I was left at the drive with the promise that if the Dean did turn up agan the officer would let me know.

◊ ◊ ◊

We had all been apprehensive about the second reading of the Badgers Bill. Not only did most MPs travel home on a Friday, but owing to the snowbound conditions, many hadn't been home for a fortnight. The two MPs representing the British Field Sports Society (BFSS), Sir Nicholas Bonsor, its chairman, and Michael Colvin, its vice-chairman, had prepared long speeches to use up the Bill's available time and so talk or filibuster it out. To prevent this, Roy Hughes, who brought the Bill, would need to move a closure motion to stop the debate and proceed to a vote. This could easily have been successful for, of those MPs present, all except the hunting lobby were in favour of it, but there were nowhere near the 100 necessary to see it voted through. If it failed to get through, as the BFSS hoped, Sir Nicholas Bonsor would submit his own bill already drafted by

them. In vain, MPs repeatedly asked Colvin to draw his speech
to a close, but he was within his rights and when he eventually
finished Bonsor would take over. (It was this Michael Colvin
who, with Sir Charles Morrison, had the previous year successfully blocked Tony Banks's Bill to protect badger setts.) So many
people, organisations and individuals had petitioned their MPs
to be present, but the Commons seemed almost empty with only
sixty or seventy members in the House that day. This Bill too
would be lost and the BFSS Bill with its loopholes to protect
hunting interests would weaken, not strengthen, existing legislation. Yet under its guise the hunting lobby could say that of
course they were concerned for the plight of the badger; hadn't
they themselves brought a Bill to protect it? The Bill looked set
to over-run its time and be lost when Simon Hughes MP
interrupted the proceedings to inform the Speaker of Saddam
Hussein's broadcast on Baghdad radio, intimating that Iraq
might withdraw from Kuwait. From the beginning, Simon
Hughes had been enthusiastic for the protection of setts. As a
lawyer, formerly prosecuting for the RSPCA with considerable
success in badger cases, Hughes used this news to its best
advantage. He asked the Speaker to inform the government and
request it to make a statement to the House that afternoon. The
Speaker agreed and although Colvin resumed his filibustering
speech the badger had won the day. As one observer in the
public gallery put it, MPs seemed to appear out of the woodwork
to take their seats; the near-empty House was steadily filling.
Colvin had no choice now but to bring his speech to a close,
though it took him another twenty minutes to do so. The Bill
was voted on to its next step, the committee stage, by most of
those present. Whilst it is true that many were enthusiastic for
the Bill to succeed, it is equally true that they also wanted to
discuss this dramatic piece of Gulf War news. Some already on
their way home and hearing of it on their car radios, turned
round to come back to Westminster. A Middle East dictator
seems a strange ally for the British badger!

That night the thaw continued and walking round to Ninepenny Wood about 11 p.m. I met Hattie grubbing about under
the beeches. She raised her snout in my direction and gazed
short-sightedly at me as I squatted down making the contact
sound. A pause, and she came right up, sniffed at my hand

resting on the ground and padded round me to trot along the poplar row, back the way I had come. I followed at a discreet distance and found both badgers and Flo at the now empty enclosure. The cat seemed to know Dean had gone, perhaps she had seen us taking him, but Hattie and Hazel called loudly and sniffed for many long moments at the big cage door. Snowdrops were out in the thawed areas of grass with daffodil greenery well advanced. That day I photographed perfect badger pawprints in the remaining snow.

Karen came to dinner; it was good to see her again. In a few weeks she would be moving to Yorkshire, but was hiring a car in the meanwhile to take some of her belongings to the house and see all was well. Would I care to go too, when the snow had all disappeared? Flo made much of Karen, playing rugby tackles with her legs as she walked by and jumping into her lap when she sat down. Whilst we laughed together, a phone call came from the local police who had been given a tip-off of badger-baiters at an event taking place that evening on the marshes. Did I know of a certain man? Were his premises suitable for holding badgers? I replied that he was too well known now to keep either brockies or fighting dogs; he preferred to farm them out with friends. Did I know of any suspect called Len living anywhere in the area? The inference being that it could be in or at his premises. I would look in my files and also ask around, then let him know. No luck, however, although Tim offered his radios, himself and members of the group to keep vigil if necessary. I phoned back with the offer to the constable who said that Steve had been alerted and might be able to use the radios and help. However, when I contacted the RSPCA Inspector, I discovered the location was far too vague and covered several square miles of marshland. A police car would go back and forth after dark and station itself on the bridge overlooking the area to radio back for help if odd lights or anything untoward occurred. When Karen left and the sun had gone, I carried round the butcher's offerings to the Poplar Sett. The butcher was very generous (I could scarcely call them scraps) and I hoped the badgers would enjoy them. The night was misty and the remaining snow frozen. Our feet and paws crunched beneath us as we walked the wood and returning later for a last look at the Poplar Sett, we found the food all gone. Flo called at the entrance, then went below and did not return. That cat really thought she was a badger!

Next evening I had a call from the city police to say that Dean was on the road again, apparently wandering, with two large, raw bites on his rump. Ken was very proud that he and Eddie had caught the boar themselves and put him in a clean dustbin, a good substitute for a holding cage. Slightly stunned, I asked how and was told 'Oh, like you did; if a little lady like you can do it, I'm darned sure we could. Just a matter of confidence,' he concluded airily. When I had picked the badger up, however, he had been barely conscious and I was tempted to point that out, but thought better of it. They were phoning from the vet's surgery where Dean had just received a shot against infection. Would I meet them at the drive to guide them in? It was evident that they intended the boar to have a permanent home here with two female badgers to keep him happy (a possible third being Flo?). And at least he hadn't been knocked down again and perhaps killed or badly maimed. Ken had the impression the boar was hoping to be picked up, and although this sounded very far-fetched I did wonder myself.

There was fresh hay in the house of the enclosure, so securing open the door, we left Dean inside; he could have his freedom or bed down there for the night. It was lovely and mild with the snow still melting and no frost, though stars pricked in a velvety sky. I lit candles in The Sett and we sat gazing out of the windows with our hands round hot mugs of coffee. Every now and again the police radio sounded, but not for Ken and Eddie. Flo had disappeared at the approach of the men, for she feared anyone she didn't know. The tabby sat outside now, delicately washing and watching the cage. At that moment, by now 9.20 p.m. a grey figure came swaying along the winding path, nose to ground, but ever and anon, her striking face raised as she scented the air – Hattie, and behind her came Hazel. They barely noticed the butcher's offerings, nor indeed did they bother with Flo. Something big and shaggy was out in the enclosure, busily washing his wounds. Ken said we shouldn't watch, they should have their sex to themselves. Eddie made no comment, but seemed to be trying not to make a noise! I noticed, however, that Ken's modesty didn't stop him gawping open-mouthed, 'God, don't they make a racket?' I remarked that we call the noise purring, for want of a better expression, and that when we should eventually leave The Sett we would notice the very strong smell of musk. This led us on to delayed implantation as we watched the sows' obvious invitation to Dean and his excited stiff-legged posture before he mounted Hattie. This took place inside the enclosure, with the sows jumping in with ease. All the while, poor little Flo sat alternately washing and mooning around. What it is to be a cat in a badger world; she really couldn't compete! Having served both sows, all three scrambled out of the enclosure, gulped down the meat and peanuts and trundled off in the direction of the empty lake and the short turf surrounding it. We trooped outside with Ken picking up his dustbin and all of us remarking on the oily musk; not unpleasant at all, but very strong on the still air. Holding Flo, I said goodbye and promised to keep them in touch. The dejected tabby accepted a stroke from Eddie and a compliment on beautiful green eyes before the policemen went on their way. Although I knew I would soon have to leave this place and the south-east where I was born, so many people here are badger-friendly that I had no real fear for the brockies, only a selfish sadness that I was losing so many good friends.

The following night I met the three badgers, Hattie, Hazel and Dean, all busy worming at a short distance from one another, along the side of Ninepenny Wood. Hattie came up and musked my boots; her sister followed. After some hesitation, Dean swayed up, had a good sniff and backed on to my boots for good measure – was he saying thanks? Flo was feeling kittenish and played 'I'll dab you, if you'll dab me' with the newest arrival. The snow was fast disappearing, leaving everywhere very wet.

Two of the dobermans had been reported digging at the sett again and Tim and I discussed the situation. He agreed to write a letter to Mrs Ellis on behalf of the group, requesting her to control her dogs. It was especially worrying now there were cubs present. He would send a copy of the letter to Oakley police. One of her dogs, Bonnie, had been rehomed some months earlier with a woman in the village. I sometimes saw the new owner out walking the doberman and a small dog. I asked her how Bonnie was progressing. The bitch had needed firmness and kindness was the reply, and above all security. It had been an uphill struggle at first, but didn't I notice the improvement already? I was happy to say that I did. Bonnie hadn't always lived with Mrs Ellis. She had been reared very happily with a family with no problems at all, until she badly bit one of their children on the cheek. The husband had asked at the local pet shop if they knew of a good home and the proprietor mentioned this to Mrs Ellis when she came to buy dog food. Her own two dogs were not typical of the breed – Butch who was so enormous and Lucky with her long tail and odd eyes. Bonnie, however, was beautiful, and without giving the matter any serious thought Mrs Ellis had taken the third dog. She couldn't be bothered to spay the new bitch (Lucky had come from Battersea Dogs' Home and was already spayed), so inevitably, pups were born, of which Bruno was the one she kept. Bonnie had come to the Big House already trained and disciplined; she was also used to affection. It was a happy ending for a dog who, through no fault of her own, had been allowed to roam with the others as a pack and become a problem. Bonnie was fortunate; she had found someone prepared to show her affection and patience; an owner who didn't see her merely as an object to guard the house. I wished the lady well and Bonnie wagged her bottom at me. To the villagers and badgers, however, that still left the other three dogs, but perhaps Tim's formal letter would give the Poplar Sett brockies some measure of security.

I would be away overnight at a conference and left at 9 a.m. having fed Flo and put more food and a large bowl of clean water for her in the small opened cage. The dogs couldn't get into this, but I showed the tabby the containers before I left. Karen had promised to come in and feed her the following day and see all was well. I left a large pile of peanuts and fresh hay by the Poplar Sett.

On my return the following evening, all the snow had finally gone. Everywhere was very damp and dismal inside The Sett and the water still gushed from the outside pipe. No electricity of course. Somehow I had hoped the miracle might have happened. Staying overnight at someone else's comfortable home had made me notice the mildew covering my walls that normally I cleaned off each day. A sinister brown fungus pushing the wallpaper away where wall joined floor seemed to have taken a hold in my brief absence and needed cutting back again. I had no sooner come in, than a miaow sounded and there was a scraping at the outside door. Opening it, Flo jumped in to greet me. I certainly had a welcome home, Flo even ignoring her food to show she was pleased to see me. Now it was raining outside, damp and miserable, but sitting in front of the gas fire, we were both warm and content. Karen phoned later to make sure everything was all right and at dusk I walked round to the Poplar Sett and found, not surprisingly, that the food and bedding had all gone. That night was very, very gusty with strong winds buffeting The Sett. Flo stayed in whilst I went walkabout and found the three badgers foraging in the comparative shelter of Ninepenny Wood. In spite of the wind there was a lovely half moon in a clear sky and it was very mild. This mildness continued with a great spotted woodpecker drumming away each morning and a green woodpecker 'yaffling' into the sunshine. Leaving the caravan door open, the sun streamed in, helping to dry out the remaining damp from the carpet and foam seating.

Karen came to stay. Mrs Ellis had phoned me, renewing her threats of arson to the caravan; she also said she 'had something else in store'. My solicitor suggested that Karen live with me till I was ready to leave, then we could both move out together. In view of its dampness, I had joked about the threats to torch my home, but in fact it was a very real possibility with the mentally off-balance woman. She knew I had all my worldly goods in this small space. Unlike her luxury mansion, there was nothing of any great monetary value, but I could never replace what I had – my natural history records contained in many volumes and sentimental keepsakes from family and friends. Twice since Christmas someone with a key had entered, ripping pictures that the Irish children had sent me from the walls and scattering papers, then left, locking the door again. Only Karen, myself and Mrs Ellis had keys to The Sett. It had been suggested that I let my landlady know I was leaving and when, believing this would pacify her. However, it had apparently had the reverse effect if her phone call was anything to go by. She seemed determined to speed the departing guest.

There was a lovely moon one night with tiny clouds in an otherwise clear sky. I went over to the Ashcroft badgers and was made much of by the mothers Crisp and Missy, for the latter had produced cubs after all, though with neither sow did I yet know how many. They were not in competition with one another for my attention and seemed very settled with only occasional visits from me. Once I left for Scotland they would soon accept that I would not return. There was much vigilance now by local people and our badger group; the police and farmers also kept a watchful eye. Ray too had a great interest and would keep me in touch. My time knowing these gentle animals was drawing to a close. I remembered the death of the badger Jessie in December 1980, when a man set his three dogs on to her. That was the turning point in my determination to help these badgers and one of the earliest entries in my first book. I knew of no badger groups then and the Wildlife and Countryside Act was not passed, nor did it come on to the statute book until the following autumn. It was some years later that John Taylor introduced me to the Surrey Badger Protection Society and so to the NFBG. There had been so much to do and there still is, but we had all come a long way since then. I returned home at first light as a faint mist shrouded the trunks and bushes leaving their tops clear. In a sense, I was saying goodbye each time I looked at a tree or beast, but I was not unhappy, for I had a home to go to and had been granted so much.

News of the Gulf War was worrying. Saddam Hussein's offer of withdrawal contained too many conditions and, whilst negotiations went on in Moscow, he was systematically practising a scorched-earth policy in Kuwait by burning the oil wells there. It was an environmental disaster on a scale as yet unknown. He was clearly determined that if he couldn't have Kuwait, no one else would. Now Desert Storm, as the land battle was known by the Allies, had begun, with the war in the air still continuing. How would it all end?

Flo was missing. Now Karen was with me, the cat regularly turned up for her dinner at 3.30 p.m. which was an hour and a half too early; it was a standing joke. It crossed my mind that perhaps this was my landlady's threat, to take my cat or shut it in somewhere to spite me, but surely not? Flo was quite capable of catching food for herself if free and often did, but it had rained steadily for two days and she was one who liked her creature comforts. I went out to see the badgers, but no tabby was amongst them. Splinter was hunting for his mate and their young family; she would not be with him. The badgers followed me home. They snuffled round the caravan and watched me go indoors, Dean rearing up on the doorstep and peering inside as if looking for his first admirer too. Where was she? That morning I walked down to the lane and searched up to the houses. The cat's territory had never extended that far and she was frightened of the noise of traffic, but I had to convince myself that her body wasn't lying around or thrown up on the bank under the hollies. I spoke to a lady living nearby; had she seen a small tabby? She promised to watch out and let me know.

I returned to Karen, who was getting ready for work, but no, the cat had not come back. Next I walked all round the empty lake searching under the hawthorns and sides of the field for snares. Was she lying somewhere shot and injured? Common sense told me this was extremely unlikely. I had already searched in the stables and stableyard, but there was nowhere really in which to shut a cat and only the lodger's tortoiseshell – Flo's arch enemy – came to my calling.

I took a deep breath and walking slowly to my landlady's garden, continued the length of it calling repeatedly until I came to the side of the Big House. I stood by the wrought-iron gate looking in at the dogs in the courtyard and called Flo by name. The dobermans pricked their ears and Lucky wagged her long tail, but no little tabby appeared. I walked right up to the huge picture window, now covered with a slatted blind and, pressing my face against it, stood there calling. Somehow I knew someone was inside and listening, though everywhere was still. Very slowly I walked up to the gate in the brick wall and so to the path and the front of the house. Her car was parked outside, so Mrs Ellis was at home and could hear me. For a very long time I stood calling in front of her house and standing by the car, then walked back to the caravan and to Karen. She too was upset and didn't like leaving for work. I had barely returned when we heard a noise and looked out. There by the step was Flo, flattened down against the ground, her ears back. She ran crouching in as I opened the door and rushed round the room, so very distressed. I picked her up and saw she must have been confined closely for she had lain in her own urine. Food was placed on the floor and she ate and drank ravenously; even for a greedy Flo that was a record. No way had she been able to hunt for herself. Gradually she calmed, washed and allowed us to pet her.

Steve came later and we caught up with events since last we met. Nothing had come of the tip-off; the informant had been too frightened to be more precise. Steve took my Scottish address and we promised to keep in touch. Searching for the cat that morning, I had missed the wonderful news – President Bush had announced 'Exactly six weeks after the declaration of war, I have ordered a cease-fire.' As one US general remarked, the Mother of All Battles had become the Mother of All Retreats. Since the beginning of the Gulf War, Baghdad had been without electricity and running water. I knew how they felt!

That evening I stood on the edge of Ninepenny Wood with Flo and Dean snuffling about my legs, looking out to Val's light, twinkling brightly from her house on the horizon. With Flo leading the way, we followed the trail we had ourselves made over the months since Legget cleared the wood, and found Hattie and Hazel also above ground. Hattie inspected Flo who walked round her purring. 'You're very sure of your welcome, aren't you?' I remarked to the cat as Hazel backed on to my boots with tail raised. Dean was skittish in marked contrast to his still soulful expression, and tapped Flo with his big snout. She patted him back with a furry paw and they were off, playing catch amongst the trees, churning up the dead leaves and doing the flowering dog's mercury no good at all!

The two sows carefully inspected my anorak; in the pockets they could smell the peanuts that I had meant to lay out earlier for them to find. I took the small kernels and spread them well over the ground so that all could take their share. Three black snouts curled back over their owners' mouths as each peanut was individually picked up delicately by front teeth. Each kernel was carefully selected – not the nearest one necessarily – and munched with much smacking of lips. For a creature with such a broad mouth they are surprisingly deft at picking up small objects. Flo sniffed a peanut with disdain, then sauntered out across the field, tail raised high like a flag. 'Give me a nice, fresh mouse any day!'

Karen had a terrible dream in which she found a sack, and opening it discovered not Flo but Splinter 'all hacked up except for his head'. It was an indication of how we felt about Mrs Ellis and the stress under which we were at present living.

◊ ◊ ◊

The Chantry fields around Ashcroft had been taken out of tenancy and returned to the district council who, with the parish council, owned the woods. Ray would be involved in their day-to-day maintenance. Little Chantry was already a wildflower meadow; Great Chantry, the largest of these fields, would possibly have a riding track around the perimeter which would be fenced off from the rest of the field. The remainder would be grass-sown and the hay from it sold. Riders wishing to use it would be licensed and charged for the privilege. This would not only help in the upkeep of the field, but also take some of the pressure of horse-riding from Ashcroft Woods. Ray had great plans for Long Field, the remaining Chantry land. He didn't want merely grass, but stands of trees such as Scots pines, as well as a pond with a hedge between it and the nature reserve itself. Ray was busy putting up bird boxes and I was asked by an officer of the county trust, who managed the woods, whether I thought dormice boxes might be a worthwhile investment. It was a good idea for I felt that dormice were still there. He then asked what I thought of the newly acquired Chantry fields. I could honestly say I was very pleased. Historically, they had always been one with Ashcroft Woods and it was right that the land should return to them.

I walked the area by night with great pleasure. Under the trees a dark shape skilfully turned and twisted on silent wings and called its quavering cry. A red eye glared between struggling clouds, then disappeared. It reminded me of the term 'hot-eye' used by scientists for a night scope with infrared light. I found the badgers feeding below the sett where it was damp; also feeding there were five Canada geese. The short, stocky badgers with their white faces and black stripes seemed to complement the taller birds with their long black necks and heads and white cheek flashes. Neither group was at all interested in the other. They brought to mind other bird/badger situations such as the woodcock probing for worms at night that the badgers here have chased; also the lapwings and gulls that their cubs enjoyed pursuing. Not that woodcock, lapwings or gulls seemed unduly bothered!

It was whilst standing by the nursery entrance in the bank that I was made aware of a small, round face, softly marked in the badger fashion, that peered out on to the great, wide world. One of Crisp's cubs! It appeared again and would have ventured further, but at that moment mother herself came by and firmly pushed it back with her snout as she followed after. The waning moon rode high in a swirling sky, but by now was its usual colour. Walking homewards, I stopped to watch near the heavy mantle of old man's beard that covered the trees of a field edge. Spectral arms raised heavenwards from the still-bare trees and the clouds fell away to reveal the pure lunar disk, as a phantom shape glided on buoyant wings to its roost. It was a barn owl and there was its mate still hunting along the hedge. The heart-shaped face came and went as it quartered the land.

At home as I boiled a saucepan of water for tea, a rather more solid shape glided by. When I opened the door, Flo turned in surprise to see me and came in with an easy leap. She had been hunting and wasn't hungry. After a fuss from me, she disappeared into the sitting room to Karen fast asleep beneath her duvet. There's cupboard love for you; Flo adores duvets!

Later that week I left for Dublin at the invitation of Badger-watch Ireland to attend the Royal Academy Seminar on the badger. The two-day seminar was intended as a review of scientific research on the bovine TB/badger issue. Ireland's Eradication of Animal Disease Board (ERAD) had maintained for many months that they were actively engaged in researching the problem. No description, however, of the nature of this research had been forthcoming, although large-scale badger culling in areas with a high incidence of the disease amongst cattle had continued unabated. This veil of secrecy, coupled with lurid anti-badger propaganda in the farming press, suggested that eradication of badgers was the total sum of the Irish government's 'research'. Indeed, the Republic of Ireland seemed determined to follow our MAFF down the same blind alleys over the TB issue.

Scientists from the UK as well as those working for ERAD were invited to speak on their research. All present were hoping ERAD would prove our doubts unfounded, but alas it was not to be. The extent of their research was a series of quotations from old reports including the largely discredited Zuckerman Report, some circumstantial case studies yet to be scrutinised by scientists and the notorious Offaly project, which was much criticised by those scientists present at the seminar. ERAD admitted that no scientific conclusions as to quantifying the role of the badger in cattle/TB transmissions could be drawn from it.

Northern Ireland was represented. Once again it pointed out that they had achieved a bovine TB level ten times lower than the south by tightening cattle-movement control and testing, without any badger killing. In England, a vaccine for badgers had already been produced and tests were currently being done on this. A vaccine for cattle would clash with the TB testing, making cows appear positive when tested for the disease. There is no recording system for cattle in the Republic of Ireland; one is urgently needed.

As one UK scientist declared to Dr Liam Downey, head of ERAD, 'Look at our and your badger populations as one population. Even if you could eradicate all badgers and recolonise with clean badgers, chances are they would become infected if only from cattle.' Talking to others during the break, I was told that Egyptian mummies have been found to have tubercular spines from drinking infected milk. Bovine TB has been around as long as bovines, but only becomes a problem when cattle are intensively kept. Since Victorian times the problem has escalated and bovine TB is now endemic. It is also endemic in many wild species apart from badgers, for example opossums in New Zealand and buffalos in Australia. In the long term, therefore, it would seem more practical to vaccinate cattle and keep records of them, whilst computerising all cattle movements.

It was a conference full of frustrations, especially for Badger-watch Ireland. Dr Downey ended it with the words 'Now we must seriously consider vaccination – whether of badgers of cattle isn't yet clear. In the meanwhile, we would be foolish not to continue to remove badger populations from cattle-infected areas.' During the discussion that followed, Badgerwatch Ireland asked if there would be a closed season for the taking of badgers or would they kill lactating sows? Dr Downey replied 'Farmers are in dire financial straits. Look at it from their position. What would you do? *Of course, we have known for years that badger control doesn't work*, but we would be foolish not to continue to take badgers all the year round.' As Dr Jim Barry bitterly remarked, 'We can take it now that this is ERAD's official policy – taking lactating sows and allowing cubs to starve to death!' Having encouraged farmers to believe badgers on their land were responsible for the spread of bovine TB, ERAD had no choice but to continue with the charade, or lose face. Indeed, ERAD and our MAFF have a great deal in common. In the words of one reporter that day 'Badgerwatch's future looks to be years of distressing battles about cruelty.'

With Karen caring for The Sett and its animals, I could stay for some days with my Irish friends. I returned via London in bright sunshine and saw blazes of crocus in the city squares. At the caravan, my primroses were palely beautiful, somehow rendering vulgar the crocus's gaudy tones. In Ninepenny Wood the growth during my absence was surprising with feathery-leaved cow parsley, goldilocks buttercups, lesser celandine and cleavers pushing through the dead leaves with the long green grass, nettles and bluebell greenery. Dublin has an amazing park of 1,750 acres and many mature trees. It has a wealth of wildflowers and a fine herd of fallow deer. It seemed strange, however, to find Scots pine and birch without woodpecker holes drummed into their trunks, but there are no woodpeckers in Ireland! Here the snowdrops' flowers were over and browning, but the dog's mercury's green, stalked tassels of petalless flowers were still fresh. Elder leaves were, as always, well advanced, but hawthorn, briar rose and many others already had their leaf buds opening. Spring seemed to have slipped in almost unnoticed and the clear air was full of birdsong.

No Flo appeared as I walked on to the sett by the poplar row, but to my delight I discovered the sows had turned out old, soiled bedding on to the spoil heap there. I gazed over the fields to the horizon; all was green under a vivid blue sky. Flo did turn up later and purred into my face with a vibration that made her stripes quiver! The night was mild and balmy, as together we walked the woodland and fields with great pleasure. I left Flo and wandered off to the Sand Pit badgers. Although I saw only three of them snuffling beneath the willows near the pond, from the fresh heaps of sandy earth and soiled bedding turned out it seemed they were thriving. At first light I returned to stand awhile in quiet content, then sat down with arms round my knees gazing at the beauty all about. Somewhere a pheasant called, which made me smile, recalling the old male near my caravan and his eccentric ways. If Karen rode along the path on her moped or I walked by during the day, he would suddenly appear alongside and slightly ahead keeping pace. If Karen or I stopped he too would stop, only to resume his pace, head jerking at each step, as we moved on. If I stopped and refused to move or sat down on the path, this appeared to confuse him and he would come nearer for a closer look. Then, bored with my inaction, he would commence feeding nearby, keeping up a continual but quiet conversation with himself as he did so.

Suddenly there was movement at the right-hand sett entrance, as first one softly rounded face and then another peered out from the pipe. Some jostling from behind as another and . . . another behind that? I couldn't be sure of the last, but certainly Hattie had three cubs. At that moment Aunty Hazel swayed up from the direction of the poplar row and, amid much contact murmuring, nosed the cubs back in. I was amazed at her familiarity with such young cubs, when a thought made me wonder. I could only see her big, grey, furry back and haunches, but was she lactating too? Hazel was more reticent than her sister and rarely knowingly came as close to me as did Hattie. It would account for the sisters denning together so amicably. Did they both have cubs? How wonderful if they should, but for a few nights longer I wouldn't know for sure. Now a light was stealing over the fields lending colour to the landscape and the badgers were gone. An owl called a faltering hoot and was silent as a skylark sang from the rows of corn.

Flo met me at the edge of Ninepenny Wood and by her heavy belly I could see she had already dined well. Something bounded across our path making the tabby start. A stoat was busy hunting, his mind and body one as he followed his prey. A great spotted woodpecker drilled loudly above us, the staccato note of his drumming telling other 'peckers that this was his domain. It might have been the First Morning.

Later that day I phoned Val and discovered there had been lamping on the farmland between us the previous Sunday at about 9 p.m. Her husband had contacted Oakley police and was pleasantly surprised to find that the young woman who answered knew all about lamping. Yes, a patrol would be along to the area shortly. He watched from a distance and, sure enough, a car did appear from the lane on to the footpath, but then it seemed to go into the field, which made him feel it wasn't a police patrol after all. The lampers' light went out, of course, but the car continued there for some while before leaving. Val asked if I thought it had been the police and I said yes, I felt sure it was. If the police couldn't find a parked vehicle, the next best thing is to turn their car headlights on to the crops, casting about. You are unlikely to apprehend such people, but at least you can make it clear you know full well they are there. Poachers are less likely to call again another night, though of course there is nothing to stop them going elsewhere. Like other forms of offence, whether petty or serious, you are unlikely to stamp them out, but you can make life difficult and move such people on.

We were not the only ones to have lampers. That March I was contacted by no less than five separate badger groups who were keeping night vigil near setts. One group had followed terrier-men into a wooded area where they were lamping amongst trees. This in itself is unusual, for tree trunks deflect the light of a beam and terriers are not really considered lamping dogs for they give voice when they scent their quarry. Many lampers are poachers and a dog 'yipping' can warn the landowner of intruders. However, though noisy and slower than lurchers, they are ideal holding dogs, and nowadays are often taken along if badgers are involved. The time was about 11 p.m. and the lampers had netted the entrances and then driven the badgers towards the sett where other men and dogs were waiting. In any case, a sow with tiny cubs underground will instinctively rush home – in this instance to find all entrances blocked. The men weren't caught, though they were obviously given a fright and no brockies were taken. Lamping badgers is becoming more and more common, for of course it is an easy way to take them with no digging involved and little likelihood of being caught in the dark.

◊ ◊ ◊

Karen and I discussed the visit to her house; we would need to be away overnight. By 3 p.m. we had reached it and carried her belongings indoors. It had been unoccupied for more than a year and jokingly, I pressed down the sitting-room light switch, never dreaming the electricity was still connected. We, who had been without it for so long, were like children in our delight. Karen put a plug on the colour TV she had brought and the vacuum flask remained unused as I filled her electric kettle for a hot drink. What luxury! Later, we bought fish and chips and sat in the well-lit room watching television. I suddenly thought of the washing that had been left to drip dry outside The Sett and convulsed my daughter by wistfully remarking how I wished I had brought it. Wouldn't it have been marvellous to be able to use an iron again!

For the first night since the previous October, my joints didn't ache when I laid down to rest. The Sett was incredibly damp now. Karen had brought a cardboard box full of china to the caravan two days ago and placed it on the floor. Lifting it to put in the car the bottom almost fell out, for it was sodden nearly halfway up from the floor. I should have thought to rest it on plastic sheeting for a continuously mouldy smell pervaded everything now in the caravan. Next morning we returned home, stopping briefly *en route* to see my Essex friend. The pussy willow catkins were in their glory with the willow leaves a lilting lime green all the way from Yorkshire and a delight to the eye. At The Sett, there was Flo to greet us. Best of all, that night I discovered that Hazel was lactating like her sister and between them they had five cubs!

Karen and I enjoyed watching the four brilliant jays, a robin and blue tits coming for the peanuts I left on the small badger cage. The jays didn't seem to quarrel, but each picked up a peanut and going to the nearest branch, held it in their claws as they pecked at it. The robin was more interested in the bird seed and remained on the cage roof industriously feeding as the others came and went. The adult badgers had been digging out their homes that mild rainy night. Worms were plentiful as well as slugs and insects. Everywhere was lush, green and growing. The geans were all in blossom with daffodils blowing gently in the long grass. The Kentish countryside seemed full of blossom, primroses and lambs. There were even black-faced sheep running with the cows and bullocks across the lane to the village.

The lambs were still very young and delightful to see as they searched under their mothers, tails awagging, to drink.

One evening I put out the dinner Flo refused to eat; she must have already killed and eaten. Much later, I happened to look over to the water bowl in the verge and there the cat was busily engaged. She wasn't eating the food, merely dragging the nearest dried grass over it with her teeth before wandering off into the night. To human eyes the food had disappeared, but to the noses of foxes and badgers it was immediately apparent. She later returned with Dean and, quite unconcerned, watched him eating what she had so carefully tupped over!

The acacia tree was alive with activity as the tawny's eggs had hatched in Steve's nest box and the male was hunting for three demanding chicks as well as his mate. Owls commence incubation with the first egg laid, so the chicks were of different ages, having hatched at five-day intervals. It was a common sight to see a tawny shape fly over the caravan with a mouse or worm dangling from his hooked beak. He would continue to hunt alone until the nestlings were sufficiently covered with down to keep warm without their mother brooding them, for the nest would be bare and unlined. Quite by chance, Flo and the hunting tawny clashed. The cat had crept stealthily over to the large badger enclosure to sit by a run that made its way through the grass and under the cement slab floor. The owl sat a dark, silent, hunched-up shape above her bent head, quite unbeknownst to the tabby. Both must have heard squeakings for the cat's ears moved forward and the owl bent lower. As a vole slipped out of cover, the tawny opened its wings to drop and the cat, sensing or seeing the movement, looked up and sprang away just in time. The owl didn't pursue or attack Flo and the vole lived to see another night. At this time of year, when mice and vole populations are at their lowest, I several times saw the owl with a very young rabbit, and once was able to watch him catch one. They are remarkably easy to catch and must have made a substantial meal for the entire family.

At the committee stage of the Badgers Bill, it was finally agreed there should be an amendment to allow foxhunts to lightly stop up sett entrances. A register of earth-stoppers would be held by the hunts themselves and these would have to be disclosed to a police officer on demand. So for the first time, earth-stoppers could be traced and made accountable for their actions if they damaged sett entrances or used unacceptable methods to close them. The definition of a sett had caused a great deal of controversy, but it was finally agreed as 'any structure or place which displays signs indicating current use by a badger'. Roy Hughes's Bill would now go on to its third reading.

Another piece of legislation known as The Badgers (Further Protection) Bill was concurrently having its committee stage and third reading too, but there was no disagreement over this. It would allow the courts to order the destruction or disposal of a dog used in badger-related cases, as well as disqualifying offenders from having custody of a dog. Yet another loophole had been plugged.*

One evening I set out for Ashcroft Woods; I did so want to see them again and most especially the badgers. To my delight the cubs were above ground; Crisp had three whilst Missy had two. It was colder than usual, so they did not stay above ground for long. Ray's pond by the car-park was half-full of water and the path beyond it was almost dry, so his idea had been a good one. The main pond was clear and full of life. I could see the frogspawn and water-weeds as if through glass. It was here a few nights later that I chanced on Mícheál, the dominant boar, swimming after frogs that had mated and spawned, but not yet left the water. He caught one and came ashore, shaking himself all over me, then ate his frog before returning for another.

I wandered happily through the woods, listening to the tawnies serenading and smelling the fresh scents of living growth. How scent is heightened at night. What a wonderful world we live in. I returned at 5.30 a.m. with the blackbirds busy in the quiet lanes ahead and mist moving over the fields. A woodpigeon cooed and distantly a cow lowed urgently to the calf separated from her in another meadow. As I neared my home-ward stretch, a glorious tawny figure slipped out to meet me

---

* The Badgers Act 1991 and The Badgers (Further Protection) Act 1991 came into force in the autumn of that year and The Criminal Justice Act 1991 now provides courts with the power to invoke custodial sentences for offences under the Badgers Act.

from the line of poplars – Splinter. On long, graceful legs he danced up to me, those great ears turning. Open-mouthed he stretched up lightly, forepaws at my waist. We touched noses, my eyes looking into the soul of the fox. My mind was attuned now to my leaving to live far away, but some things I would miss greatly and this was one of them. Together we walked into Ninepenny Wood along a path lined with the living spring and tumultuous birdsong all around. At the boar's sett I paused fascinated as a mole digging below ground sent up showers of bright, brown earth. Something rufous sprang and dug down with great speed; it grasped, shook, dropped and bit again. Movement activates the fox's instinct to kill, though moles, with their musky scent, aren't popular food. Oddly though, foxes will kill and carry them back for their cubs to eat at times. I picked up the still-warm owner of the finest fur you will ever find. The mole has no nap to its fur, the dirt falling away as it tunnels, which is why the mole stays clean underground. I looked round to discover Splinter had disappeared as silently as he came. Further on by the beeches, a striped figure yawned and stretched. I had come home at last, and about time, my furry feline seemed to say. 'Now what about a nice drink of milk?'

It was a joy to steal out of the caravan to see the Ninepenny badger cubs at play. I took to scrambling up into the tree near the Poplar Sett where I could watch unknown to the youngsters themselves. Hattie and Hazel would leave their home to forage across the farmland or in the wood itself and soon two, three, four and five cubs appeared to play. The last was a tiny creature. It made me determined to continue feeding the mothers in the hope that it too would survive and Dave had promised to look after the setts as much as he could when I left. I never did decide which cubs belonged to who, for the moment a sow approached all five would begin to nuzzle under – they even tried it with Dean! Fatherhood, even if adopted, seemed to suit him well. Some nights, Flo would appear and lie in the soft earth of the spoil heaps inviting the cubs to play. Long after the four largest had grown too big for the tabby, the wee one remained hers to be championed. If the others bullied or harried it, she was there to arch her back and spit in its defence. A spayed tabby could never have kittens, let alone cubs, of her own, but this cub in its early weeks seemed to satisfy her maternal desire. I longed to take a photo of the cat washing it, but knew this would disturb and frighten them both; sufficient to retain the picture in my mind. Hattie and Hazel seemed to accept Flo's interest in their offspring. If she had been capable of producing milk and suckling them, I believe they would have accepted this too.

The Ashcroft cubs were also entertaining to watch. At eleven weeks old, Crisp's three would groom themselves, sitting back on their haunches only to keel over slowly with a squawk, very much like puppies. One night there was Crisp lying by a sett entrance as they played over her body, climbing on to her big, grey shape and sliding down. One larger than the rest (male I think, though he hadn't yet grown his cheek tufts), scrambled on top and dared the others to dethrone him, till Crisp slowly rolled over and he flopped off. Later, the sow went out to forage and this same cub began exploring the very steep sett slope in the hedgerow. He fell down on to the field below and cried and cried from the bottom with the other two looking down at him. Eventually their mother, who had been collecting fresh bedding for them, returned. She grasped him by the scruff and carried him inside. I could almost hear her sigh 'Kids!'

That night I returned to find that Splinter and Fran had moved their cubs from the den under the Japanese knotweed to a fresh one dug out in the roots of a gale-felled gean near the badger cubs' home. Unlike badgers, they are not good house-keepers, and once one site has become fouled from droppings and discarded food, they will move to another. The four cubs were old enough to follow Fran and not be carried.

I left very early for that last day in Ashcroft Woods. At the six-wents clearing I made to sit on an old coppiced stool, its gnarled sides covered in mosses. A squirrel had peeled a chestnut case and left the shiny exterior in neat strips there. The thin morning sunshine lit the slender green hornbeams' trunks, surrounded by fine, green filigree tracery of the new year's leaves. At the base of one fine oak, a rich bush of evergreen butcher's broom moved stiffly in the breeze. A tree-creeper stole flittingly up an ancient trunk, probing the bark with a small, curved beak. Mouse-like it ascended with pauses to inspect the next cranny for insects, then continued to the first stout branch high above. As I waited, the light slowly crept over the barred ground as the sun rose higher in the sky. A bird was exploring one of the warden's nest boxes – an open-fronted one. The robin disappeared inside just as a kestrel's pointed shape appeared over the treeline. Soft greens were everywhere, with the newly opening bluebells showing, whispers of blue amongst the grass.

Ray arrived and together we walked the woodland doing a nest box check. On a spray of cherry blossom five magnificent peacock butterflies fed and as our way led us further, orange-tips, commas and brimstones appeared along the path. I had a long, last look at Little Chantry Field, the wildflower meadow that had once been merely a dream. Three months later, Ray was to phone Scotland telling me of the orchids appearing on its woodland edge.

On my return to Ninepenny Wood, something moved along the trail towards me, its head briefly glimpsed above the living green. Flo was coming to meet me. Sitting down, she sprung into my lap purring and I thought how much I would miss her when we moved. The household in Scotland already had a cat and two dogs; my tabby would hate it there. Karen, however, had a long garden and no animals apart from her terrapin. She would be very much on her own and glad of the cat's company. There was a wood and a large, untended field nearby and although she was unlikely to find badgers, Flo would certainly discover a fox to befriend. Walking home through Ninepenny Wood, I noticed shining lesser celandine's yellow stars underfoot and the poplar row's young leaves had their incense smell. Flo ran ahead and up a trunk, then dropped and dashed to me. Picking her up, I recalled how often she played with Karen.

Inevitably, perhaps, the Ninepenny badger cubs soon found they had new neighbours. The fox cubs' red guard hairs were beginning to show through their chocolate woolly coats, for they were about six weeks old. Fox cubs develop much faster than badgers: the latter's eyes open at about five weeks old, whereas fox cubs' do so at ten days. What advantage the badgers had from their greater size and weight, was well matched by the little foxes' turn of speed. One badger cub stood on top of a rotten hollow tree stump with a bedraggled bluebell in his mouth, daring the others – foxes and badgers – to topple him. A young fox sprang up and the badger disappeared backwards into the hollow with a bark. Moments later, his face reappeared over the rim of the stump and he was still holding the stem of the bluebell in his mouth, although the flower had given up! This youthful innocence would not last. There comes a time in the relationship when each species goes its own way and ignores the other. I have a feeling this may be linked to the foxes' developing scent glands, when suddenly they smell very pungently, which badgers find distasteful; but for whatever reason, the idyll is short-lived.

I came upon Hazel at first light playing with all five young badgers, leaping through the bluebells like a joyful dog as they scampered after, then racing back again to roll over and over with them tumbling about her larger shape. Hattie and Dean came upon the scene and the flower-scented air was filled with excited barks, yaps and whickers. Just as suddenly they were gone as the game moved deeper into the wood. I sat there for a time in a haze of musk, holding a trampled bluebell, alone with my thoughts.

That final morning I went out again – such a lovely day – to look at the Poplar Sett and Flo asked to come too. Without her knowing, I slipped the camera into my pocket and carried her along the path to Ninepenny Wood for the last time. How she always loved this. It was one of those moments, full of tenderness, as if she knew we were soon to part. She nestled lovingly in my arms and patted my face with velvet paws. In the wood now, she gazed up at the leafing trees and a mist of green. My friend had told me that Scotland is some weeks behind Kent, so I would have another spring in store. Flo jumped down to investigate the rich badger musk amongst the bluebells. I was able to take photos of her without her being aware. She didn't follow, so I walked on only turning back near the curve of the path. She was crouched on the fallen beech that straddles the way. The morning sun stroked her striped coat as she watched something farther along the trunk. I took a last photo of her in the sunlit wood, then moved on to check the sett. Fresh grass blades lay in the entrance; sure sign that clean bedding had been taken down by a hardworking parent that night. All was serene and quiet till walking back to where I had left Flo, I heard, then saw, a cuckoo displaying from the old, decaying crab apple tree. The cat miaowed to be carried back and we arrived at The Sett to find Karen up and busy packing. Flo promptly took her place under the duvet and went to sleep until it was time to leave.

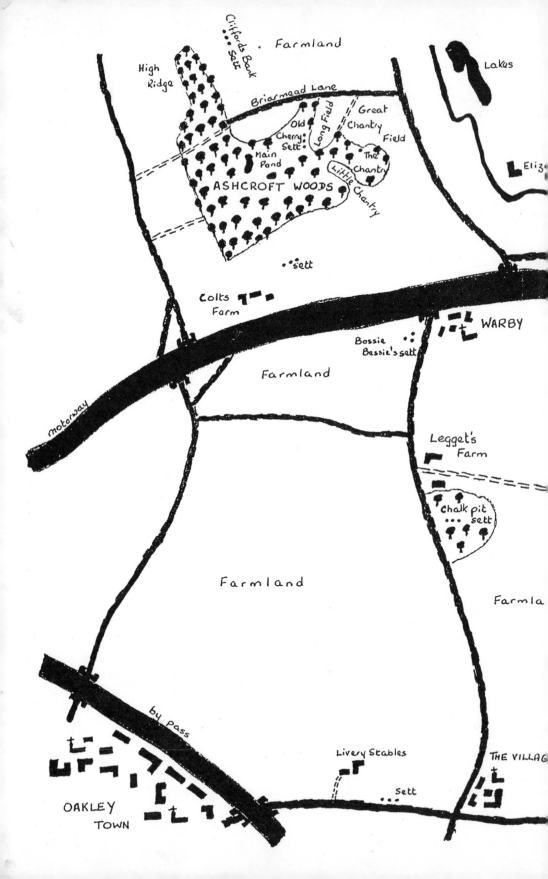